PUBLIC CHOICE ESSAYS IN HONOR OF A MAVERICK SCHOLAR:

Gordon Tullock

PUBLIC CHOICE ESSAYS IN HONOR OF A MAVERICK SCHOLAR: GORDON TULLOCK

Edited by

Price Fishback

Gary Libecap

Edward Zajac

Department of Economics
University of Arizona

Springer Science+Business Media, LLC

Library of Congress Cataloging-in-Publication Data

Public choice essays in honor of a maverick scholar : Gordon Tullock/edited by Price Fishback,Gary Libecap,Edward Zajac.
p.cm.
Research summaries discussed at a conference held at the University of Arizona to honor Gordon Tullock,professor,Economics Department.
Includes bibliographical references and index.
ISBN 978-1-4613-7060-4 ISBN 978-1-4615-4563-7 (eBook)
DOI 10.1007/978-1-4615-4563-7
1.Social Choice--Congresses.2.Tullock,Gordon. I. Tullock,Gordon. II.Fishback,Price Van Meter.III.Libecap,Gary D.IV.Zajac,Edward E.

HB846.8.P832 1999
302.13--dc21 99-048299

Printed on acid-free paper.

CONTENTS

FIGURES

TABLES

ACKNOWLEDGMENTS

We dedicate the book to Gordon Tullock, our friend and colleague. The editors gratefully acknowledge the contributions and cooperation of the authors. The editors and the authors all thank Susan Isaac for her editorial assistance and her skill at typesetting the book. We thank Ranek Jasani, our editor at Kluwer, for her help and enthusiasm for the project. Mark Zupan, Dean of the College of Business and Public Administration at the University of Arizona, was the originator of the idea to honor Gordon. He and the college provided extensive support throughout for the project. David Kennedy and the Earhart Foundation gave us the financial means to host the conference. Fred Boice generously donated funds that helped make the conference a success. Financial support for the conference was also provided by the Center for Public Choice at George Mason University, while general support was provided by the Economics Department at the University of Arizona. Kathy Wiener and the staff at the Hacienda del Sol provided a wonderful environment for discussing the research summarized in the papers in the volume. Viola Furry helped organize the conference and provided secretarial support for Gordon for years. Merrilee Holmes handled many of the financial arrangements. Finally, we would like to thank all of the scholars who attended the conference and provided comments and intellectual stimulus that improved the work in this volume: Dagibert Brito, Jeff Clark, Roger Congleton, James Cox, Domenico da Empoli, James Davidson, Michael Ghiselin, Bob and Mary Lou Gunderson, Douglass Hibbs, Jack and Phyllis Hirschleifer, Harold Hochman, Soo Young Hwang, Keith Jakee, Haengbum Kim, Samson Kimenyi, Daniel Klein, David Laband, Sumner Lacroix, Janet Landa, Peter Mayer, Brint Milward, Bettina Monissen, Jose Casas Pardo, Charles Plott, Stan Reynolds, Colin Robinson, Jane Shaw, William Shughart, Alexander Tabarrok, Betty Tillman, Mark Toma, Charlotte and Richard Twight, Akihito Udagawa, and Mr. and Mrs. John Virgo.

INTRODUCTION: PUBLIC CHOICE ESSAYS IN HONOR OF A MAVERICK SCHOLAR: GORDON TULLOCK

Price Fishback, Gary Libecap, and Edward Zajac
Department of Economics
University of Arizona
Tucson, AZ 85721
U.S.A.

In May 1999, over 50 distinguished scholars from all over the world gathered to honor Gordon Tullock, one of the most prolific, original, and versatile scholars of his generation. Gordon is best known for his pioneering work in Public Choice, the study of how self-interested individuals interact with governments. Gordon's research in public choice has contributed to our understanding of the decisions made by elected officials and bureaucrats, as well as knowledge about how individuals and pressure groups both inside and outside the government seek to shape it. Yet Gordon's work ranges well beyond Public Choice. He has made significant contributions to political science, law, military strategy, and conflict resolution as well. He is one of the few, perhaps the only, economist who has published in the *American Naturalist*, one of the top-ranked journals in biology.

His scholarly productivity is astounding; as indicated by the fact that he is one of the most widely cited economists in the world. This productivity has shaped the course of public choice and has resulted in many honors. Gordon has been named a Distinguished Fellow of the American Economic Association and is a member of the American Political Science Review Hall of Fame. He has received an honorary Doctor of Law degree from the University of Chicago, the Adam Smith Award, and an Award for Outstanding Contributions in the Field of Law and Economics from the George Mason University Law School. He has been appointed to chairs at the Virginia Polytechnic Institute and State University, George Mason University, and the University of Arizona. Gordon has been elected President of the Public Choice Society, Southern Economic Association, Western Economic Association, and Atlantic Economic Association. He is a member of the Council of the American Political Science Association. Gordon served as the editor of *Public Choice* for over two decades, and has been a member of too many editorial boards to mention.

Gordon's professional work has influenced so many scholars that there is little wonder that so many people came together to honor him. In this introduction we try to give the reader a sense of who Gordon is, an idea of the individual with whom we have conversed almost daily for the last dozen years (except when Gordon had flown off to yet another location to be honored or to present his work). We also try to convey how Gordon approaches research. Finally, we try to give a sense of what Gordon has been up against. For, his has not been an easy research life. He truly has been a maverick scholar and therefore has met more than his share of rejection of the products of his efforts—products that sometimes were later rightly recognized as path breaking. He has persevered in spite of many obstacles (see Brady and Tollison [1994], for more on Gordon's difficulties in getting published). Yet his persistence has paid ample dividends, which can best be illustrated by the written versions of the nine papers presented at the conference. Each of the papers was strongly influenced by Gordon's work.

GORDON TULLOCK THE INDIVIDUAL

To meet Gordon Tullock for the first time is an experience. He may ask you to name your specialty. Your answer will be followed by an oral examination on the topic, reminiscent of your PhD defense. You will, of course, fail. Alternatively, he may present you with the economic puzzle he is currently pondering and demand that you solve it. Your solution will be one that Gordon has considered and has rejected out of hand. Gordon will promptly so inform you.

If you live in the same city as Gordon, you may be surprised that, after this initial treatment where you have seemingly miserably fallen short of Gordon's expectations, he has invited you and your spouse to dinner. It will be at one of the city's most expensive restaurants, with wines from the portion of the wine list that you never look at because of the stratospheric prices. At dinner, the intellectual thrust and parry will continue, and you will realize that Gordon has not singled you out for special treatment. Rather, Gordon is like a precocious fourteen-year-old who has just discovered the joys of life of the intellect and of intellectual jousting. The way you can best please Gordon is to join in the fun and give as well as you get.

How is it that, in his 70s, Gordon still has the irrepressible intellectual curiosity and enthusiasm of a teenager and still delights in intellectual combat? We will never know. Perhaps it's in his genetic makeup. Or, perhaps it's because he was on the debate team both in high school and in college. Or, perhaps it's because of his unusual academic training.

For, as Gordon Brady points out in this volume in his biographical sketch of Gordon, Gordon's formal post-high school academic training consisted of five years at the University of Chicago. During this time he did not receive an undergraduate degree (he refused to pay the $5 fee necessary to get it) but did complete law school. Law school was followed by nine years in the U.S. State Department and an academic appointment not in an economics department, but in a newly-formed Department of International Studies at the University of South Carolina.

Gordon was thus spared the usual servitude of a half dozen or so years in a PhD program plus another half dozen or so years in the tenure track trenches—a servitude that can beat the intellectual curiosity out of all except the most stalwart.

Whatever the forces that molded Gordon, we can be grateful that they did their job. Although Gordon loves to fire off "what ought to be done about it" letters to the editor of newspapers and periodicals, his scholarly output is focused on positive science—Gordon directs his major energies at understanding what *is* rather than preaching what *ought to be*.

The result is a scholar of awesome productivity; his vita lists 26 books and over 500 published papers. His footprints are to be found all over the landscape, not only in economics but in political science, law, biology, military strategy, and conflict resolution.

Most importantly, his contributions are at the frontiers. One is reminded of Schumpeter's assertion that capitalism progresses not because of advances at the margins but because of the creation of new innovations and inventions, new methods of organization, and new industries. Gordon has been the consummate Schumpeterian of academia, and has often been called a maverick because his publications are invariably original, unique, and deviate from standard theory or wisdom.

GORDON TULLOCK'S CONTRIBUTION TO THE STUDY OF BUREAUCRACY

Gordon Tullock has made so many contributions to economics, political science, and legal study that it is difficult to select any one area to illustrate Gordon's originality and maverick attacks on sacred cows. Perhaps a good illustration is his work on bureaucracy, work that is neither his most cited nor his most influential, but work that has the hallmarks of both the triumphs and problems with Gordon's research. The study of bureaucracy was the subject of the first book Gordon ever wrote. It was ahead of its time. As a result, Gordon had great difficulty in getting it published, succeeding only after publication of *The Calculus of Consent*.

Historically (and even today) bureaucracy has attracted little attention from economists. Bureaucrats were perceived as responding to the directives of politicians who had various means of insuring compliant behavior. Of course, until the implications of public choice were broadly recognized the economics profession viewed politicians merely as the agents of voters, and hence not too worthy of analysis. In the heyday of Keynesian Theory from the end of World War II through the early 1970s, government "failure" was not seen as an important problem. Market failure was the object of concern. But just as public-choice theorists argued that politicians might have interests separate from voters and be motivated by self-interest, Gordon Tullock asserted that the bureaucracy should be viewed as a third party in political transactions, along with voters and politicians. If information were limited and monitoring costs were high, then bureaucrats might adjust the policies adopted by politicians for their own purposes. Just what motivated bureaucrats, however, remained (and has remained) subject to debate. But the notion that a principal/agent problem might exist and that bureaucrats might play a separate role in molding policies, affecting economic performance, and possibly, encouraging the growth of government was the key insight.

Gordon completed a draft of *The Politics of Bureaucracy* in 1957 or 1958 (Gordon does not remember the exact year), but it was not published until 1965. Its publication followed Anthony Downs's *An Economic Theory of Democracy* (1957), but predated William Niskanen's better-known book, *Bureaucracy and Representative Government* (1971) by six years. In *The Politics of Bureaucracy*, Tullock described bureaucrats as self-interest maximizers who could influence political decisions as a separate and well-organized constituency and who could adjust policy administration to further their interests. The debate as to just how far the bureaucracy could stray from the objectives of politicians remained unresolved (Weingast and Moran [1983]). Nevertheless, Gordon was one of the first to identify the potential for bureaucratic opportunism and to argue that bureaucrats could be a source of the observed growth of government in the United States and western Europe.

After straying from the topic for some time, as has been his style, in 1974 Gordon returned to the issue of what might motivate bureaucrats with his short paper, "Dynamic Hypotheses on Bureaucracy" (*Public Choice* [1974]). If bureaucrats had separate interests from politicians and voters, what might those interests be and what might the consequences of bureaucratic maneuvering be for the political process and economic performance? William Niskanen had posited that bureaucrats were budget maximizers. Gordon presented a theoretical rationale for such an objective function that also would provide for internal demand for larger government. Basically, although citizens would demand a certain level of government services, bureaucrats as a separate constituency would demand even more because larger bureaucracy and greater budgets would lead to higher salaries. But the process was more complex, according to Gordon. Incumbent bureaucrats would prefer that budget allocations for approved policies go to higher salaries than for hiring more bureaucrats and providing more services. Hence, the effect of bureaucratic lobbying would be to raise the cost of programs. Gordon hypothesized, however, that if the number of bureaucrats were successfully held down in this rent-seeking activity that bureaucrats as an interest group would suffer because their size would decline. The predicted pattern then would be for bureaucrats to raise program costs, but the size of bureaucracy would decline over time. This size decline could in turn reduce the ability of the bureaucracy to raise their wages through the political process.

As with much of Gordon's scholarship, his arguments were provocative and they stimulated empirical work on the relationship between the size of government, the bureaucracy, and bureaucratic wages (Blais and Dion [1991], and Johnson and Libecap [1994]). Gordon has since turned his attention to other issues. The debate over the growth of government and its sources has quieted. At the same time, however, the performance of the bureaucracy and its impact on the efficiency of government ("government failure") has become the focus of discussion. As in other areas of research, this debate owes much of its basic framework to Gordon's pioneering work.

Gordon's prescient late-50s manuscript had one salutary effect—it helped him get a research fellowship at the Thomas Jefferson Center for the Study of Political Economy and Social Philosophy at the University of Virginia (see Gordon Brady's chapter in this volume). However, Gordon's efforts to get the manuscript published were frustrated for quite some time. Even though James Buchanan wrote a forward, academic publisher after academic publisher turned down the manuscript. Only in 1965 was Gordon able to publish *The Politics of Bureaucracy*, and even then, only by partially funding the publication costs out of his own pocket.

METHODOLOGY AND REPRISE OF GORDON'S WORK

Gordon's methodology consists of no high-powered mathematics or econometrics. Instead, he rigorously applies verbal reasoning, as might be expected of an accomplished debater and one trained in the law. What he has to say is expressed in simple, straightforward English that is easy to read and comprehend. At issue will be an insight, usually a simple one, but one that has eluded everyone else. Some insights, such as his rent-seeking insight, have created a whole new scholarly industry.

The straightforwardness of his prose and the simplicity of his results have perennially presented the problem encountered in his attempt to publish *The Politics of Bureaucracy*. Editors and referees have often treated Gordon's insight as something odd, simplistic, unimportant, or as something everyone has known all along. In order to be published, a number of his important papers have required the same determination and persistence that Gordon displayed in getting *The Politics of Bureaucracy* published. Chapters 2 and 4 of *On the Trail of Homo Economicus* (Brady and Tollison [1994]) give a number of examples.

Gordon's method of operating also makes it difficult to summarize his life's work. As Hans Monissen in this volume points out in citing Mark Blaug, "It is not always easy to see a common thread in Tullock's work; he is almost too fertile and throws off so many ideas in all directions that the connecting links between them threaten to disappear from view." Blaug then goes on to suggest that a possible common thread "is the view that human behavior must be viewed in all circumstances as a 'rational' response to the twin constraints of the physical environment and the prevailing social institutions; people will always strive to maximize their satisfactions in the face of these constraints, taking due account to the costs of alternative choices."

It is certainly true that Gordon is a member in good standing of the "rational choice" school of social sciences. But, perhaps another common thread going through Gordon's work is his preoccupation with governance—of society and of private and public institutions—and the design of institutional arrangements to achieve it effectively. It is the subject matter of *Calculus of Consent*, coauthored with James Buchanan, his most famous book. It is also the subject matter of all of his solo-authored books, as is apparent from their titles:

The Politics of Bureaucracy
The Organization of Inquiry
Towards a Mathematics of Politics

Private Wants, Public Means: An Economic Analysis of the Desirable Scope of Government
The Logic of the Law
The Social Dilemma: The Economics of War and Revolution
Trials on Trial: The Pure Theory of Legal Procedure
Economics of Income Redistribution
The Economics of Wealth and Poverty
Autocracy, Wealth, Poverty and Politics
The Economics of Special Privilege and Rent Seeking
Economic Hierarchies, Organization, and the Structure of Production
The New Federalist
The Economics of Non-Human Societies
On Voting: A Public Choice Approach

SUMMARIES OF THE CONFERENCE PAPERS

Gordon's influence on studies of governance is well illustrated by the nine papers in this volume. The papers were presented in May 1999 in Tucson, Arizona at a conference sponsored by the Earhart Foundation, Fred Boice, the Economics Department at the University of Arizona, the College of Business and Public Administration at the University of Arizona, and the Public Choice Center at George Mason University. Over 50 people attended the event to honor Gordon, the vast majority at their own expense. The discussions were lively. The papers were distributed in advance, and each author was given only five minutes to present his main findings. We chose this format so that Gordon would have an opportunity to tell each paper presenter what was "wrong" with his paper soon after the speaker began. Of course, Gordon would have jumped in within five minutes even if the speaker had had an hour to present, as he has in many workshops. We sought to institutionalize his interruptions. The papers and the discussion touch upon a broad array of aspects of public choice and of Gordon's research. Amazingly, the breadth of topics still does not come close to covering the enormous range of topics on which Gordon has written.

Perhaps Gordon's most influential insight was his discussion of rent seeking and the consequences of people competing to use government for their own ends. At one time Gordon thought this insight might be doomed to obscurity. The paper had been rejected by several major journals and was not often cited in the early days after its original publication in the *Western Economic Journal*. However, Robert Tollison helped Gordon to publicize how rent seeking can lead to extensive waste of resources.

In his chapter in this volume, Robert Tollison explores "The Rent Seeking Insight" further. He starts by making the notion of rent seeking precise. What is essential is the "social cost in terms of the foregone product of the resources employed in rent seeking." One must be careful not to confuse competitive profit seeking and entrepreneurship with rent seeking, since these do not result in social costs but rather in the expansion of output and the creation of value—for example, new products. Nor is rent seeking the result solely of governmental activity—rivalry among siblings for an inheritance can result in rent-seeking activities within families. Likewise, a pure transfer such as a bribe is not rent seeking. As Tollison puts it, "Hiring a lawyer or a lobbyist to obtain a favorable law is rent seeking; bribing a legislator for the same law is not."

As Tollison reviews the theory of rent seeking, it becomes clear that rent seeking is a slipperier concept than is suggested by simply considering Tullock rectangles. The idea of rent seeking implicitly assumes that there is an ideal standard that can be used to measure rents, and that "rents" are the resource costs that exceed ideal resource costs because of faulty institutional arrangements. Determining the ideal and measuring the resource costs of deviating from it is far from trivial.

Numerous scholars have found Gordon's rent-seeking concept useful in examining various political economic regimes. Charles K. Rowley in his chapter "Political Culture and Economic Performance in Sub-Saharan Africa" applies the insights of rent seeking and rent extraction to the tragic economic and social performance of post-colonial regimes in sub-Saharan Africa. "Rent-extraction" is a term coined by Fred McChesney who, as Rowley points out, "suggested that payments often are made to politicians not to secure political favors, but rather to avoid threatened political harm. In essence, rent-extraction is a euphemism for a system of political extortion." Sub-Saharan African dictators have used rent seeking and rent extraction to loot their countries, with the loot ending up in numbered foreign bank accounts. Rowley argues that appalling governance has made Sub-Saharan Africa a trivial force on the international economic scene, and has made it unlikely that outside intervention will solve a Sub-Saharan country's problems. The solution can only come from an internal purge. Rowley concludes "that such a purge is an essential pre-requisite for Sub-Saharan Africa if they are to restore civil society and, for the first time, to become a functioning part of an increasingly global world economy."

Gordon, himself, has used the rent-seeking insight as part of his explanation of a recent puzzle in world economic history that he addresses in a recent paper called "Why Europe" that he has been circulating. Gordon and recent students of Chinese history believe that China in the late eighteenth century had levels of per capita income and technological capabilities similar to those found in Europe at the time. The major puzzle then is why Europe and not China developed into an industrial giant during the nineteenth century. Jürgen G. Backhaus in "Constitutional Causes for Technological Leadership: Why Europe?" outlines the major factors that Gordon addresses as important to the issue and then fleshes out Gordon's brief discussion of the political and military competition among states in Europe and the development of "cameralism" as a multi-disciplinary science and practice of public administration. He claims that the political and military competition was the fallout of the constitutional system created by the Treaties of Westphalia of 1648 in central Europe. The constitution set the stage for political competition among small states that led many to adopt policies to attract and develop human capital, in part through the development of universities. A number of university professors became political economic advisors to their princes, as they developed the doctrines of cameralism. The cameralists saw the household as the primary component of the political economic system, and scholars such as Christian Wolff pressed for government policies that provided basic features that the households could not provide for themselves, including defense, police protection, education and universities, and some forms of social insurance. The cameralists argued for many policies that we see in place today.

Gordon's interest in history is matched by his interest in theories of voting. Throughout his career Gordon has developed verbal and simple arithmetic examples that show the pitfalls of various forms of voting rules. One example of this modeling style was his famous discussion (in Chapter 10 of *The Calculus of Consent*) of how a simple majority rule voting procedure would lead to inefficient over-provision of government services. Gordon illustrated this concept with an example of 100 farmers living on secondary roads bargaining for road maintenance and upkeep. James M. Buchanan and Yong J. Yoon develop "Variations on Tullock's Road Model" in which they show how a slight change in assumptions leads to a slightly different result. Buchanan and Yoon consider the case in which members of the initial minority, who were shut out of receiving services, sequentially bargain with members of the initial majority to form a new majority that will provide services to those initially shut out. The sequential bargaining converges to a new equilibrium which, in terms of taxes paid and upkeep level, is not far from the initial majority state. Buchanan and Yoon conclude that their extension confirms Gordon's basic hypothesis but differs from his original results as well. They also show that their problem relates to the problem of the commons. In limiting cases, the two are in fact the same. In a sense, Gordon's original model is a more-refined posing of the problem of the commons, with in both cases the result of inefficient over-consumption.

Theoretical discussions of various voting rules suggest that majority-rule voting can lead to unstable, cyclically dominated results, i.e., each voting outcome is dominated by at least one other outcome preferred by a different majority. Yet Gordon Tullock and many others have noted that although the theory predicts instability, we see examples of substantial stability of political outcomes all around us. Peter Bernholz throughout his own career has analyzed various decision procedures used by decentralized agents, who have been assigned the right to decide different issues. He has shown that for several issues negative externalities as well as contracts (of which logrolling is one example) among groups or individuals controlling different issues are a necessary condition for cyclically unstable social preferences.

Bernholz summarizes the most important insights that he has derived in his chapter on the "Instability of Voting Outcomes, Logrolling, Arrow, Coase, and All That." In this chapter he develops an elegant model—exposited by using the simple case of two issues and three voters—that is more general than previous voting models since it includes vote-trading, logrolling, and all other kinds of contracts among groups deciding different issues. In doing so he exposes various phenomena that cast light on the stability issue and develops a series of propositions. Besides the relationships already mentioned, he demonstrates that a generalized Coase Theorem holds: If contracts are binding and no transaction costs are present, a stable Pareto-optimal outcome will be reached, whatever the assignment of rights to groups or individuals to decide issues and whatever decision rules are used. Though Arrow's Impossibility Theorem thus covers all cases of decentralized decision-making, including logrolling and other settings in which agents conclude contracts benefitting them, it becomes irrelevant if contracts are binding. The same is true for Sen's Impossibility of a Paretian Liberal, which is just a special case of Arrow's Theorem. Bernholz also shows that the Paradox of Voting for two or more issues is identical with the cycles caused by explicit or implicit logrolling. Finally, it is demonstrated that cycles of voting outcomes can also arise if individual preferences are identical, but the restrictions (e.g. disposable incomes) faced by them are different.

Public-choice theory is not confined to analysis of the internal decision process. It has also been used to address issues related to size of government. In "Reflections on the Optimal Size of Government" Hans Monissen puts a public-choice twist on optimal taxation theory. He formulates a simple general-equilibrium model containing a representative private consumer and a complementary private firm, with a government-produced public good that enhances the consumer's utility and increases productivity in the private sector. This basic model yields a number of interesting results. For example, it shows that when organized labor succeeds in fixing real wage rates over the efficiency level, the size of government increases. This Leviathan result obtains whether we assume that the government is being run by a budget-maximizing bureaucrat or a surplus-maximizing selfish dictator. Monissen concludes that the explosive growth of almost all Western countries "would certainly suggest the need for bureaucratic (and legislative) reforms on a constitutional level" and that "taxing activities as proposed by Buchanan and Brennan are without a doubt a most effective recipe for taming Leviathan." He also concludes that further progress requires "opening the 'black box' called government and analyzing the internal organization of government." Further, "the main theoretical avenue seems clear: Constitutional reforms should start from a behavior model of the politician-bureaucrat."

One of the hallmarks of Gordon's career has been his ability to develop a simple insight that no one has developed before, but that in turn seems obvious in hindsight. Sometimes these insights can lead to a reversal of standard theories. Dwight R. Lee and Richard B. McKenzie develop just such a ju-jitsu style insight in their discussion of "Monopoly as a Coordination Problem." They argue that it's not easy for a firm's owners to fully capture monopoly rents, even when there are complete barriers to entry into the firm's markets. All firms of any appreciable size are faced with principal-agent problems because the owners find it costly to monitor their employees. Thus, workers and managers are often in positions where they make decisions that do not maximize the owner's profits. Using a simple model they show that the presence of these monitoring and agency costs can lead managers to choose lower prices and higher output levels than those that maximize profits for the owners. Therefore, the monopolization of an industry could well lead to lower prices and higher output than what is predicted by the standard economic theory of monopoly behavior. In essence, the monopolist may face an internal problem of "over-production" similar to the problems faced by cartels. This internal cartel problem mitigates some of the efficiency losses associated with the formation of monopolies.

In a similar reversal of the standard economic model, Richard L. Stroup in "Free Riders and Collective Action Revisited" offers an interesting insight on another market "failure," the provision of public goods. The standard economic discussion of public goods points out that private entities face problems in providing goods such as national defense or saving the whales. Since it is hard to exclude users from the benefits of these goods, and use by one person does not prevent use by others, everybody has an incentive to free ride and let others provide the good. When everybody acts this way, a less than optimal amount of the public good is provided. Economists have long argued that the government can solve this problem by forcing potential users to pay taxes. Stroup argues that this description is too simplistic. The problem of providing the public good does not end when the government states that it will use taxes to provide the public good. Stroup identifies what might be considered as the second-order free rider problem, a problem that Gordon first pointed out. In providing a public good, a public or private entity can't just stop at passing a law, it has to make numerous decisions on what to provide, and how much; and it must convince society of its importance. This process gives rise to all sorts of information gathering, decision-making and organizational activity, the provision of which is itself a public good. Of special concern is the ongoing monitoring and supervision of the projects to see that they are designed and performed in the interest of the diffuse public rather than to benefit the concentrated special interests such as input providers or other direct recipients of special benefits. If people free ride on the provision of this type of information and supervision, then the public good will still be under-provided. Stroup notes that the second-order public good problem arises in both the public and private sector, and then argues that in many cases the private sector is better equipped to handle it. He gives the example of provision of religious services, which turn out to be more adequately provided where religion is a private matter rather than a state-sponsored activity.

The chapters described above give a sense of how Gordon's work has influenced the work of others. Yet Gordon himself was influenced by the work of other scholars and his own experiences and training. In "Gordon Tullock: His Development as an Unconventional Economist, 1947–1962," Gordon Brady offers a biographical sketch of Gordon's early career. Gordon was educated in the legal profession with very little formal economic training. His aborted legal career might suggest that he learned the lessons of economics far better than he did the law. Nine years of service in the U.S. State Department exposed him to a wide variety of experiences in Asia that influenced his views of government and bureaucracy. In the late 1950s Gordon entered the academic world with a fellowship at the University of Virginia and an assistant professorship in international studies at the University of South Carolina. Discussions with his colleagues lead to some of his most productive work, including his co-authorship with James Buchanan of *The Calculus of Consent* in the early 1960s. Throughout his early career Gordon interacted with and learned from some of the leading scholars of our time. As befits a maverick scholar, at times Gordon also dismissed some of the ideas of these great scholars, and what resulted were new insights that opened up whole new realms of scholarship.

REFERENCES

Blais, Andre, and Stephane Dion, eds. (1991). *The Budget Maximizing Bureaucrat: Appraisals and Evidence*. Pittsburgh: University of Pittsburgh Press.

Brady, Gordon L., and Robert D. Tollison (1994). *On the Trail of Homo Economicus*. Fairfax, VA: George

Mason University Press.
Downs, Anthony (1957). *An Economic Theory of Bureaucracy*. New York: Harper and Row.
Johnson, Ronald N., and Gary D. Libecap (1994). *The Federal Civil Service System and the Problem of Bureaucracy*. Chicago: University of Chicago Press.
Niskanen, William A. (1971). *Bureaucracy and Representative Government*, Chicago: Aldine-Atherton.
Tullock, Gordon (1965) *The Politics of Bureaucracy*, Washington, D.C.: Public Affairs Press.
______ (1974). "Dynamic Hypotheses on Bureaucracy." *Public Choice* 16, 127–31.
Weingast, Barry, and Mark Moran (1983). "Bureaucratic Discretion or Congressional Control? Regulatory Policymaking by the Federal Trade Commission." *Journal of Political Economy* 91 (5) 765–800.

THE RENT-SEEKING INSIGHT

Robert D. Tollison
School of Business Administration
University of Mississippi
University, MS 38677
USA

METHODOLOGY AND STYLE

Before addressing Gordon Tullock's work on rent seeking, one should say a brief word about his general approach to economic analysis and his writing style. In fact, Tullock has shown far more interest in obtaining useful results than he has in how he happened to go about obtaining them. In this way he has been a methodological anarchist, operating under the general maxim that in science anything goes and results count. His well-known papers generally rely upon simple price-theoretic or spatial constructs and perhaps a little algebra and game theory. Where he has found a need for more formidable tools, he has generally acquired them through coauthors. This "anything goes" approach does not seem to have hampered his work. He has shown a talent for getting at the essence of problems and avoiding clutter in his work. Moreover, he has shown almost no penchant for methodological exegesis in his work, with the major exception of his general insistence that rational economic man models are the best description of behavior. On this point he has been steadfast. In fact, Buchanan (1987) uses Tullock's emphasis on the *homo economicus* assumption to describe Tullock as a "natural economist." I think this is an accurate interpretation of Tullock. We have all known people who are naturally good at things, such as playing shortstop or the piano, and in this sense it is analogous to say that Tullock has a natural inclination toward economic reasoning and behavior.

Tullock is not a great stylist. His normal routine is to dictate the first draft of his papers and work through them from there. This allows him to make his point, but sometimes not very eloquently or clearly. The real question about scientific writing style is whether it matters or not. There are protagonists on either side of this issue. Empirical research (Laband and Taylor [1992]) suggests that style has no marginal impact on citations. This result can be interpreted in various ways, but perhaps the most appropriate interpretation is that researchers have not yet found the margin on which writing style matters. Nonetheless, D. N. McCloskey lists Tullock along with several other modern economists as a good writer. To wit, "when you read any of these in economics, pay attention: this is as good as it gets" (1987: 9).

RENT SEEKING

Rent seeking is the socially costly pursuit of transfers. The concept of rent seeking was introduced to the economics profession by Tullock (1967). In his original presentation the basic idea that transfer seeking could lead to social costs was so simple that it has been automatically assumed that the idea had to have clear precursors in the literature. Nonetheless, even though one can find vague resemblances to the idea in many earlier writings, no one has uncovered a forerunner to Tullock's idea. His 1967 paper represents an original and important development in economic theory.

The early doctrinal development of the theory of rent seeking proceeded as follows. A. O. Krueger (1974) gave the field a name in her paper on "The Political Economy of the Rent-Seeking Society." For better or worse this terminology has stuck. J. N. Bhagwati (1980, 1982) made an attempt to rename the field as Directly Unproductive Profit-Seeking (DUP), but the language of "rent seeking" has carried the day. Although it presented some of her empirical estimates of the costs of rent seeking, Krueger's paper was primarily theoretical in nature, showing how rent seeking can lead to social costs in the adoption of policies to restrict international trade. Krueger was unaware of Tullock's paper. Posner (1975), who was aware of Tullock's paper, wrote out the first formal model and presented the first empirical estimates of the costs of rent seeking. His estimates suggested that the social costs of rent seeking in the regulated sector of the U.S. economy were substantial. Finally, in an effort to solidify the earlier contributions and to stimulate work in the field, J. M. Buchanan, Tullock, and R. D. Tollison (1980) published a collection on rent seeking which has been widely cited and used in the subsequent development of the field.[1]

Definitions and Semantics

Tullock originally framed the theory of rent seeking in contrast to the prevailing wisdom in the late 1950s and early 1960s that the deadweight costs of monopoly and tariffs were empirically quite small. A. C. Harberger's (1954) famous calculations on the extent of monopoly power in the United States, and discussions of how little British economic welfare would be increased if the United Kingdom joined the Common Market, are good examples of this type of thinking (Mundell [1962]). Microeconomics was on the verge of being trivialized. Tullock's insight in this context was to advance an argument that rectangles as well as triangles (or trapezoids) matter in the calculation of the social costs of such policies as tariffs, monopolies, and crime.

Tullock's point was simple, but full of potential pitfalls. He argued that expenditures made to capture a transfer were a form of social cost. The social cost arises because the resources used for transfer seeking have a positive opportunity cost elsewhere in the economy with respect to engaging in positive-sum activities. Transfer seeking is at best a zero-sum activity in that it simply shuffles dollars among people and groups, and is probably negative-sum if traditional deadweight costs are a by-product of such activities (Tullock [1980b]). Social costs arise in the process by which resources are shifted from positive- to zero- and negative-sum activities. Rent seeking embodies a social cost in terms of the foregone product of the resources employed in rent seeking.

Several points should be kept in mind at this juncture. The theory of rent seeking does not condemn all types of profit seeking. As Buchanan (1980) articulated clearly, traditional competitive profit seeking or entrepreneurship in the competitive model (seeking quasi-rents) does not qualify as rent seeking. Such profit seeking is productive; it expands output and creates value in the form of such things as new products. Rent seeking is unproductive; it destroys value by wasting valuable resources. Market-based entrepreneurs are generally socially productive; political entrepreneurs are generally socially destructive.

In a way, Buchanan has rearticulated an old point. Rent seeking and profit seeking arise from the same motive—the individual's attempt to make himself better off. The difference is due to the environment in which the individual is operating. A fundamental insight of economics is that if property rights are not well specified, individual maximization will lead to rent dissipation, or rent seeking in Tullock's definition. Y. Barzel (1974) and S. N. S. Cheung (1974) provide excellent examples of the rent-dissipation model.

Normally, the concept of rent seeking is applied to cases where governmental intervention in the economy leads to the creation of artificial or contrived rents. Seeking such returns leads to social costs because output is fixed by definition in, for example, a government regulation. Entrepreneurship in this setting can only be said to be negative; it will simply dissipate rents and lead to no increase in output. Nonetheless, it is quite possible to conceive of rent seeking as taking place in a non-governmental setting. Buchanan (1983), for example, argued that the rivalry of siblings for an inheritance can lead to rent-seeking activities within families, and R. H. Frank (1986) has shown how certain labor markets involving competition for position (the rat race, tournaments) generate costly rent-seeking activities by participants.

Another point to keep in mind is that to the degree that the process of rent seeking involves the provision of utility or real income to participants in the process, these benefits should be netted out against the cost of rent seeking. As R. D. Congleton (1988) has argued, if the rent seeker takes the regulator out to dinner, the value that the regulator places on the dinner must be subtracted from the social costs of rent seeking.

A final definitional point to bear in mind is that bribes are technically not a rent-seeking cost. A bribe is a transfer, and as such, it represents a method of influencing governmental behavior that does not involve explicit rent-seeking costs. Recall that rent seeking involves the expenditure of costly resources to procure a transfer. Hiring a lawyer or a lobbyist to obtain a favorable law is rent seeking; bribing a legislator for the same law is not. This is not intended as a defense of bribery; it is simply an analytical distinction.

Moving beyond bribes, however, once artificial rents have been created, it is hard to avoid the implication that rent seeking will occur along some margin. If a tax deduction is offered, tax shelters will be created. If civil servants are paid a wage in excess of their marginal revenue products, queues will develop for government jobs. All of these processes involve the use of scarce resources to seek transfers; the process is relentless.

Theory

Any pool of rents will do for analytical purposes. Normally, the exposition of rent seeking stresses rents arising from regulation, monopoly, or tariffs. Standard economic analysis treats such rents as pure transfers, with no effect on the economy. Tullock's insight converted such transfers into potential social costs.

R. A. Posner (1975) stated the first version of a rent-seeking game. His procedure was to describe a constant-cost game in which the probability of winning is proportional to investment and the available rents are exactly dissipated. He posited risk-neutral bidders, a fixed prize, and a given number of bidders. Where, for example, the pool of rents equals $100,000, and there are ten rent seekers, each bidder will offer or expend resources of $10,000 to capture the rents. In Posner's model rent seeking is analogous to buying a lottery ticket with a one in ten chance of being successful. Under such conditions rents are exactly dissipated; $100,000 is spent to capture $100,000.[2]

Posner's exact-dissipation hypothesis is popular in the literature because it makes empirical work easier. A rectangle is a definite area with a value that can be reasonably estimated. Moreover, Posner's model is robust with respect to the free entry and exit of bidders (Corcoran [1984]; Higgins, Shughart, and Tollison [1985]). That is, it naturally generalizes to a concept of a long-run equilibrium of bids and bidders. Rents are perfectly competed away with an endogenous number of bidders, and the prize to the winning rent seeker represents only a normal rate of return on her rent-seeking investment.

Two points about this exact-dissipation result should be kept in mind. First, it is important to understand that this is an equilibrium result under the postulated conditions. Government cannot simply put the regulatory favor or monopoly right up for rebidding and expect that bidders will not adjust their bids for such unexpected takings. If takings are expected, the original bids will reflect the relevant probabilities. Either way, instability in government policy comes to be reflected in a rent-seeking equilibrium outcome. Government cannot simply endlessly bid off regulatory favors. Second, the concept of an equilibrium in a rent-seeking contest does not mean that an incumbent possessor of a monopoly right will not make expenditures to defend and protect his monopoly. But this behavior does not defeat the concept of an equilibrium in the original rent-seeking game; initial bids will be deflated to reflect the expected costs of defending the monopoly right.

The constant-cost rent-seeking game represents a popular equilibrium hypothesis. The exact dissipation model is like the model of perfect competition; it is a useful, though not necessarily descriptive, analytical construct for increasing our understanding of how the world works.

This does not mean, however, that all or even most rent-seeking contests are perfectly competitive in nature. Tullock (1980a) presented classes of models where rent seeking is imperfectly competitive in the sense that the competitive process for rents leads to over- or under-dissipation of the available rents. That is, more or less than the value of the rents is expended to capture them. Rent seeking in these models does not take place under constant-cost conditions. These cases are interesting, and they are generated by assumptions about risk aversion, limitations on the number of bidders, imperfect information, and so on. They are not very popular, however, because imperfect dissipation makes the problem of deriving reduced-form equations with which to estimate rent-seeking costs much more difficult and case-specific (Fisher [1985]). One can no longer simply estimate the area of a trapezoid; rather, the task is to estimate the area of something more or less than a trapezoid that is a function of behavior in the economy. This is clearly a harder modeling problem.

As between Tullock's analysis of over- and under-dissipation possibilities, the over- dissipation possibility does not seem to be very plausible. In this case rent seekers are somehow led to bid more than the value of the prize. That is, they would be better off by not playing the game in the first place. While this is perhaps possible once, through the distortion of information to favor-seekers about their expected chances of winning, such behavior should not persist for long. The regulator/ bureaucrat should be able to mislead only once. In the next round of rent seeking, bids will be adjusted to reflect "true" probabilities of winning; bureaucratic prospects will be properly discounted.[3]

The best known version of a maximalist hypothesis about rent seeking is the black-hole tariff result of S. P. Magee, W. A. Brock, and L. Young (1989). They devise circumstances under which the rate of return to lobbying switches in such a fashion as to lead to huge (proportionately) amounts of the resources in an economy being devoted to lobbying. Indeed, in the black-hole case, almost 100 percent of the economy is devoted to lobbying. This result is driven by assumptions under which the returns to capital from lobbying (versus production) became magnified or arbitrarily large, so that it becomes rational for capital to invest nearly all its resources in redistributive competition. By symmetry, labor follows suit. The returns from lobbying are magnified because of the assumption that changes in product price have very large effects on factor prices. Lobbying consumes almost all productive activity in this stylized economy. This is an important result that deserves further study. A central issue in this regard will be the empirical relevance of the black-hole model. Economic historians may be able to find examples of such cases; the only one that comes immediately to mind is the case of hyperinflations. In general, however, over-dissipation results would seem to be rare, given the theoretical preconditions on which they are based.

Underbidding, where rent-seekers in the aggregate spend less than the value of the prize, is another matter. There are several plausible bases for underbidding equilibria, including risk aversion (Hillman and Katz [1984]), comparative advantage among monopolizing inputs (Rogerson [1982]), and game-theoretic considerations (Tullock [1980a, 1985]). As stressed above, such considerations make the problem of analyzing the costs of rent seeking more difficult and case-specific, but be this as it may, under-dissipation seems to be an intuitively more plausible description of the real world.

A related point is that rent-seeking models may be based on incomplete models. For example, B. M. Owen and R. R. Braeutigam (1978) argue that individuals are willing to pay a lot to reduce risk and attain stability in their lives. This helps explain why, for example, European countries are willing to bear high "rent-seeking" costs in order to finance their social programs. A formal model that incorporates the preference for risk avoidance may thus end up with lower rent-seeking costs.

The minimalist hypothesis is that rent-seeking costs are approximately zero. W. R. Dougan and J. M. Snyder (1993) have argued that there are powerful and plausible incentives to convert rent-seeking costs into transfers. Something close to this same result seems to underlie G. S. Becker's (1983) work on pressure groups, though it is not explicit in his theory. The problem is complex. Obviously, recipients of transfers would prefer to receive them as transfers. If not, rent seekers will find out what the recipients prefer, and give it to them (fishing trips?). Dougan and Snyder argue this point well. They stress that transfers are endogenously determined, and so the social costs of transfers are minimized by successful interest groups.

It will also be generally more efficient for rent seekers to deal in money transfers (bribes). Nonetheless, there is no competitive mechanism that guarantees such a result. If rent-seeking inputs are able, by acting as an interest group themselves, to control the processes of rent assignment, then bribes and auctions for regulatory and other governmental favors will be illegal, and the demand for rent-seeking inputs to compete for such favors will be pervasive. These inputs become, through their own influence, a necessary cost for doing business with the government, and the interest of the rent-seeking inputs resides in maximizing the costs associated with transfers.

The minimalist approach basically implies that the world is efficient. Indeed, the pleas of economists to the contrary are simply part of whatever rent-seeking equilibrium that exists. But how do you test this hypothesis? This is the key.

All this is to say that exact dissipation appears to be a useful general conjecture about equilibrium in rent-seeking contests, but this theory must be adapted to the circumstances of any particular case of rent seeking. Like the model of perfect competition, the model of exactly dissipated rents is a vehicle and starting point for helping us to understand actual rent-seeking processes.

Measurement of Rent-Seeking Costs

There are numerous empirical results on the social costs of rent seeking, depending on the methodology, coverage, and economy analyzed by the author. Krueger (1974) suggested that 7 percent of Indian GNP was wasted in rent seeking and 15 percent of Turkish GNP was lost due to rent seeking for import licenses. Posner (1975) estimated that as much as 3 percent of U.S. GNP was lost due to the social costs of monopolization through regulation. These are obviously substantial amounts of resources in any economy.

Subsequent empirical work in this area has proceeded along a variety of routes. A reasonable amount of work has followed the lead of Krueger in seeking to examine the rent-seeking costs of trade intervention in various economies. In general, these works come up with higher numbers than Krueger. Magee, Brock, and Young (1989, Ch. 15) provide a survey of this research. V. B. Ross (1984), for example, estimated that trade-related rent seeking accounted for 38 percent of GDP in Kenya in 1980.

Other work has attempted to estimate the costs of rent seeking for economies as a whole. This analysis has taken two general forms. First, there are the lawyer regressions. Various authors, including D. W. Laband and J. P. Sophocleus (1985), Magee, Brock, and Young (1989), and K. M. Murphy, A. Shleifer, and R. W. Vishny (1990), have included lawyers in various regression formats set up to explain GNP or rates of growth in GNP, both in the United States and across countries. The robust conclusion of this work is: more lawyers, lower growth, lower GNP. Some of these admittedly simplistic regression estimates suggest that lawyers reduce aggregate income by as much as 45 percent.

Eschewing a regression-based approach, Laband and Sophocleus (1992) attempted an aggregate, sector-by-sector accounting of rent-seeking costs in the U.S. economy. They counted expenditures on such items as locks, insurance, police, and military expenditures as being driven by rent-seeking or rent-protecting incentives. On this basis they estimated that almost one-half of the U.S. GNP in 1985 was consumed by such costs. Their approach will surely be controversial. A small sample of the categories that they treated as rent-seeking/rent-protecting costs include crime prevention (FBI), police (corrections), restraint of trade (FTC), residential investments (locks), commercial investments (guards), educational (library theft), property rights disputes (tort litigation), and government (defense, lobbyists, PACS). Following an accounting-like procedure, these authors go sector-by-sector to obtain their estimates of rent-seeking costs.

The results of the various studies are summarized in Table 1. In one sense, the table shows the importance of the rent-seeking insight. No longer can the costs of tariffs, monopolies, and theft be called a trivial issue in virtually any economy.

Table 1. Estimates of the Costs of Rent Seeking

Study	Economy	Year	Rent-Seeking Costs
Krueger (1974)	India	1964	7 % of GNP
Krueger (1974)	Turkey	1968	15 % of GNP (trade sector)
Posner (1975)	U.S.	various years	3 % of GNP(regulation)
Cowling and Mueller (1978)	U.S.	1963–1966	13 % of GCP* (private monopoly)
Cowling and Mueller (1978)	U.K.	1968/69	7 % of GCP* (private monopoly)
Ross (1984)	Kenya	1980	38 % of GDP (trade sector)
Mohammand and Whalley (1984)	India	1980/81	25 to 40 % of GNP
Laband and Sophocleus (1992)	U.S.	1985	50 % of GNP
Regression-based studies	various countries	various years	Up to 45 % of GNP

* Cowling and Mueller (1978) use gross corporate product as the basis of their calculation.

As with all empirical work, these various approaches are only as good as the theories and models upon which they are based. Buying a lock is a response to the security of property rights in a society. This security can be produced in a variety of ways, including moral exhortation, but in the face of the relevant probabilities, buying a lock can hardly be seen as an unproductive investment. Given the prevailing ethos, a lock protects property rights, and the protection of property rights enhances the productivity of resources over what they could produce without the lock. To argue that one can be wealthier without locks and lawyers implies that there are feasible reforms in behavior that will reduce such costs. This is certainly believable, but this is exactly the burden that estimators of the costs of rent seeking face. The lock and the lawyer are only wasteful to the extent that these resources can be feasiblely reallocated to more productive uses. Alternatively, contributions to churches can be regarded as substitutes for locks.

In principle, the cost of rent seeking is simply the increase in GNP that would result if a feasible way to reallocate resources from locks and lawyers to more productive uses could be found by a political entrepreneur. This figure could be high or low, but it is probably low given the ability of rent-seeking inputs to resist such reallocations. And the mere resistance of the inputs is yet another reason not to waste resources attempting such a reallocation (Wagner and Tollison [1991]).

The bias of this argument is apparent—the range and extent of feasible reform in the rent-seeking society is not large, and the logic of this argument is inherent in the theory of rent seeking. Reform will be resisted, and this resistance is one-for-one a social cost of reform. When one says that rent seeking costs an economy X percent of GNP, this is tantamount to saying nothing of particular importance. Perhaps more fairly, one is reminded of F. M. Fisher, Z. Griliches, and C. Kaysen's (1962) estimates of the costs of automobile styling charges. These authors did not present their estimates as social costs, but simply as a type of "bill" that the consumer had to pay. As with all such bills, the question was simply, is it worth it? This is the spirit in which estimates of the costs of rent seeking should be understood.

Rent Protection

Not only do individuals use real resources to seek transfers, but as noted previously, they also sometimes use real resources to protect their rents from encroachment by other rent seekers. In contrast to rent seeking, this behavior is called rent protection. The basis for such behavior is clear. Not all "suppliers" of wealth transfers find it economically rational to allow their wealth to be taken away (why spend a dollar to save a dime?). However, some will find it worthwhile to fight back (spend a dollar to save two dollars).

The simple example of an excise tax on a competitive industry will illustrate the concept of rent protection. In Figure 1, as a result of an excise tax on the industry's product, the industry supply curve shifts from S to S'. The traditional analysis of this case stresses three basic results: (1) ABG is the deadweight cost of the tax; (2) EAGF is the tax revenue that is transferred to the government; and (3) the incidence of the tax is split between consumers (C) and producers (P) as a function of the elasticities of demand and supply.

Assume that consumers are unorganized and have no rational incentive to organize to resist the loss of consumer surplus that the tax imposes on them. However, let producers be organized and prepared to lobby against the tax. In the case at hand, producers may rationally spend up to their loss of producer surplus, P_CBGF, to resist the tax or to keep it from being higher than it is. These expenditures are a rent-seeking (rent-

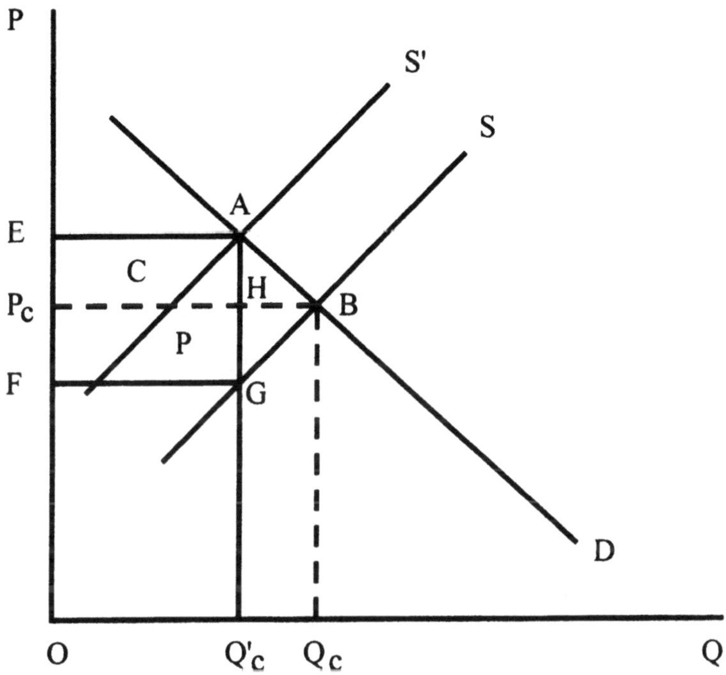

Figure 1. Rent Protection and Excise Taxation.

protecting) cost in Tullock's terms, and so they must be added to the traditional cost of the excise tax, ABG, to obtain the total social cost of excise taxation in this case, P_CBGF plus ABG.[4] Obviously, if consumers organize to resist the tax, the social costs of tax resistance rise even further.

It is a mainstay of optimal taxation theory that the excess burden imposed by selective excise taxation (ABG) is minimized, for a given amount of revenue raised, when such taxes are placed on commodities with relatively inelastic demand curves. Unfortunately, this rule cannot stand up to the above analysis. It is quite easy to show that when P_CBGF is counted as part of the social cost of excise taxation, taxing an industry with a more elastic demand curve, but with no organized, rent-protecting opposition to the tax, is socially preferable. Moreover, considerations of monopoly only strengthen the analysis.[5]

Virtually all welfare analyses of monopoly and regulation ignore rent-protection activities of organized opponents of such governmental programs. A more general welfare analytics will include traditional deadweight costs, rent-seeking costs, and rent- protecting costs. An important contribution to this literature in recent years is F. S. McChesney's (1987, 1997) concept of rent extraction. In these works he derives results on rent seeking in which regulation or legislation is threatened and then withdrawn as a way to stimulate the formation of interest groups from which politicians can exact tribute.

Rent Seeking and the Distribution of Income

Before Tullock, the effect of monopoly on the distribution of income was clear—the monopolist got richer and consumers got poorer (Comanor and Smiley [1975]); monopoly rents were simple transfers. In the rent-seeking approach, the impact of monopoly on income distribution is a more complicated issue. Of the original formulators of the theory, only Posner relates his analysis to the distribution of income. He states: "There is no reason to think that monopoly has a significant distributive effect. Consumers' wealth is not transferred to the shareholders of monopoly firms; it is dissipated in the purchase of inputs into the activity of becoming a monopolist" (1975: 821).

Posner's argument seems logical. Rent seeking dissipates monopoly rents, translating potential transfers into social costs. The effect of monopoly on the distribution of income in the rent-seeking society would thus appear to be nil. However, the argument needs to be scrutinized further.

Using the simple example employed by Posner, suppose that there are $1 million in rents to be captured and ten risk-neutral bidders for a monopoly right. Each bidder bids $100,000 for the franchise; $1 million is spent to capture $1 million; at a social level the monopoly rents are exactly wasted. The example, however, embodies a distributional consequence. Clearly, one of the ten bidders wins the competition, and receives a net return on his efforts of $900,000. Without more information, one cannot clearly say in this stylized example whether rent seeking increases or decreases the degree of inequality in the distribution of income. The most logical presumption, given that rent seekers earn normal rates of return on their investments in rent seeking, is that consumers (poor?) are worse off and rent seekers (rich?) are no better off than before. A type of low-level, wasteful inequality is thereby generated. It seems a little far-fetched, however, to think that rent seeking generally promotes a leveling or only a mild inequality in the income distribution. Set in a world of tradition, class, privilege, power, and differential organization costs, rent seeking likely promotes significant inequalities in the distribution of income.

Perhaps more realistically, there will not be an equal distribution of rent- seeking ability in a society. Thus, the mechanism by which rents are assigned is likely to affect the distribution of wealth to the extent that Ricardian rents are earned in rent seeking. Consider a regulatory hearing mechanism for assigning rents, and suppose that some lawyers or economists earn inframarginal rents in rent seeking. On average, these individuals will be wealthier than their marginal competitors and wealthier than they would be without a rent-seeking mechanism of the particular type that rewards their skills. The choice of such a transfer mechanism increases the demand for lawyers (and possibly economists) above that which would hold with (say) an auction mechanism for assigning monopoly rents. So, first of all, the mechanism will alter the distribution of wealth by occupation. Moreover, if the requisite talents of the favored occupation cannot be reproduced at constant costs, the inequality of wealth in society may be further affected. For example, suppose the qualities of a good businessman/speculator are more fungible among the population than the qualities of a good lawyer. Then, inframarginal rents will accrue to the best of the legal profession in regulatory hearing cases, whereas with an auction no Ricardian rents would be earned. The distribution of wealth would differ between these two societies as a consequence.[6]

Reform in the Rent-Seeking Society

Once the Pandora's box of rent seeking has been opened, great difficulties confront any theory of economic reform. The reason is simple—the objects of reform (monopolists and transfer recipients in general) will spend resources to resist reform and to protect their transfers. As stressed above, these rent-protecting expenditures are the simple analogues of rent-seeking expenditures—they are one-for-one social costs just as rent-seeking expenditures are. And the point is not just that such expenditures will defeat reform initiatives in a political setting, it is that such expenditures defeat the utilitarian rationale for such deregulatory effects. An incumbent monopolist will easily find it worthwhile to defeat a utilitarian reformer by spending enough of its monopoly rents to make deregulation socially unprofitable (Tollison and Wagner [1991]). This is the difficulty in achieving any analytical rationale for reform in a rent-seeking society.

The presumption of a passive monopoly underlies typical discussions of the social value of economic reform. But such passivity is implausible in most circumstances. For an intentional monopolist who sought actively to secure a monopoly position, sudden passivity when confronted by a reformer is inexplicable. But it is the same for an accidental monopolist. To come into a position of receiving *T* per period without having had to expend anything to get the transfer does nothing to make the recipient more eager to relinquish the transfer. A monopolist will resist the reformer's efforts in any event.

To assess the gain from economic reform in the presence of an active monopoly, the gain in the case of a passive monopoly (*H* [Harberger costs]) must be reduced by the cost of bringing about and maintaining the reform. The reformer must expend resources in trying to secure the reform. But the reformer's efforts to do so will induce the monopolist to resist. A utilitarian reformer will count both his costs in trying to secure reform and the monopolist's costs in resisting reform as subtractions from the potential gain from that reform (*H*).

There are several ways of showing that a utilitarian reformer would not try to reform an active monopolist. One way is simply to ask how much the monopolist would be willing to spend to avoid being reformed into a competitive industry. The answer here is "up to *T*," which exceeds *H*. Any expenditure less than *T* will leave the monopolist better off than she would be if she were reformed into a competitive industry. And any expenditure in excess of *H* by the monopolist will render the value of the reform negative to the utilitarian reformer.

To be sure, this simple formulation of the matter begs some pertinent questions. The monopolist would spend up to *T* if he were assured of success, but would spend less if the reformer had some likelihood of success. But how much would the reformer spend in trying to secure reform? It would normally be expected that both the reformer and the monopolist would make some expenditure in securing and resisting reform, the result being that each side has a chance of winning. One simple way to model this process is to assume that both the monopolist and the reformer are risk neutral, with each side's chance of success being equal to its spending as a share of total spending. In this setting the monopolist can induce the reformer to choose alternative employment by spending H in defending his monopoly. Thus, for an expenditure of H, the monopolist can be certain of retaining $T - H$.

There are, of course, alternative ways to model this process. Moreover, reform may still proceed under a distributional rationale about monopoly, regulation, and transfers; but this is a different story. The moral of this story is not completely nihilistic. The important point is to prevent the emergence of socially unproductive transfers in the first place. This falls into the realm of constitutional economics and the prevention of certain types of transfers (tariffs) from arising through the operation of ordinary politics (Buchanan, 1980a). And, finally, the discussion here is perhaps too static. If reform and deregulation stimulate entrepreneurship and higher productivity, the compound effects of economic growth clearly tilt any social calculus such as this one toward economic reform.

The Positive Economics of Rent Seeking

The theory of rent seeking has been advanced as an evaluatory theory. It is a procedure to evaluate reforms that can lead to potentially lower social costs in the economy. In this sense the theory of rent seeking is a normative theory. The idea that political behavior is motivated by wealth transfers also has a long tradition as a positive economic theory of regulation and government.[7] A thumbnail sketch of this theory will round out this essay on rent seeking.

One way to think about legislation is in terms of the interest group theory of government. Individual citizens can want or demand laws for any reason—for example, the law makes the world a better place, the law promotes the production of a public good, the law makes them wealthier, and so forth—but will generally act in some group context to obtain the passage of a desired law or the defeat of an undesired law.

A basic principle as well as a basic conundrum underlies the demand for legislation. The principle is that groups who can organize for less than \$1 in order to obtain \$1 of benefits from legislation will be the effective demanders of laws. The conundrum is that economists have little idea about how successful interest groups are formed. That is, how do groups overcome free-rider problems and organize for collective action so as to be able to seek \$1 for less than \$1? The plain truth is that economists know very little about the dynamics of group formation and action. Olson (1965) offered a by-product theory of interest group formation in which a private good was provided to members at a monopoly price, with the monopoly profit being used to finance interest group activities. G. J. Stigler (1974) later criticized this theory on the grounds that there was no reason to assume that the interest group had any monopoly power over the sales of the by-product. What has not been generally recognized is that this is a testable proposition. The Sierra Club, for example, may very well face a downward sloping and inelastic demand curve for its calendars.

Indeed, for whatever reason that organization is undertaken, lobbying for special interest legislation becomes a relatively low-cost by-product of being organized. Lawyers may agree collectively to a code of ethics to address such matters as attorney-client privilege and then proceed to adopt provisions in their code that restrict competition among lawyers. A firm is an example of an organization that can be used for lobbying purposes at very low marginal cost, and so is a labor union.

In the interest group theory, the supply of legislation is an inverse demand curve. Those who "supply" wealth transfers are individuals who do not find it cost effective to resist having their wealth taken away. In other words, it costs them more than $1 to resist having $1 taken away.[8] This concept of a supply curve of legislation or regulation suggests that the costs of political activity to some individuals exceed the potential gains (or avoided losses). The supply of legislation is, therefore, grounded in the unorganized or relatively less-organized members of society.

The individuals who monitor the supply-demand process are politicians, bureaucrats, and other political actors. These individuals may be conceived of as brokers of legislation, and they essentially act like brokers in a private context—they pair demanders and suppliers of legislation. That is, they seek to pair those who want a law or a transfer the most with those who object to it the least. In the usual logic of the interest group theory, brokers will concentrate on legal arrangements that benefit well-organized and concentrated groups for whom the pro-rata benefits are high at the expense of diffuse interests, each of whom is taxed a little bit to fund the transfer or legislation. By efficiently pairing demanders and suppliers of legislation, political brokers establish an equilibrium in the market for legislation, and this equilibrium is disciplined by periodic elections.

Perhaps the most basic issue related to the demand for legislation is how to explain why laws persist over time. That is, why is the work of one legislature not overturned by the next legislature? W. M. Landes and Posner (1975) sought to answer this question by addressing the role of the independent judiciary in promoting durable legislation. Their analysis was framed in terms of the interest group theory of government. Obviously, an interest group would not bid very much for a protective statute if it lasted only for the current legislative session and was repealed by the next legislature. To be worth anything to the interest group, a law must be durable—that is, it must have a present value of benefits that exceeds the costs of obtaining it.

Landes and Posner focused on the role of the independent judiciary in this regard. They posited that the institutional arrangements surrounding judgeships lead judges to behave so as to resolve legal disputes in terms of what the propounding legislature actually intended. Given that independent judges actually behave in this manner, the present value demand curve for legislation rotates to the right, and laws become more valuable because they last longer. The enacting legislature's intent is upheld in this theory of the independent judiciary, making each legislature's actions more durable and worth more to interest groups.[9]

Other margins of the political process can be extended to increase the durability of legislation. The institutions of the legislature can make it costly to repeal a law once it is passed, and interest groups can seek their rents through constitutional provisions (hence, more durable) rather than ordinary legislation. Bicameralism, constitutional amendments, the committee system, and majority size are just a few of the ways in which the durability of legislation can be increased. The point is that the independent judiciary is not the only institutional margin by which the value of the legislative system as an "exchange process" can be maximized. And, indeed, one can argue that the system was designed and has evolved through time to solidify an exchange process between interest groups and political brokers.

As noted previously, this is just a sketch of the positive economic theory of rent seeking. Suffice it to say in closing that this is a testable (and tested) theory of government and political behavior, which is gaining more adherents over time as scholarly theories of the state begin to square up with the daily newspaper headlines and stories about government.[10]

I thank Price Fishback, Gary Libecap, William Shughart, and Edward Zajac for helpful comments. The usual caveat applies.

[1] For related surveys of the theory of rent seeking, see Tollison (1982, 1987, 1997, 1998).

[2] Keep in mind the previous point that rents here are not transfers or bribes, but must be expended in real resources devoted to regulatory favor seeking.

[3] Casual evidence can be gathered by playing the so called "Brennan Game" with your class. Offer $5 as the prize. Ask the students to write down their bids for the $5 and seal them without communicating with their fellow students. All bids must be paid to the professor; the professor funds any losses and pockets any profits from the contest. Collusion among bidders can also be allowed. Results vary, but the contest illustrates in a practical way the complex nature of rent-seeking contests.

[4] Note that there is no double-counting involved in this calculation; the triangle, HBG, enters twice.

[5] For more analysis along these lines, see Lee and Tollison (1988).

[6] For more discussion along these lines, see Higgins and Tollison (1988).

[7] See Stigler (1971), Peltzman (1976), McCormick and Tollison (1981), and Becker (1983).

[8] "Supply" as used in this context is not the ordinary concept of voluntary supply at higher prices. It is voluntary in the sense that giving up $1 is cheaper than spending $10 to resist giving up $1. It is not voluntary in the sense that the state is a coercive set of institutions.

[9] Note that the judiciary is not really "independent" in this theory.

[10] See Tollison (1988, 1991) for surveys of the positive economic theory of rent seeking.

REFERENCES

Barzel, Y. (1974). "A Theory of Rationing by Waiting." *Journal of Law and Economics* 17: 73–96.

Becker, G. S. (1983). "A Theory of Competition among Pressure Groups for Political Influence." *Quarterly Journal of Economics* 97 (August): 371–400.

Bhagwati, J. N. (1980). "Lobbying and Welfare." *Journal of Public Economics* 14 (December): 355–63.

______. (1982). "Directly Unproductive Profit-seeking Activities." *Journal of Political Economy,* 90 (October): 988–1002.

Buchanan, J. M. (1980)." Rent Seeking and Profit Seeking." In J. M. Buchanan, R. D. Tollison, and G. Tullock (Eds.), *Toward a Theory of the Rent-Seeking Society,* 3–15. College Station: Texas A&M University Press.

______ (1983). "Rent-Seeking, Noncompensated Transfers, and Laws of Succession." *Journal of Law and Economics* 26 (April): 71–86.

______ (1987). "The Qualities of a Natural Economist." In C. K. Rowley (Ed.), *Democracy and Public Choice*, 9–19. Oxford: Oxford University Press.

Cheung, S. N. S. (1974). "A Theory of Price Control." *Journal of Law and Economics* 17: 53–72.

Comanor, W. S., and R. H. Smiley (1975). "Monopoly and the Distribution of Wealth." *Quarterly Journal of Economics* 89 (May): 177–94.

Congleton, R. D. (1988). "Evaluating Rent-Seeking Losses: Do the Welfare Gains of Lobbyists Count?" *Public Choice* 56: 181–84.

Corcoran, W. J. (1984). "Long-Run Equilibrium and Total Expenditures in Rent-Seeking." *Public Choice* 43: 89–94.
Cowling, K., and D. C. Mueller (1978). "The Social Costs of Monopoly Power." *Economic Journal* 88: 727–48.
Dougan, W. R., and J. M. Snyder (1993). "Are Rents Fully Dissipated?" *Public Choice* 77: 793–813.
Fisher, F. M. (1985). "The Social Costs of Monopoly and Regulation: Posner Reconsidered." *Journal of Political Economy* 93 (April): 10–16.
Fisher, F. M., Z. Griliches, and C. Kaysen (1962). "The Costs of Automobile Model Changes since 1949." *Journal of Political Economy* 70 (October): 433–51.
Frank, R. H. (1986). *Choosing the Right Pond*. Oxford: Oxford University Press.
Harberger, A. C. (1984). "Monopoly and Resource Allocation." *American Economic Review* 44 (May): 77–87.
Higgins, R., W. F. Shughart, and R. D. Tollison (1985). "Free Entry and Efficient Rent- Seeking." *Public Choice* 46: 247–58.
Higgins, R., and R. D. Tollison (1985). "Life among the Triangles and Trapezoids: Notes on the Theory of Rent Seeking." In C. K. Rowley, R. D. Tollison, and G. Tullock (Eds.), *The Political Economy of Rent- seeking*, 147–57. Boston: Kluwer.
Hillman, A. L., and E. Katz (1984). "Risk-Averse Rent-Seekers and the Social Cost of Monopoly Power." *Economic Journal* 94 (March): 104–10.
Kreuger, A O (1974). "The Political Economy of the Rent-Seeking Society." *American Economic Review* 64 (June): 291–303.
Laband, D. W., and J. P. Sophocleus (1992). "An Estimate of Resource Expenditures on Transfer Activity in the United States." *Quarterly Journal of Economics* 107 (August): 959–84.
______ "The Social Cost of Rent Seeking: First Estimates." *Public Choice* 58 (September): 269–75.
Landes, W. M. and R. A. Posner (1975). "The Independent Judiciary in an Interest-Group Perspective." *Journal of Law and Economics* 18 (December): 875–901.
Lee, D. R., and R. D. Tollison (1988)." Optimal Taxation in a Rent-Seeking Environment." In C. K. Rowley, R. D. Tollison, and G. Tullock (Eds.), *The Political Economy of Rent-Seeking*, 339–50. Boston: Kluwer.
Magee, S. P., W. A. Brock, and L. Young (1989). *Black Hole Tariffs and Endogenous Policy Theory*. Cambridge: Cambridge University Press.
McChesney, Fred S. (1987). "Rent Extraction and Interest-Group Formation in a Coasean Model of Regulation." *Journal of Legal Studies* 20: 73–90.
______ (1997). *Money for Nothing*. Cambridge: Harvard University Press.
McCloskey, D. N. (1987). *The Writing of Economics*. New York: MacMillan.
McCormick, R. E., and R. D. Tollison (1981). *Politicians, Legislation, and the Economy*. Boston: Kluwer.
Mohammed, S., and J. Whalley (1984). "Rent Seeking in India: Its Costs and Policy Significance." *Kyklos* 37: 387–413.
Mundell, R. A. (1962). "Review of L. H. Janssen: Free Trade, Protection and Customs Unions." *American Economic Review* 52 (June): 622.
Murphy, K. M., A. Schleifer, and R. W. Vishny (1991). "The Allocation of Talent: Implications for Growth." *Quarterly Journal of Economics* 106 (June): 503–31.
Olson, M. (1965). *The Logic of Collective Action*. Cambridge, MA: Harvard University Press.
Owen, B. M., and R. R. Braeutigam (1978). *The Regulation Game: Strategic Use of the Administrative Process*. Cambridge: Ballinger.
Peltzman, S. (1976). "Toward a More General Theory of Regulation." *Journal of Law and Economic* 2 (August): 211–40.
Posner, R. A. (1975). "The Social Costs of Monopoly and Regulation." *Journal of Political Economy* 83 (August): 807–27.
Rogerson, W. P. (1982). "The Social Costs of Monopoly and Regulation: A Game-Theoretic Analysis." *Bell Journal of Economics* 13 (Autumn): 391–401.
Ross, V. B. (1984). "Rent-Seeking in LDC Import Regimes: The Case of Kenya." Discussion Papers in International Economics: No. 8408. Graduate Institute of International Studies: Geneva.
Stigler, G. J. (1971). "The Theory of Economic Regulation." *Bell Journal of Economics and Management Science* 5 (Spring): 321.
______ (1974). "Free Riders and Collective Action." *Bell Journal of Economics and Management Science*

5 (Autumn): 359–65.

Tollison, R. D. (1982). "Rent Seeking: A Survey." *Kyklos* 35 (4): 575–602.

_____ (1987). "Is the Theory of Rent Seeking Here to Stay?" In C. K. Rowley (Ed.), *Democracy and Public Choice,* 143–57. London: Blackwell.

_____ (1988). "Public Choice and Legislation." *Virginia Law Review* 74 (March): 339–71.

_____ (1991). "Regulation and Interest Groups." In J. High. (Ed.), *Regulation: Economic Theory and History,* 59–76. Ann Arbor: University of Michigan Press.

_____ (1997). "Rent Seeking." In D. Mueller (Ed.), *Perspectives on Public Choice,* 506–25. Cambridge: Cambridge University Press.

_____ (1998). "The Theory of Rent Seeking." In P. Newman (Ed.), *The New Palgrave Dictionary of Economics and the Law,* 315–22. London: MacMillan.

Tollison, R .D., and R. E. Wagner (1991). "Romance, Reality, and Economic Reform." *Kyklos* 44 (1): 57–70.

Tullock, G. (1967). "The Welfare Costs of Tariffs, Monopolies, and Theft." *Western Economic Journal* 5 (June): 224–32.

_____ (1980a). "Efficient Rent-Seeking." In J. M. Buchanan, R. D. Tollison, and G. Tullock (Eds.), *Toward a Theory of the Rent-Seeking Society,* 97–112. College Station: Texas A&M University Press.

_____ (1980b). "Rent-Seeking as a Negative-Sum Game." In J. M. Buchanan, R. D. Tollison, and G. Tullock (Eds.), *Toward a Theory of the Rent-Seeking Society,* 16–36. College Station: Texas A&M University Press.

_____ (1985). "Back to the Bog." *Public Choice* 46: 259–64.

POLITICAL CULTURE AND ECONOMIC PERFORMANCE IN SUB-SAHARAN AFRICA

Charles K. Rowley
Department of Economics
George Mason University
Fairfax, VA 22030
U.S.A.

INTRODUCTION

The second half of the twentieth century has been a period of economic stagnation if not decline throughout most of sub-Saharan Africa (henceforth abbreviated to Africa). As recent statistical studies show, many Africans are worse off than they were at the commencement of independence, afflicted with serious health and nutrition problems and with a badly eroded economic infrastructure. Furthermore, many Africans are less economically free now than their predecessors were prior to independence.

The dismal economic performance of much of Africa since independence can be explained only in part by conventional economic analysis. At least of equal importance are malignant political institutions that have their genesis in the Treaty of Berlin (1884), whereby the continent was divided into colonies that were shared out among the major European imperial powers party to that Treaty. The colonial powers conferred economic and educational privileges on elite African tribes, using the latter to maintain internal order often under relatively loose imperial supervision.

At independence, such *elites* assumed political power and quickly subverted fragile democracies into autocracies as they pursued policies of overt rent-extraction similar to those that had been deployed by their imperial predecessors. African leaders consolidated malignant political cultures hostile to economic development in order to loot their countries of the rents that these adverse economic and political institutions created.

This essay will argue, (following Ake, 1996), that the ready assumption among development economists that there has been a failure of development in Africa is misleading. Development has not failed. Rather, it has rarely been on the agenda of the governments that succeeded the imperialist powers. Responsibility for this failure of development is shared among the African leaders, the *elites* that have maintained them in power, the evolving institutions, and the political organizations deliberately fashioned to promote rent-seeking and rent-extraction policies.

In short, the economic problems of Africa and the absence of economic freedom there have their roots in public-choice impediments. Because these impediments have lasted so long, it is inappropriate to explain them as the consequence of error. The thrust of this essay is to explain them as the consequence of deliberate design, not by outsiders, but by dominant *elites* within their respective indigenous populations.

THE EVIDENCE

The lowering of the British flag and the raising of the flag of the new nation of Ghana at midnight on March 6, 1957 is generally recognized as the beginning of the independence period in Africa. By 1965, much of the rest of Africa had gained its independence. In these early years, Africa as a whole, rich in natural resources, was compared favorably with East Asia as a promising development region. Yet, by the late 1980s, when real per capita income in South Korea had increased by 700 percent, average real per capita income in Africa had not increased at all and in many countries had actually declined.

This stunning outcome was the result of two trends in Africa: very low overall economic growths rates combined with high rates of population growth (Lancaster, [1999] 19). From 1973 to 1980, the annual economic growth rate for Africa was 2.5 percent. From 1980 to 1990, the annual average economic growth rate declined to 0.5 percent. Throughout this period, population growth rates accelerated, rising from an average of 2.5 percent in 1960 to more than 3 percent per annum in the late 1980s. These rapid increases in population increasingly overwhelmed income growth during these decades leading to significant declines in real per capita income throughout the 1980s.

During the 1980s, per capita GDP declined by 1.3 percent per annum, a truly appalling record, 5 percentage points below the average for all low-income countries. During the period 1990–1994, this decline accelerated to 1.8 percent per annum, and the gap between Africa and all other low income countries widened to 6.2 percentage points per annum (Collier and Gunning [1999] 64). In consequence Africa as a whole remains by far the poorest area in the world at the closing of the twentieth century even though annual growth rates in per capita GDP have struggled into the positive range since 1994 (Lancaster [1999] 19).

Economic poverty in Africa is accompanied by an acute absence of economic freedom. In 1998, of 42 sub-Saharan African countries graded in terms of economic freedom (Johnson, Holmes and Kirkpatrick 1999) not one received a rating of "free." Only seven countries received a rating of "mostly free," while 27 countries were rated as "mostly unfree," and eight were rated as "repressed." Furthermore, economic freedom actually declined across the sub-continent during 1998 as African leaders continued to invade such property rights as their citizens had struggled to stake out in environments alien to the rule of law. A few African countries still tolerate slavery despite widespread international repugnance concerning this odious practice.

It is not surprising, in such circumstances, that Africa is viewed as the "Dark Continent" and is largely written off as a non-player in the newly emerging global world economy.

CONVENTIONAL RATIONALIZATIONS OF ECONOMIC MALFUNCTION IN AFRICA

The problems of African poverty and economic stagnation have attracted a great deal of attention in the literature of development economics. Much of this discussion has done little more than scratch the surface of the problem, often in an extremely misleading way.

One set of rationalizations has focused on the environmental inheritance of Africa. Apologists argue that the physical characteristics of much of the region—a harsh and unpredictable climate, non-navigable rivers, weathered and often fragile soils, and the high incidence of debilitating diseases—make development an especially difficult challenge (Lancaster [1999] 21). This inheritance is made worse by the fact that most African countries gained independence at an early stage of development, with a limited infrastructure, few educated nationals, subsistence agriculture, and almost no other industries.

Many other countries have overcome similarly unpromising inheritances and have not found them to represent insuperable obstacles to economic progress. Most of East Asia has overwhelmed such initial handicaps as their populations have become relatively wealthy. South Korea, for example, was confronted in the mid-1950s with few natural resources, little industry, and a war-devastated infrastructure.

The colonial inheritance has also been advanced as an explanation for economic stagnation in Africa. Marxist scholars, in particular, attribute African underdevelopment to the alleged colonial exploitation of the region. It is argued that the region is peripheral and economically weak because it was forced by the colonial powers to export primary products at relatively low prices and to import manufactured goods from capitalist countries at relatively high prices. As a result, capital effectively was withdrawn from the region, dooming it to perpetual poverty.

Even if this account is correct—and it is not uncontroversial—past colonial exploitation can hardly explain the continued absence of economic growth in the region some forty years after its political independence. The evident economic success of formerly poor and economically peripheral countries in Asia and Latin America undercuts the force of such rationalizations, even if plain commonsense does not.

The relatively low levels of investment and of saving evident in Africa are also advanced as an explanation of economic stagnation. Development economists argue that poor countries must invest roughly a quarter of GDP in order to achieve rates of growth that will raise them from poverty. In fact, the rate of investment in the region has fallen well short of this objective, averaging 20 percent over the period 1960 to 1980, and then declining to 16 percent throughout the 1980s. Despite recovering to 18.5 percent by the mid-1990s the rate remains little more than half that maintained by low-income countries worldwide in 1995. Despite the low value of the capital stock, available data show a low and declining rate of productivity of investment in Africa (Lancaster [1999] 20).

Savings rates have also been low across Africa, averaging 19 percent of GDP between 1965 and 1973, 23 percent between 1974 and 1980 ,and 16 percent during the 1990s. Only 12 of 42 sub-Saharan countries recorded savings rates in excess of 15 percent in 1996, and four of those were petroleum exporters (Lancaster [1999] 20). Undeniably, the data on investment and savings rates suggest that important elements in the growth equation have long been weak within the region. The data themselves do not explain why this chronic weakness continues to manifest itself.

The difference between savings and investment rates is made up with foreign aid, foreign borrowing, and foreign investment. Attempts have been made to rationalize African economic stagnation in terms of the failure of the aid program. Such attempts are ludicrous. Over the past five decades, it has been unusual for foreign aid to exceed 2 percent of any country's GNP. For 35 countries in Africa, foreign aid has exceeded 5 percent of GNP throughout the past twenty years and has tended to increase over that period reaching more than 10 percent in a number of countries. In the singular case of Somalia foreign aid in 1990 equaled 237 percent of GNP.

Development economists usually emphasize the importance of foreign aid as the key to sustaining high rates of investment in poor countries. In 1992–1993, aid amounted to 50 percent or more of total investment in 29 sub-Saharan African countries. In 13 of those countries it was equivalent to more than 100 percent of investment. We shall argue in this essay that far too much aid has gone to Africa, with alarming implications for both economic performance and political culture. Such arguments take us beyond conventional economic analysis into the economic analysis of politics.

THE POST-COLONIAL POLITICAL INHERITANCE

The present political situation in much of Africa has its roots in the international conference held in Berlin in 1884 under the chairmanship of Otto von Bismarck when Belgium, France, Britain, Germany and Portugal were staking out their respective colonial stakes on the African continent (Rowley 1998). On February 26, 1885, the Berlin Act was promulgated, laying down the rules of partition for the continent. On this basis, Africa was divided up into colonies and transformed into appendages of the leading European imperial powers. Boundaries were drawn up with little regard for demographic and tribal configurations, usually to facilitate colonial development of natural resources (Mbaku [1993] 24). By 1910, the partition of Africa was complete and, for the following 45 years, only Liberia and Ethiopia remained independent nations (Kimenyi [1997] 12–14).

Africa's colonial experience is an important factor to be taken into account in analyzing the nature of the political institutions and the broader political culture that emerged following grants of independence (Rowley [1998]). First, the colonists coercively integrated different ethnic and tribal groups, ignoring differences in culture and social systems. Second, in order to maintain internal stability, the colonial powers only rarely encouraged the development of participatory forms of government prior to independence.

Third, in order to divide and rule, the colonial powers failed to treat different ethnic and tribal groups equally, with damaging consequences for the post-independence era. Most of the educated, skilled members of the indigenous populations, at independence, had been cultivated in the European languages and had embraced elitist aspects of the European culture. They would seize the apparatus of government and dominate many of the post-independence political markets. This concentration of political power would have damaging consequences for the emergence of efficient political systems (Mbaku [1993]).

Fourth, the potential leaders who had been educated in European (and especially in British) elite universities had been indoctrinated in socialist political philosophy and in the economics of John Maynard Keynes. This disastrous colonial legacy accentuated the immediate post-independence drift towards pan-African socialism, characterized by highly centralized governments and by highly politicized economic markets (Rowley [1998]).

With few exceptions, Africans gained their independence not by defeating the colonial regimes, but as a gift (albeit often a reluctant gift) from their colonizers. The imperial powers essentially handed over power to their chosen African successors, successors educated in their systems and supposedly attentive to their interests (Ake [1996] 3). The *elites* that inherited such political *largesse*, moved quickly to consolidate it, attempting to marginalize economically and to disenfranchise politically those who might compete with them for the apparatus of government.

In many instances—for example, Nigeria, Ghana, Ivory Coast, Sierra Leone, Cameroon, Zambia, Uganda, and Zaire—centrifugal forces were so pronounced by the date of independence as to threaten the political viability of the new governments. As coalition partners withdrew, the battle for control over the apparatus of government assumed an importance out of all proportion to Western experience as tribes, ethnic groups, and regional interest groups vied for the rents that political control was seen to offer. Political leaders seized upon such centrifugal tendencies to create sectional support for their own programs, thereby further weakening already fragile national bonds.

The new African leaders typically were neither personally wealthy nor were they experienced in protecting the economic rights of others. In many instances, they succumbed to the temptation to use government power as a basis for the personal accumulation of wealth. Since they had no entrepreneurial experience, the only basis for such wealth accumulation was the diversion of resources, too often provided in the form of international aid, away from processes of economic development into personal numbered bank accounts in Switzerland and elsewhere.

For the most part, the European powers prior to independence had behaved like bandits, extracting the wealth of sub-Saharan Africa for the benefit of their own peoples. However, because the territories allocated among them by the Treaty of Berlin remained in their possession over lengthy periods of time, the colonial powers viewed themselves as *stationary bandits* in the sense of M. C. McGuire and M. Olson (1996). Because stationary bandits enjoy a monopoly of theft, they have a stable and encompassing interest in the domain over which their power is exercised. For this reason, their selfish economic incentive is to improve productive capacity in order to raise the stock of wealth available as the basis for their thieving.

Rational stationary bandits limit their rates of theft in order to create an environment in which society's production will increase. To this end, they endorse minimalist laws designed to protect the property rights of their subjects from internal anarchy. They defend their monopoly of theft against potential internal and external aggressors. They even provide a limited social infrastructure of public goods designed to augment the productivity of their subjects. The European Empires were differentially rational in this regard, with the British Empire markedly more far-sighted than the rest.

With few exceptions, the autocratic leaders of post-independent African countries quickly discovered that they did not possess a durable monopoly in theft. As dictator after dictator succumbed in a rapid sequence of *coups d' etat*, governance in Africa rapidly began to resemble that of a *roving bandit* in an environment of anarchy (McGuire and Olson [1996]). The relative absence of wars between neighboring African countries further weakened nationalistic incentives for African countries to unite behind a stationary bandit in order to improve their respective military prowess.

By definition, the roving bandit does not exhibit a stable and encompassing interest in the domain over which he rules. In such an environment, there is little incentive for the bandit to invest in improving future productive capacity, and, therefore, little indigenous wealth to steal. However, as the bandit leaders quickly recognized, senior, budget-maximizing bureaucrats in the World Bank and other grant-making agencies were only too willing to provide foreign aid for grandiose, often ill-thought-out programs of economic development.

Independence, therefore, did not lead to major changes in the form and function of African politics. State power remained, for the most part, as absolute and arbitrary as that of the colonial powers that had preceded it. Political behavior became even more myopic as the monopoly in theft began to erode and as roving bandits began to displace the stationary bandits of the colonial era. This was not and is not a political environment conducive to good economic performance.

PUBLIC CHOICE IMPLICATIONS

The Vote Motive

In varying degree, the departing Imperial Powers set in place rudimentary democracies across Africa. In the case of former British colonies, these embryonic democracies were designed in accordance with the Westminster, two party, parliamentary model. Only rarely would such two-party parliamentary systems survive for very long before they were subverted by ruling *elites* into single party presidential oligarchies, if not into outright dictatorships. It is important to understand why such two-party democracies failed to thrive in Africa.

The two-party democracies imposed by the departing empires upon their former colonies bore little resemblance to the idealized consensual democracies analyzed by Buchanan and Tullock in *The Calculus of Consent* (1962). In no sense were these democracies created by unanimous consent to provide governance over a distribution of endowments that enjoyed widespread support. Without exception, the democracies created by the imperial powers were oligarchic in nature, often with restricted franchises reflective of the colonial experience. Typically, the elected government governed society exclusively in the minority interest of the favored ex-colonial *elites*.

According to McGuire and Olson (1996), *redistributive democracies* predictably tend to enhance economic performance more effectively than is possible under a stationary bandit. In justification of this claim, McGuire and Olson (1996) focus upon three fundamental features of redistributive democracies only one of which was characteristic of the early African experience.

The first fundamental feature, present only in a fragile form in Africa, is competition for votes to determine who controls the government. Although technically this existed at the outset of independence for most African countries, the electoral playing field was never level. Differential degrees of literacy, differential access to relevant information, and differential access to the polling booths ensured that the favored colonial tribal *elites* would dominate elections at least during the initial post-independence period.

The second fundamental feature, which was characteristic of post-independence Africa, was the ability of governments to redistribute income and to provide public goods. In principle, at least, this places redistributive democracies on a par with the stationary bandit in terms of incentives to promote economic performance. Whether or not such democracies will out-perform the stationary bandit then depends crucially on the third fundamental feature, namely the share of the economy that the government includes in its decision-making calculus.

McGuire and Olson's case rests on the judgment that a democratically elected government has a more encompassing interest than an autocracy because its members earn income in the market, whereas the autocrat does not. For reasons outlined above, this simply was not the case in post-independence Africa, where the political *elites* started out with little private wealth and no prior entrepreneurial experience in private markets.

Because two of the three necessary conditions outlined by McGuire and Olson (1996) failed to hold, the early African democracies failed to create environments conducive to economic progress. Given the presence of powerful forces favoring the one-party presidential system, this doomed experiments in two-party democracies to an early grave.

Because post-independence African states were completely politicized, the seeking of wealth through politics absorbed the energies of all the *elites*, whether in or out of power. In such a politicized environment, it was dangerous for individuals to channel their activities into the pursuit of private market success. Individuals who became wealthy independently of state patronage were viewed as a direct threat to the ruling elite. State patronage was the foundation on which the ruling dictators and oligarchs attempted to secure themselves against competition.

At independence, the new African nations confronted important decisions concerning the nature of their political systems. They did so within an environment of widespread illiteracy and of virtually no experience of participatory politics. Because of the centrifugal pressures of ethnic and tribal differences, most African leaders argued persuasively in favor of single-party systems of government as a powerful unifying agent. Such single-party systems in reality were to limit expressions of group differences and to become a conduit for corruption. Those leaders who rose to power through popular elections quickly outlawed opposition parties and squashed the development of democratic political systems (Kimenyi [1997] 12–17).

This hostility to democracy on the part of African *elites* was to prove a long-lived implication of the transition from colonial dominance. Until 1990, when the tide slowly began to turn against autocracy, virtually all of Sub-Saharan Africa remained under either military or civilian dictatorship (Kimenyi [1998] 12–18).

Rent Seeking

The theory of rent seeking, initiated by Gordon Tullock in 1976 (but see also Tullock 1971, 1975, and 1993), focuses attention on the rational behavior of interest groups under conditions of democracy. The theory has been adapted to encompass interest group behavior under conditions of dictatorship or one-party oligarchy (Tullock [1987]).

In essence, rent seeking focuses attention on the resources expended by competing interest groups in order to persuade governments to provide returns higher than they could earn in the absence of government protection. In the stylized Western model, politicians act as brokers, distributing rents in return for rent-seeking outlays, while securing brokerage fees for themselves. The extent to which such activity dissipates rather than transfers wealth is a matter of scientific controversy (Posner [1975], Cowling and Mueller [1978], Tullock [1980 and 1989], Becker [1983], Crew and Rowley [1987 and 1988], and Laband and Sophocleus [1988]). Estimates of rent-seeking waste in the Western democracies range from 3 percent of GDP to 45 percent of GDP.

Rent seeking takes a radically different form in Africa. For the most part, African political markets are not openly competitive. There exists instead a marked tendency toward *Leviathan* forms of government, dominated by either a military or a civil dictatorship. There is no rule of law and private property rights scarcely exist. In analyzing rent seeking under such conditions, it is important to note two distinguishing characteristics of the countries under review, namely their ethnic and tribal pluralism and the instability of their dictatorships.

Rent seeking under such conditions is more complex than under conditions of democracy. Initially, the ruler obtains his position through rent seeking, purchasing the support of the military/police establishment in order to access the rents available to dictatorship. However, just because the ruler has rent sought his position does not mean that this position is stable. The fact that he is earning rents renders him vulnerable to overthrow by competing would-be rulers. In Africa, such competition is fierce and tends to come from within the country and not from outside.

In order to protect himself from such forces, the rational dictator is forced to continue rent seeking by making financial appropriations to the military/policy establishment. He must also shore up support within his preferred ethnic or tribal group by providing such groups with rents, sometimes in the form of direct subsidies, but often through complex and costly networks of economic regulation. In extreme circumstances, such outlays may fully dissipate the gains from dictatorship, though even then dictators find it dangerous to relinquish office and to expose themselves to the wrath of their former subjects.

Where the dictatorship takes the form of the roving bandit, the brand of rent seeking that dominates the Western democracies, in which competing interest groups expend resources on the government in pursuit of long-term rents that only government can provide, is extremely rare. For the roving bandit is interested only in extracting immediate rents, not those that are available only from stable government.

Where the dictatorship takes the form of the stationary bandit, the opportunity for more conventional rent seeking exists, but even in such circumstances rent seeking will differ from that in the Western democracies. Even the stationary bandit must continuously favor those tribes and ethnic groups whose support deters the *coup d' etat*. He cannot respond even-handedly in response to rent-seeking outlays by groups that do not constitute his core support. Recognizing this, outside groups rationally will not seek rents from the current dictator, but instead will direct their outlays as clandestinely as possible to rivals for the dictatorship. To the extent that such anti-establishment rent seeking is effective, stationary bandits are transformed into roving bandits with potentially harmful consequences for economic development.

Rent Extraction

The original rent-seeking insight placed politicians in the role of passive agents in wealth redistribution, responding as brokers to the competing bids of rent-seekers. Politicians were not modeled as portraying entrepreneurial initiative in exploiting rent opportunities for themselves. In 1987, Fred McChesney extended the rent-seeking insight to incorporate a more active role for politicians as rent extractors.

McChesney suggested that payments are often made to politicians not to secure political favors, but rather to avoid threatened political harm. Rent-extraction so defined, is a euphemism for blackmail or political extortion. Politicians extract political contributions from interest groups in return for promises not to introduce measures harmful to their members.

The extraction of private rents and the creation of political rents through rent seeking need not be mutually exclusive strategies for politicians. Indeed, for politicians to maximize their gains typically they must combine the two activities. At first sight, rent extraction appears to impose a lower burden of resource waste on society since it does not involve lobbying outlays. However, this appearance is false. Rent-extraction induces significant resource misallocation and unambiguously lowers the wealth of a nation (McChesney [1997] 33).

First, the prospect that government is prepared to reduce returns to capital unless paid off reduces firms' ex ante willingness to invest, *ceteris paribus*. Second, firms that are alerted to this prospect will divert assets to less productive but more politically salvageable forms as a protection against expropriation. "If you own nothing, you have nothing to lose" (McChesney [1997] 33).

Third, rent extraction diverts scarce political resources away from potentially productive activities, notably defense, law and order, and the provision of public goods. The opportunity cost involved in this unproductive diversion constitutes a social cost. Fourth, if politicians are able to accumulate campaign funds from rent-extraction, this raises the electoral stakes, channeling scarce resources into political campaigns.

Rent extraction is the *raison d'etre* of African dictatorships. Private property rights either do not exist or are unenforceable against the dictator. Within the limits imposed by the threat of *coups d'etat*, dictators are able to extract wealth by direct expropriation, by accepting payoffs in return for restraining from expropriation, by manipulating complex networks of regulation, and by entering into private markets as a discriminatory monopolist (North 1981). Figure 1 illustrates the way in which dictators in sub-Saharan Africa create excess demand as a basis for rent extraction.

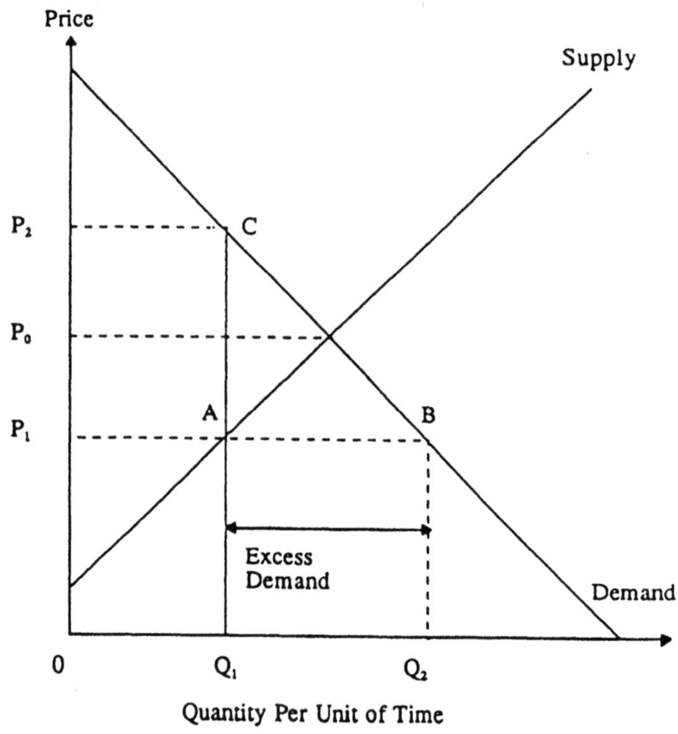

Figure 1. Excess Demand as a Basis for Rent Extraction

In Figure 1 an excess demand, AB is created by a government-imposed price ceiling P_1 designed to keep the legal price below the market-clearing price $0P_0$. The existence of this excess demand implies that buyers are willing to pay in excess of the legal price $0P_1$ for the quantity $0Q_1$ released to the market. The dictator can expropriate rents equal to the present value of the rectangle P_1ACP_2 simply by selling OQ_1 units of output on the black market. Although the details vary, Figure 1 encapsulates the behavior of rent-maximizing African dictators.

African dictators make extensive use of this and other similar devices, regulating commodity prices and interest rates, foreign exchange rates, and import licenses in order to create opportunities for black-marketeering. Such interventions impose high excess burdens on the productive sector and are a prominent reason why African economic performance is so poor.

THE EVOLUTION OF AN ADVERSE POLITICAL CULTURE

In his 1981 book entitled *Structure and Change in Economic History* Douglass North discarded his earlier presumption that political institutions are always efficient. He acknowledged that rulers devise property rights to serve their own interests and that high transaction costs result in such inefficient property rights prevailing even where opportunities for mutual gain clearly exist. In 1981 North had no explanation why competitive forces frequently fail to eliminate inefficient institutions.

In his 1990 book entitled *Institutions, Institutional Change, and Economic Performance* North developed an answer to this paradox that hinges on the difference between institutions and organizations and the interaction between them that shapes the direction of institutional change. Institutions, together with the standard constraints of economic theory, determine the opportunities in society. Organizations are created to exploit these opportunities. As these organizations evolve, they alter the institutions of society and change the incentive structure that the institutions provide. This process of interaction may be positive or negative with respect to economic efficiency.

With respect to non-developing third world countries, North argues that this symbiotic relationship is unambiguously negative. The opportunities for political and economic entrepreneurs have not disappeared. However, they overwhelmingly favor activities that promote redistribution rather than productive activity; that create monopolies rather than competition; that restrict choices rather than extend them. The organizations that develop in this adverse institutional framework become increasingly efficient at making society even more unproductive. In doing so, they render the institutional structure even less conducive to productive activity (North [1990] 9). North's analysis is particularly pertinent to the African dictatorships.

The governments that came into power in post-independence Africa were drawn from a tiny *elite* of educated young men and so were separated from the mass of the population. This lack of representation rapidly became institutionalized (Collier and Gunning [1999] 67). Within a decade after independence, the fragile democratic political institutions put in place by the departing colonial powers had been discarded by military *coups* or undercut by constitutional changes that banned opposition parties and controlled or suppressed most independent organizations in the name of ensuring national unity. By 1975, most sub-Saharan African states lacked a legislature, and most chief executives were not elected. In excess of 60 percent of the population lived under such regimes.

From the outset of independence, the relatively modern, industrial sectors of African economies were in the hands of these privileged ethnic minorities. With the rapid centralization of government, these sectors became the private resources of the ruler, sources of patronage for influential groups or for the corrupt personal uses of powerful politicians who were soon called "Big Men."

The "Big Men" provided their supporters with access to the resources of the state, hiring them into the civil service and appointing them to government boards and public corporations. They channeled low-interest loans and contracts from public agencies to such supporters. They encouraged supporters with opportunities for illicit gain from public office, thus introducing a culture of corruption into the machinery of government. They tolerated or encouraged the theft of public property and the illegal appropriation of public revenues among their supporters much as they indulged in such activities themselves.

The "Big Men" did not restrict such activities to the public sector. They rewarded their supporters also by granting preferential access to resources outside the public sector. For example, aspiring businessmen were required to obtain licenses and permits to enter into almost every avenue of trade and commerce. Supporters were provided with licenses at low fees and with minimal bureaucratic delay. Outsiders confronted extensive bureaucratic obstacles and heavy license fees. Allocations of such non-governmental benefits became counters in a sophisticated game of factional maneuver (Lancaster [1999] 28).

This widespread use of public institutions as vehicles for patronage and rent extraction eroded the already weak capacity of those institutions to perform effectively and imposed a severe drag on economic development. Control over the state became the principal vehicle for gaining access to economic resources. The rulers and their supporters became rich as the wealth of their nations declined. Not surprisingly, the beneficiaries supported existing institutions and organizations even when the negative economic consequences became undeniable.

The divorce of African governments from the general population and the lack of ownership by the general population of industrial assets encouraged a widespread policy of taxing exports to finance the expansion of industry. As the government expanded its own employment, and as its industrial supporters grew in number, the rulers also developed a political interest in cheap urban food. Subsidies for industry and for urban food were financed by the explicit and implicit taxation of exports of minerals (where these were available) and of agricultural products.

This bias against exports and in favor of import-substitutes was common both to the socialist regimes (Ghana, Tanzania, Zambia, Uganda, Ethiopia, Mozambique, and Angola) and to the more market-oriented regimes (Nigeria, Zaire, and Zimbabwe). It was a bias that found ready endorsement from international organizations like the World Bank anxious to boost their own annual budgets by engaging in grandiose industrial ventures. Running directly contrary to comparative advantage in international trade, such policies contributed to African economic stagnation and decline.

Because they were insulated from the mass of the rural population, and because they were endowed with only limited legitimacy, African governments were extremely exposed to pressures exerted by their own narrow base of supporters. In consequence, much of the industrial sector became entirely reliant on subsidies and controls, with up to 25 percent of manufacturing output producing a negative value added at world prices.

Because the state was weak as well as autocratic, corruption was uncoordinated and highly competitive. Such corruption is much more costly to society than the centralized monopolistic corruption characteristic of Asia because bribes in Africa frequently exceed revenue-maximizing levels and even eliminate transactions (Collier and Gunning [1999] 69). This is yet another example of how organizations become increasingly efficient at making society unproductive as they evolve in an adverse institutional framework.

THE DESCENT INTO KLEPTOCRACY

The Oxford Dictionary defines *kleptocracy* as "government by a ruling body of thieves; a nation ruled by thieves." This section will trace the rapid post-independence descent from representative democracy to kleptocracy of four African nations—Ghana, Nigeria, Kenya, and Zaire (now renamed the Democratic Republic of Congo). It is worthy of note that of these countries only the Democratic Republic of Congo truly represents the bottom of the African barrel as measured in terms of per capita GNP and economic freedom. Beneath the others, in deteriorating order are Malawi, Congo, Chad, Sierra Leone, Burundi, Zimbabwe, Mozambique, Rwanda and Somalia. The role of adverse political cultures in facilitating their descents into kleptocracy corresponds precisely to Douglass North's 1990 analysis of institutional change and economic performance.

Ghana

Prior to independence in 1957, the Gold Coast was under British colonial rule. Its population comprised a diverse mixture of ethnic and tribal groups combined more for the purposes of empire than on the basis of cultural and social homogeneity. The British authorities relied on the status and authority of local patrons as buttresses for their system of governance. The anti-colonial struggle that culminated in independence challenged the legitimacy of colonial governance without offering a viable democratic alternative.

On March 6, 1957, Kwame Nkrumah, the so-called father of African socialism, became Prime Minister of Ghana as leader of the Convention People's Party (CPC), victorious in the pre-independence elections. The CPC quickly moved to consolidate its political base, systematically redistributing income from the unorganized small-scale farmers in favor of the more effectively organized urban interest groups that constituted its core support base.

Nkrumah quickly cracked down on the scattered and ineffective political opposition, and stimulated the growth of the urban sector by expanding the government bureaucracy. The CPC taxed cocoa producers heavily to finance grandiose, ill-fated programs of public investment. Within little more than three years of independence, Nkrumah emerged as the first of the "Big Men" of Africa, designating himself as President of the Ghanaian Republic in July 1960.

Nkrumah's "development" strategy in the immediate post-independence period was based on state-led import substitution. The rhetoric supporting this strategy was the eventual establishment of an industrialist socialist state. The reality was a cynical process of setting in place the organizational basis for systematic rent-extraction.

In order to expand his urban support base, Nkrumah increased government expenditures, running down inherited reserves of foreign exchange on investments high in import content. With foreign reserves declining sharply and budget deficits out of control, taxes were sharply raised and exchange controls introduced in July 1961. By December 1961, comprehensive import licensing was introduced and the organizational structure for rent-extraction was fully operational.

The result of these policies, despite the high rate of public investment, was a decline in the growth performance of the economy. Over the period 1957–1961 Ghana's GDP grew at an average rate of 5 percent. Between 1962 and 1966 the growth rate in GDP decelerated to an average of 2.4 percent at a time of escalating population growth.

By February 1966, when he was deposed by a military *coup* Nkrumah had effectively exhausted the rents then available to his regime. The $400 million of foreign reserves bequeathed to him by Britain had been converted into a foreign debt of $858 million. Only three out of 64 state enterprises that he had created proved to be economically viable. His state farms barely produced enough food to feed their own workers, let alone the nation, and manufacturing output was running at less than 20 percent of available capacity (Ayittey [1992] 168). More fatal to his regime was the collapse in his principal sources of taxation. The cocoa tax base declined from 16 percent of GDP in 1958 to 7.7 percent in 1966 and the import tax base declined from 35 percent in 1961 to 20 percent in 1966. Without rents to disperse, the power base of his regime eroded.

An army *coup* removed Nkrumah from office in February 1966, replacing his regime with the government of the National liberation Council. The "father of African socialism" was investigated and was found to have deposited more than $5 million of his people's assets in numbered accounts in foreign banks. Small as this discovered theft now appears to be, it was a shattering blow to the faith of the simple Ghanaian peasant in the ethic of African socialism.

The adverse political culture bequeathed by Nkrumah to Ghana had its immediate aftermath in the systematic abuse of Ghana by the military regime for personal gain (Chazan [1992]) as the stationary bandit model quickly evolved into the roving-bandit model of dictatorship.

As economic performance continued to worsen, military governments further tightened the controls necessary to extract rents. In 1982, the kleptocratic military dictatorship led by Flight Lieutenant Rawlings, relying for its support on the previously dispossessed interest groups, plumbed such depths as to force the Ghanaian economy into a black hole with per capital GNP collapsing to the level of the worst performing African nations. (Hodder-Williams [1984]).

Ghana is only now struggling to emerge from the adverse political culture created by its first "Big Man" (Rowley [1999]). Despite liberalizing its economy since 1993, and elevating its growth rate in GNP, Ghana still achieved a real per capita income of less than $1000 in 1998 and ranked only 74 out of 150 countries on the index of economic freedom (Johnson, Holmes and Kirkpatrick 1998).

Nigeria

Ethnic consciousness was generated in Nigeria during the period of colonial rule as the British authorities brought together some 250 variously defined linguistic groups under one administration. Distinct ethnic groups emerged as potential political actors as enterprising ethnic leaders rallied tribes into cultural consciousness, much as interest groups are formed in the Western democracies. This process intensified following independence in 1960 (Williams [1992] 99).

The First Republic provided in 1960 for a considerable degree of regional autonomy. Although Nigerian democracy was based formally on the Westminster parliamentary model, national politics centered on inter-ethnic relations between the three largest tribes—Hausa-Fulani, Igbo, and Yoruba—each of which enjoyed hegemony in its own region over other ethnic minorities. The federal government possessed few constitutional powers and depended on the loyalty of key regional governments.

The regions controlled almost 50 percent of total fiscal outlays and exercised complete control over marketing boards and law enforcement. From this position of strength they threatened the federal center in order to extract wealth. The federal government was dominated by politicians representing the most highly populated Northern region—the most backward, ill-educated, Islamic section of the population. The two regions of the South, in contrast, although endowed with relatively well-educated populations and more favorable opportunities for diversified economic development found themselves in the political minority (Williams [1992] 100).

The central government, under pressure from the local and regional authorities, acquiesced in redistributing wealth to the Northern region through preferential job placement policies in the federal bureaucracy and in the military officer corps. In part because the federal government was weak, corruption exceeded its revenue-maximizing level with harmful consequences for economic performance.

In 1966, the armed forces effected a successful *coup*, replacing democracy with a military dictatorship. Desire for rents fueled this intervention: "the dominant concern of the vast majority of participants in politics at all levels during the early 1960s was the receipt of the largest share of benefits in the shortest period of time" (Post and Vickers [1973] 47). The bitter regional factionalism that pursuit of rents accentuated culminated in the Biafran war which raged from 1967 to 1970.

During the thirteen years of military rule, the state governments were subordinated to federal control, as the latter added to its exclusive control of such important areas as education, petroleum production, and the coordination and direction of development plans. The large post-1974 windfall in petroleum revenues concentrated financial power in the hands of the central government, with federal outlays increasing from 60 percent of all outlays in 1968 to 87 percent in 1980 (Williams [1992] 103).

In the late 1970s yet more favorable market conditions yielded oil revenues averaging $29 billion per annum. This led to a frenzy of rent extraction on the part of the military elite that culminated in civil rebellion leading to the collapse of military rule in 1979.

With the ending of military rule, the Westminster parliamentary model of the First Republic was abandoned by the Second Republic in 1980 in favor of a more centralized federal arrangement that included a strong presidential chief executive. The president was mandated to appoint at least one minister from each of the nineteen states as members of his cabinet. President Shagari, conforming to this provision, chose his entire cabinet from his own supporters in the National Party of Nigeria and the Nigerian People's Party, thus consolidating around him individuals from the political class of all the key ethnic groups.

The opportunity thus provided to accommodate ethnic diversity in fact was sacrificed on the altar of rent extraction by the elite political class, comprising a mixed group of bureaucrats, politicians, and members of the bourgeoisie. This group, aided by its access to immense personal wealth fueled by the oil boom, acted cohesively to further its collective interests.

From 1979 through 1983, scandals involving billions of dollars dominated the newspaper headlines. Import licenses were illicitly auctioned, and some $50 million per month allegedly disappeared to ghost workers and in other forms of federal payroll fraud. Senior Nigerian ministers allegedly smuggled $7 billion into numbered bank accounts during the short-lived second republic (Ayittey [1992] 252).

Within the political culture of Nigeria, politicians rest for their popularity upon their ability to reward their own constituents through preferential access to the national treasury. They accomplish this either through legal transfers in the form of community patronage projects or through illegal disbursements to private citizens. The decline in economic performance due to looting and gross mismanagement weakened the civil government which was overthrown in 1981 by a military *coup*.

Thereafter, Nigeria was ruled by a sequence of military dictatorships. Corruption has continued throughout the 1990s at a high level. In 1990 it was estimated that the "Big Men" have smuggled some $33 billion out of Nigeria into numbered accounts in foreign banks. This sum is equivalent to Nigeria's large foreign debt. In 1992, President Babangida refused to account for the $10 billion in oil windfall profits that had been occasioned by the onset of the Gulf War in January 1991 (Ayittey [1992] 252–53).

Although the current military government is committed to a transition to democracy its corruption and its human rights abuses are so serious that all international aid has been cut off. Nigeria is currently characterized as a highly repressive military dictatorship. It is a major center both for the narcotics trade and for international crime. In 1998, Nigeria ranked 94 out of 150 countries on the index of economic freedom (Johnson, Holmes, and Kirkpatrick [1998]).

Despite its rich resource endowment, Nigeria remained in 1998 one of the poorest countries in the world, with a per capita GNP of only $240. Economic growth continues to be impeded by structural bottlenecks and by political uncertainties regarding the transition to civilian rule. Almost exclusively, this outcome is the consequence of an adverse political culture introduced by the First Republic in the heady post-independence years of the early 1960s (Rowley [1999]).

Kenya

In contrast to Nigeria and Ghana, a significant minority white settler community was located in Kenya prior to independence. These settlers resisted the rise of African nationalism during the period when many other Sub-Saharan African colonies were in transition to independence, thus stimulating, in 1952, an armed insurrection known as the Mau Mau rebellion. The British Empire put down the insurrection within two years and declared a state of emergency which lasted until 1960, jailing Jomo Kenyatta and other nationalist leaders during the state of emergency and banning the Kenya African Union and all other nationwide political organizations (Barkan [1992] 168). Nevertheless, the British government committed itself to the eventual independence of Kenya.

As usual, the British government sought to transfer political power to an indigenous elite in Kenya by phasing in a parliamentary system of government. The procedure adopted was that of holding a series of elections designed to transform the Legislative Council (LEGCO) from an appointed and advisory body into an elected legislature.

Through these elections the proportion of LEGCO members elected on the basis of universal suffrage would rise until it exceeded 90 percent. At this point a provisional government would be formed by the leader of the majority party or majority coalition. Independence would then quickly follow. The first elections were held in 1957, providing African representation for eight out of 32 seats and a second round in 1958, providing for six additional African seats. In both cases, candidates were allowed to form campaign organizations only at the district level.

Individual candidates for political office created district organizations as a means of mobilizing ethnic support (Barkan [1992] 169). Thus, when nationwide political parties were legalized at the end of the emergency in 1960, the leaders of the new parties were faced with a wide array of district organizations representing distinct ethnic groups. In anticipation of the British intention to hold a third round of elections for33 seats in 1961, two nationwide coalitions of district organizations formed—the Kenya African National Union (KANU) and the Kenya African Democratic Union (KADU).

KANU was the professed heir to the Kenya African Union and comprised a coalition of districts that had provided KAU with its support prior to the emergency. These areas included the districts of Central Province, the eastern part of Rift Valley Province, both populated mainly by the Kikuyu people, the districts of Eastern Province, populated by the Embu, Meru and Kamba peoples, and the districts of Nyanza Province, populated by the Luo and Gusii peoples. KANU drew most of its support from four of Kenya's five largest ethnic groups, represented some 60 percent of the total population, and found its base support among groups that were the most prosperous and politically well organized (Barkan [1992] 169).

By contrast, KADU was composed of the less prosperous, less well-organized small ethnic groups located in relatively undeveloped geographical areas. These included the Abaluhya peoples in Western Province, the Kalenjin peoples of the western side of Rift Valley Province, the Mijikenda peoples of Coast Province and the semi-nomadic peoples scattered across northern and northeastern Kenya. Although its geographic base was vast, the support base for KADU amounted to barely one-third of Kenya's population.

In the February 1961 elections, KANU won 19 out of 33 seats with 67 percent of the vote. The British government, in response to this victory, released Jomo Kenyatta who assumed the presidency of KANU. A new Constitution was negotiated between KANU and KADU providing for a bicameral legislature with members of the lower chamber (The House of Representatives) to be elected from single-member districts. Under pressure from the British government, KANU acquiesced to a federalist arrangement, known as *Majimbo*, to protect members of KADU's minority coalition.

A fourth election, held in May 1963 under this Constitution confirmed the 1961 result with KANU winning 71 out of 129 seats with 54 percent of the vote as compared with KADU winning only 32 seats with 26 percent of the vote. KANU formed the first elected Kenya government, with Kenyatta as Prime Minister, in June. Independence followed in December 1963.

The Westminster two-party model established at independence was not destined to last. Representatives both of KANU and KADU focused attention on the issue of wealth distribution, with KANU seeking to consolidate the dominant position of the prosperous *elite*, and with KADU seeking to defend the weak positions of the less well-off. The outcome was predictable.

Once in power, Kenyatta's government refused to implement federalism and by the middle of 1964 Kenyatta and KANU effectively shut KADU out of the political process. As members of a minority coalition in a unitary state, KADU politicians folded their party into KANU. Kenya had become de facto a one-party state under the personal rule of Jomo Kenyatta.

A new Constitution was passed eliminating *Majimbo* and providing for a presidential form of government, with Kenyatta at its head and with Daniel arap Moi, formerly deputy leader of KADU as Vice President. KANU became Kenya's sole political party (Barkan [1992] 171). The scenario for the rent-seeking and rent-extracting model of Sub-Saharan African politics was clearly set.

Although Kenyatta clearly was a "Big Man," and although his regime became increasingly authoritarian, he was not especially corrupt by African standards. There is no evidence that he moved rents out of Kenya into foreign bank accounts. Yet, in his attempts to forge winning political coalitions through the allocation of rents to his supporters, Kenyatta set in place the institutional and organizational basis upon which less scrupulous successors quickly forged an adverse political culture following his death in August 1978.

Daniel arap Moi, Kenyatta's corrupt Vice President, succeeded to the presidency in accordance with the Constitution and quickly replaced the governance system established by Kenyatta with a spoils system. Moi began his presidency in 1978 with an attempt to undermine the political power of the dominant Kikuyu tribe, signaling a shift in the rent-seeking equilibrium.

Henceforth, resources would be redistributed to Kenya's former have-nots, the core of the old KADU coalition of which Moi had been a leader. Moi's populist approach—*Nyayo* or "peace, unity and love" - evidently was not to be extended to the Kikuyu tribe, whether relatively rich or relatively poor (Barkan [1992] 179).

In 1982, Moi introduced a series of institutional changes that entrenched *Nyayo* essentially as a rent-extraction program. First was a constitutional amendment to make Kenya under KANU *de jure* a one-party state. To be eligible to vote, citizens were forced to pay to register as KANU members, under threat to their jobs and personal security. To work for the Kenya government, one had to be a KANU member. The repression that went with this amendment provoked an unsuccessful *coup d'etat* by the Kenya Air Force in August 1982.

Second, was a shift of policy that treated prominent elected officials not as supporters but as rivals to his regime. A number of significant elected officials were drummed out of KANU into the political wilderness. Third was a policy of systematic intervention in the election of regional leaders, declaring those he distrusted to be ineligible for KANU, and forcing open rather than secret balloting upon the electorates.

The Moi era has been characterized by the systematic looting of Kenya by a corrupt administration. Between 1978 and 1989 it has been estimated that members of Moi's regime shifted $5 billion into numbered accounts in foreign countries (Ayittey [1992] 243). That sum exceeded the total of Western investment and aid provided to Kenya over the period in question and was larger than the total foreign debt of Kenya.

President Moi's personal wealth is estimated to be in excess of $3 billion. In addition to moving wealth into foreign bank accounts, Moi has developed an economic empire in Kenya, forcing the government to make purchases from his businesses. The escalating greed of the president and his cronies coupled with the repressive regime necessary to extract such wealth is largely responsible for the collapse of the Kenyan economy into a black hole

In 1997 the per capita GNP of Kenya was less than $300. In terms of the economic freedom index Kenya was ranked 77 out of 154 countries in 1998 (Johnson, Holmes, and Kirkpatrick [1998]). Despite these statistics, Moi has managed to retain the presidency following the resumption of limited democracy in Kenya. This achievement indicates the influence that a rent-dispersing 'Big Man' possesses over an ill-educated and often simple African electorate even under conditions of democracy (Rowley [1999]).

Democratic Republic of Congo (Formerly Zaire)

The Congo obtained its independence from Belgium in 1960 in an extremely acrimonious atmosphere. Its peoples had enjoyed no prior experience of even limited self-government. The region quickly fell into turmoil as various regionally based ethnic groups fought for control over a weak central government and as the Congo became a Cold War battlefield between the United States and the USSR.

In 1965 the United States Central Intelligence Agency, with the connivance of President Lyndon Johnson, participated in a successful plot to assassinate the pro-USSR "Big Man," President Patrice Lumumba, and to replace him with a Western puppet, Mobutu Sese Seko. Mobutu signaled the change in political direction by renaming the Congo Zaire.

President Mobutu would quickly become the biggest of all the "Big Men" of Africa, a stationary bandit who imposed decades-long policies of repression upon his subjects and who established an extensive network of economic regulations exclusively as the basis for rent extraction (Ayittey [1992] 233). Secured in his office by a sequence of Cold War–obsessed U.S. governments, Mobutu was able to ignore entirely any responsibility for the provision of public goods and to devote his regime entirely to the securing of maximal short-term rents.

Presiding over an "empire of graft and venality" (Ayittey [1992] 233), Mobutu bragged on U.S. national television in 1984 that he was the second richest man in the world with more than $8 billion dollars in a numbered personal account at a Swiss bank (Ayittey [1992] 254). Throughout his rule, it is estimated that 60 percent of the annual budget of Zaire was diverted into the personal accounts of himself, his families and his cronies (Ayittey [1992] 252). Until the end of the Cold War in 1989, Zaire received some $70 million per annum in aid from the United States, most of which went into numbered accounts and the rest of which was dissipated.

With his U.S. patron no longer interested in protecting him, following the end of the Cold War, Mobutu confronted growing internal unrest and presided precariously over an increasingly rent-sacked economy. In May 1997, physically ailing and increasingly isolated, he was forced to flee the country as his poorly organized army collapsed before rebel forces led by Laurent Kabila.

Kabila immediately pronounced himself President of the newly named Democratic Republic of Congo. His accession was not met with the joyous cries of a liberated people. For the population at large was fully aware that the cycle of corruption would not be broken by the emergence of a new "Big Man." Kabila's government, if such it can be called, has lived down to its expectations.

It has gained international infamy by the slaughtering of Rwandan refugees and by its habit of arresting arbitrarily all those who oppose it. It has further raised trade barriers and has increased government intervention in what little is left of the domestic economy. It is now little more than one out of a growing number of competing roving bandits that myopically loot what is left of a sacked economy.

The per capita income of the Democratic Republic of Congo is too small to measure. In terms of economic freedom The Republic was ranked 147 out of 154 in 1998, its rating lowered from that accorded to Mobutu's regime in the final year of his oppressive dictatorship (Johnson, Holmes, and Kirkpatrick [1998]).

Rent Extraction and Foreign Aid

Rents in excess of $15 billion per annum are removed from Africa each year by the "Big Men" and their cronies and transferred into numbered bank accounts in foreign countries (Ayittey [1992] 335). This flight of wealth exceeds the total annual aid received by Africa from all foreign sources. Much of the foreign aid in fact never moves beyond the treasuries of the "Big Men." It is treated, so to speak, as their private pocket money.

Aid to Africa has been largely ineffective, certainly less effective than aid to any other part of the globe. On average, only one out of five projects and programs endures after aid funding is terminated (Lancaster [1999] 2). There is compelling evidence that large and continuous aid flows have exerted negative effects on economic development. In part, the failure of the aid program is the responsibility of corrupt African regimes. In part, however, the responsibility lies with the technical incompetence of bureaucrats in the grant-giving institutions, combined with their zeal to spend the moneys entrusted to their governance.

There is a real sense, therefore, in which foreign aid has become the fuel that drives the engine of adverse political culture in Africa. In this sense, the World Bank is properly viewed as a Stagnation Bank rather than as a Development Bank. The closure of the Africa Division of the World Bank and the cessation of all international aid to Africa must be viewed as a first priority for the concerned international community if the peoples of that region are ever to take realistic steps towards reforming their institutions and their organizations.

THE PROSPECTS FOR INSTITUTIONAL AND ORGANIZATIONAL CHANGE

Institutions are the rules of the game in a society, the constraints that shape human interaction. These rules of the game structure incentives in human exchange, whether political, social, or economic. Institutions may evolve informally in the shape of conventions and codes. Or they may be created formally by conscious human design. As North (1990) emphasizes, institutions whether formal or informal, and the effectiveness with which they are enforced provide the framework within which societies function.

Organizations are to be distinguished from institutions in the same sense that players are to be distinguished from the rules in a competitive game. Organizations include political bodies, economic bodies, and social bodies. They are groups of individuals bound by some common purpose to achieve objectives. Both the pattern of organizations that come into existence and the way in which they evolve are influenced fundamentally by the institutional framework. In turn, the organizations themselves influence the institutional structure.

The institutions of sub-Saharan Africa bequeathed by the imperial powers provided disincentives to productive activity and incentives to inefficient programs of wealth redistribution. The organizations and interests that emerged to exploit these opportunities assumed a stake in extending the perverse institutions under which they prospered. This symbiosis between institutions and organizations has impacted upon human nature itself, eroding virtuous qualities such as trust, tolerance generosity honesty and loyalty in favor of non-virtuous qualities such as distrust, intolerance, greed dishonesty, and disloyalty—characteristic of mankind in the Hobbesian jungle.

Inefficient institutions and organizations, once they are in place, are not easily disturbed, even when the adverse economic consequences are there for all to see. The principal obstacles to the reform of perverse institutions and organizations are increasing returns and transaction costs (North [1990] 95).

With increasing returns, institutions are resistant to change even when they are widely perceived to be inefficient. Where transaction costs are also high, reforms cannot be instituted through Coaseian bargains. The path-dependent route to an adverse culture cannot easily be retraced. In such circumstances, cultures will not typically reform themselves by a process of marginal adjustment. More discrete, revolutionary changes may be required.

Those African countries that have descended into kleptocracies are immune to economic help from outside. Reform must be initiated from within. *Coups d'etat* are unlikely to provide the basis for reform. They simply restructure the ruling coalition. Popular revolutions offer a more likely avenue for removing the prevailing institutions and organizations, but these are difficult to coordinate, given the free rider problem, and where successful, too often disintegrate into dictatorships.

The "Big Men" of Africa clearly have placed themselves in a state of war with the people. Whether the people can exercise their natural rights to bring them down is the unanswered question. Ironically, the solution most likely to prove successful is politically impossible: for the former colonies to return themselves to their masters in return for a covenant of enlightened administration. There can be no doubt that the British governance of Hong Kong through the second half of the twentieth century was far superior to the governance provided by any of the "Big Men" of Africa following independence.

ACKNOWLEDGMENTS

Charles K. Rowley thanks Maria Pia Paganelli for research assistance. The chapter has benefited greatly from comments provided by participants at the Conference on Economic Policy and Political Culture held at the Tinbergen Institute, Erasmus University in February 1999 and at the Conference in Honor of Gordon Tullock held in May 1999 at the University of Arizona. In particular, I am grateful to Peter Bernholz, Price Fishback, Arye Hillman, Jack Hishleifer, Gary Libecap, Martin Paldam and Ludger Schuknecht for valuable suggestions.

REFERENCES

Ake, C. (1996). *Democracy and Development in Africa.* Washington, D.C.: The Brookings Institution.

Ayittey, G. B. N. (1992). *Africa Betrayed.* New York: St. Martin's Press.

Barkan, J. D. (1992). "The Rise and Fall of Governance in Kenya," in G. Hyden and M. Bratton (eds.), *Governance and Politics in Africa,* pp. 167–92. Boulder, CO and London: Lynne Reiner Publishers.

Becker, G. S. (1983). "A Theory of Competition Among Pressure Groups for Political Influence." *Quarterly Journal of Economics* 63 (3) pp. 371–400.

Collier, P., and J. W. Gunning, (1999). "Explaining African Economic Performance." *Journal of Economic Literature,* March, 37 (1) pp. 64–111.

Cowling, K., and D.C. Mueller (1978). "The Social Costs of Monopoly Power." *Economic Journal* 88, pp. 727–48.

Chazan, N. (1992). "Liberalization, Governance, and Political Space in Ghana," in G. Hyden and M. Bratton (eds.), *Governance and Politics in Africa,* pp. 121–42. Boulder, CO and London: Lynne Rienner Publishers.

Crew, M. A., and C. K. Rowley (1987). "Dispelling the Disinterest in Deregulation," in C. K. Rowley, R. D. Tollison, and G. Tullock (eds.), *The Political Economy of Rent-Seeking.* Boston: Kluwer Academic Publishers.

______ (1988). "Toward a Public Choice Theory of Monopoly Regulation." *Public Choice* 57 (1) pp. 49–68.

Hodder-Williams, R. (1984). *An Introduction to the Politics of Tropical Africa.* London: George Allen and Unwin.

Johnson, B.T., K. R. Holmes, and M. Kirkpatrick (1998). *1998 Index of Economic Freedom.* Washington, D.C.: The Heritage Foundation.

Kimenyi, M. S. (1997). *Ethnic Diversity, Liberty and the State.* The Shaftesbury Papers, 12, Cheltenham and

Northampton: Edward Elgar Publishing.
Laband, D. W., and J. P. Sophocleus (1988). "An Estimate of Resource Expenditures on Transfer Activity in the United States." *Quarterly Journal of Economics* 107, pp. 959–84.
Lancaster, C. (1999). *Aid to Africa: So Much to Do So Little Done*. Chicago: University of Chicago Press.
Landau, D. (1990). "The Pattern of Economic Policies in LDC's: A Public Choice Explanation." *Cato Journal* 10 (2) pp. 573–601.
Locke, J. (1690). *Two Treatises of Government*, edited by P. Laslett and republished in 1960. Cambridge: Cambridge University Press,
Mbaku, J. M. (1993). "Rent Seeking and Democratization Strategies for Africa." Ogden, UT: Weber State University Working Paper.
McChesney, F. S. (1987). "Rent Extraction and Rent Creation in the Economic Theory of Regulation." *Journal of Legal Studies* 16, pp. 73–90.
______ (1997) *Money for Nothing*. Cambridge, MA: Harvard University Press.
McGuire, M. C., and M. Olson, Jr. (1996). "The Economics of Autocracy and Majority Rule." *Journal of Economic Literature*, March, 34 (1) pp. 72–96.
North, D. C. (1981). *Structure and Change in Economic History*. New York: Norton.
______ (1990). *Institutions, Institutional Change and Economic Performance*, Cambridge: Cambridge University Press.
Posner, R. A. (1975). "The Social Costs of Monopoly and Regulation." *Journal of Political Economy* 83, pp. 807–27.
Post, K. W. J., and M. Vickers (1973). *Structure and Conflict in Nigeria 1960– 1966*. Madison: University of Wisconsin Press.
Rowley, C. K. (1998). "Institutional Choice and Public Choice: Lessons for the Third World," in J. Dorn, S. Hanke, and A. Walters (eds.), *The Revolution in Development Economics*. Washington, D.C.: Cato Institute.
______ (1999). "Rent Seeking and Rent Extraction from the Perspective of Africa," in J. M. Mbaku, and M. S. Kimenyi (eds.), *Institutions and Collective Choice in Developing Countries: Applications of the Theory of Public Choice*, pp. 223–54. Brookfield: Ashgate Publishing Company.
Tullock, G. (1967). "The Welfare Costs of Tariffs, Monopolies and Theft." *Western Economic Journal* 5, pp. 224–32.
______ (1971). "The Cost of Transfers." *Kyklos* 24, pp. 629–43.
______ (1975). "Competing for Aid." *Public Choice* 21, pp. 41–52.
______ (1980). "Efficient Rent-Seeking," in J. M. Buchanan, R. D. Tollison, and G. Tullock (eds.), *Towards a Theory of the Rent-Seeking Society*. College Station: Texas A&M University.
______ (1987). *Autocracy*. Boston: Kluwer Academic Publishers.
______ (1989). *The Economics of Special Privilege and Rent-Seeking*. Boston: Kluwer Academic Publishers.
______ (1993). *Rent Seeking*. The Shaftesbury Papers 2, Aldershot and Brookfield: Edward Elgar Publishing.
Williams, D. C. (1992). "Accommodation in the Midst of Crisis? Assessing Governance in Nigeria," in G. Hyden and M. Bratton (eds.), *Governance and Politics in Africa*, pp. 97–120. Boulder, CO and London: Lynne Rienner Publishers.

Northampton: Edward Elgar Publishing.

[illegible]

CONSTITUTIONAL CAUSES FOR TECHNOLOGICAL LEADERSHIP: WHY EUROPE?

Jürgen G. Backhaus
Maastricht University, AE
P.O. Box 616
6200 MD Maascricht
The Netherlands

INTRODUCTION

In a paper circulated since the end of 1997 Gordon Tullock poses a simple but provocative question. Why did the technological take-off marking the start of the industrial revolution take place in Europe rather than in Asia in the 19th century. Until shortly before that time other parts of the world and notably China looked much better equipped for sustained intellectual, scholarly and technological leadership and the wealth that technological leadership can bring about. Drawing on his extensive expertise on Chinese history and culture and on his longstanding interest in the *Organization of Inquiry* Tullock argues that Europe assumed the technological leadership towards the end of the eighteenth century due to a set of unique constitutional factors not present anywhere else in the world.[1]

This essay examines Tullock's discussion of Europe, particularly, the role played by cameralism. Thus, the discussion offered here is focused on only one part of the larger mosaic of Tullock's explanation. Tullock's discussion can be categorized into seven elements. These elements are by no means accidental aspects of European history but are related to issues of the constitutional design arising out of the Peace of Westphalia of 1648. The economic and political structure that arose out of the Peace of Westphalia led to the development of the political-economic doctrine of Cameralism, which competed with mercantilistic doctrines that influenced so many western countries. Many of the constitutional principles underlying cameralism were developed by the German scholar and political advisor Christian Wolff, who established many foundations found in modern political-economic thought.[2]

A RESTATEMENT OF THE TULLOCK HYPOTHESIS

Europe towards the end of the eighteenth century became an excellent candidate for a leadership position in technology and took advantage of this opportunity. Tullock's hypothesis about Europe's technological leadership position can be stated as a function of at least seven different factors: 1) the absence of a universal state in Europe with only Spain as a technological laggard; 2) the peripheral role of Russia as a large centralized system of despotism, despite the high quality of its Academia of Science; 3) the imminence of war and the necessity of military preparedness, which required technological insight in various military-related fields such as the scientific aspects of sieging, artillery, naval matters, as well as financing, logistics, food and health, sanitation, and population development; 4) the specific doctrine of Cameralism as a multidisciplinary science and practice of public administration: 5) systematic attempts at avoiding unproductive rent seeking and using rent seeking as an arrangement to foster development; 6) low levels and further reductions of transactions costs notably in maritime travel; and 7) the development of science, notably as a dynamic process with possibilities for exponential growth.

True enough, Tullock mentions other aspects and focuses his attention on the technological aspects of military matters (at the expense of the other ones mentioned). Yet, these seem to be the leading elements in Tullock's discussion, which he regrets to be somewhat ad hoc. My purpose in this chapter is to show that the discussion is not ad hoc, once we consider the overall context in which Europe's specific position developed. My discussion centers on the peculiar doctrine of Cameralism that developed on the European continent and apparently nowhere else.

In 1648 the First Treaty of Münster ended 80 years of conflict and the Second Treaty of Münster and the Treaty of Osnabrück concluded 30 years of conflict. These treaties created a unique political and economic system in Central Europe that was to have an impact on all the other elements in Tullock's explanation. The system certainly made a universal state impossible; therefore, there would be no successor to the Holy Roman Empire as it had been founded on Christmas night in the year 800. Rather, a complex system of competing, but also co-operating, states bound together in the Empire formed the core of the system with larger states such as Sweden, France, Spain, Russia, and Britain on the periphery. Meanwhile, the Ottoman Empire also remained a threat. The Treaty system involved these peripheral states in different ways and established rules of a competitive game among the member states forming the empire. All of the states had received through the Treaty system a modicum of sovereignty never enjoyed before. The preceding wars had brought enormous losses, particularly in Central Europe, which lost about four-sevenths of its population and sustained extensive losses in property, cultural heritage, cultivated land, and infrastructure. A daunting task of reconstruction brought about a specific doctrine for economic and cultural development, i.e. Cameralism (Tullock's element 4) and an emphasis on the role of sciences more generally (element 7). The war had created an acute awareness of military requirements and a need for preparedness on the part of all the rulers involved (element 3). The newly sovereign Central European states, principalities, monasteries, bishoprics, free cities, and the like were allowed to enter into defensive treaties with foreign neighbours as long as those treaties or alliances were not directed against the unity of the Empire in general or the Emperor in particular. An important element of the treaties was an emphasis on the issue of trade. The First Treaty of Münster is based on the rule of Law on the Free Seas (with the notable exception of the port of Antwerp). Neighboring states were granted access to all of the major German waterways, i.e. the rivers Rhine, Ems, Weser, Elbe, and Oder. Although the interest of neighboring states in securing control over these rivers was not so much to promote trade but to reap the major benefits from it, the ultimate outcome necessarily was an increase in the volume of trade. With more trade there might have been a reduction in transactions costs, including both transport costs and the costs of resolving legal issues in international trade. Thus, we see attempts to limit rent seeking (element 5) while reducing trade costs (element 6).

The absence of a universal state (element 1) had substantial repercussions for economic policy, including policies of economic development, warfare, and the constitutional principles that governed relationships between different public bodies. The interplay between center and periphery was particularly important with respect to the sciences. Among the constitutional principles, the principle of subsidiarity played a specific and important role. The restrictions imposed upon the princes by the Peace of Westphalia and the concomitant Constitutional doctrine allowed the peculiar political-economic doctrine of Cameralism to arise, in contrast with the rise of mercantilism in the areas where the peace treaty did not apply.

THE PEACE OF WESTPHALIA OF 1648

The Peace of Westphalia of 1648 consisted of three treaties. The first treaty between Philip the Fourth, King of Spain and the United Provinces of the Low Countries was signed at Münster on the 30th of January of 1648 and ended the 80 Years War of the Dutch Republics against Spanish rule. The background of this war in which France at times sided with the Dutch was eminently religious. The Protestant Dutch fought their Catholic rulers. Yet, the war was also fought over trade and financial resources. Despite Spain's control over the Americas, the Kingdom derived by far the largest part of its tax revenues from the Low Countries. In addition to the Treaty of Münster, the combatants signed two further documents dated the 8th of January of 1647 and the 27th of December concerning the relationship between the House of Nassau, Orange and the King of Spain, which dealt with the return of property and fortifications.

On the 24th of October 1648, two further treaties were signed in Münster and Osnabrück, respectively. The Treaty of Münster was signed on 24th October by the most Christian King of France and Navarre, Lewis the Fourteenth and Ferdinand the Third, elected Roman Emperor, King of Germany, Hungary, Bohemia, Dalmatia, Croatia, Slavonia, Arch-Duke of Austria, Duke of Burgundy, etc.[3] The revolt that actually sparked the war took place in Bohemia, where the King of Bohemia was an elector of the Roman Empire. It was then rapidly fed by older conflicts and grievances, which turned the revolt against the Catholic Emperor under the leadership of the Protestant electors, notably the elector of the Palatinate. Ostensibly, France entered on the side of the Catholics, but it ultimately secured a Peace Treaty in which the Emperor in his capacity as Duke of Luxembourg and Landgrave of Alsace ceded territories to the King of France. This cession is remarkable in that the Emperor was thereby violating his own oath of preserving the unity of the Empire. Of course, he could cede territories to another prince provided that other prince would henceforth function as a member of the Empire and if that cession and endowment had taken place according to the rules of the Empire. These rules, through the 30 Years War, had clearly broken down and the Peace Treaties were an attempt to create a new system of such rules.

The Third Treaty, which was agreed upon in Osnabrück on 24 October 1648 between the Emperor and Gustavus Adolphus—the King of the Swedes, Goths, and Vandals as succeeded by Queen Christina—was a very different document again. While France was interested in pushing its eastern border towards the Rhine through annexations, the Swedish Queen Christina's instructions show that she was primarily interested in obtaining as large a cash payment for "demobilization" as possible, while retaining her territorial gains.[4] According to paragraphs 8 and 9 of Article XVI of the Treaty of Osnabrück, the seven northern German imperial circuits of the Rhineland, Upper Saxony, Frankonia, Suabia, Upper Rhine, Westphalia, and Lower Saxony were to pay a total of 5 million Thaler in three installments. Christina's instructions called for twice that amount, and it is clear that her haggling substantially prolonged the war. As for the territorial concessions, the Swedish Crown was willing to renounce annexation and rather take its possessions as fiefdoms within the Empire, honoring rules of succession, rules of decision making in collective bodies, and all the feudal rights and responsibilities according to the specific estate received. For instance, the Duchy of Pommerania was being divided, the elector losing the western part and retaining only the eastern one. This concession actually made the peace ultimately possible, and the elector was richly compensated with the rich Abby of Magdeburg, Halberstadt, and Minden. However, where the Duke of Pommerania had the chair in the College of Knights, the chairmanship would alternate between the Swedish King and the elector of Brandenburg.

This kind of provision is typical of the spirit of the Treaty of Osnabrück. In trying to bring about peace between Catholics and Protestants in their daily life, the Treaty abounds with specific rules governing decision making. Typically, a collective body was assigned specific rights and operated by a rule of parity, as the chairmanship alternated between the two parties.[5] In this context there is an amazing provision about the Bisdom of Minden where the elector of Brandenburg essentially received the secular part of the Bisdom (i.e. the See) with the revenues, while the clerical part was split between various chapters and the knights along confessional lines. Likewise, in the case of the Bisdom of Osnabrück with two confessions present, the acting bishop had alternate titles; one year he was the Arch Bishop of Cologne, the next he was Duke of Brunswick. Similar examples abound.

We can interpret the treaties in the light of economics as a science, which involves understanding the human condition and seeking in a narrower sense to increase welfare. An increase in welfare is the punch line behind Gordon Tullock's research questions: 1) Why was Europe scientifically so far ahead of China?[6] And 2) Why had this advantage led to such a relatively small effect on the living standards and the level of development of the mechanical side of civilization for such a long period? The standard interpretation of the Treaties of Westphalia is that France, England and Sweden took control over Germany by imposing an unworkable chaotic system. France had pushed its border far to the west, Britain was aiming to sustain a balance on the Continent and allowed a sovereign entity to control the mouths of the rivers Scheldt and Rhine. Meanwhile Sweden effectively took control of the mouths of the rivers Weser, Elbe, and Oder, and Prussia (i.e. Brandenburg) gained a foothold on the mouth of the river Ems in Emden side by side with a Dutch garrison. While this interpretation is not incorrect and it clearly reflects the intentions of the foreign parties mentioned, it does not quite capture the full impact of the Treaty system. The Treaty with its many complicated decision-making rules is an unbelievably complex legal document that creates a constitutional framework in which a large number of different parties had to operate. By virtue of its conflict-resolution procedures, it typically establishes "games" whereby rulers could only make progress by cooperating with otherwise opposing interests; noncooperation would entail a loss for both parties.

By granting the constituent members of the Empire a modicum of sovereignty, certainly an avenue was opened for foreign interventions in the affairs of the Empire.[7] However, what did this mean in practice? France took full advantage of the possibilities created by Cardinal Mazarin and actively participated in each Imperial election until the demise of the Empire in 1803. Also, France succeeded in creating the Rhine Federation and thereby created a military buffer against potential aggression from Germany. Although chances for such a military move were extremely dim, the policy required France to maintain embassies in a large number of territories, and to maintain well-stocked large embassies in each of the seven electorates. The expenditures necessary to maintain this diplomatic effort, which included bribes of the electors in order to swing the electoral decision for the Emperor, and substantial subsidies to military campaigns, is estimated to have drained about 5 percent of total outlays of the French Kingdom annually. The drain on French resources this arrangement brought about can hardly be overestimated. It is generally believed that the burden of taxation (and the fact that these taxes brought little of value for the taxpaying Frenchmen) contributed to the French Revolution of 1789.

Nor did the Swedes gain much from their enormous war bounty, which resulted in little beyond some rather impressive architecture in Sweden and Norway. Meanwhile, in the seven German circuits, where the taxes had to be levied from an exhausted tax base, much experience was gathered in assessing taxability and processing tax claims and payments. The large number of jurisdictions that had to participate in this endeavor, which was accepted only as a means to get rid of the hated occupation army, underscores the complexity of the administrative task to be accomplished.

One of the surprising features of the Treaty, which was intended to follow the old maxim of *divide et impera*, was the agglomeration of different landholdings of different status bound together only by the hereditary legal person of the prince and in some cases his personal charisma. Brandenburg, for example, now held territories all the way from the river Maas to the river Memel, but most of it was noncontiguous. Similarly, the Palatinate stretched from the Danube all the way along the Rhine river (see the map in Figure 1), yet purposefully managing this far-flung set of holdings must have been

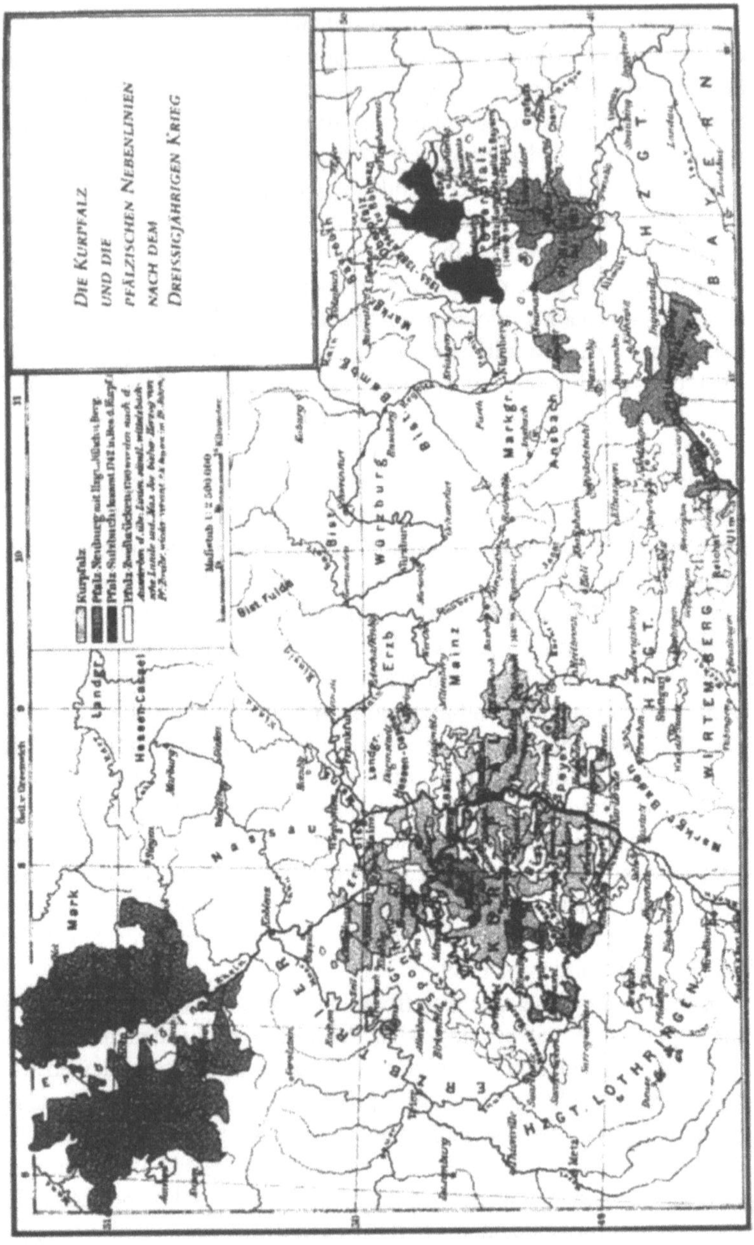

Figure 1. The Palatinate after the Thirty Years' War

anybody's nightmare. Given the many hereditary lines of succession and the vicissitudes of life, sickness, and death, marriage, birth, and male or female succession, the task of managing one of these hereditary principalities was indeed a challenging one.

Additional problems were created by the extreme poverty that had befallen the Holy Roman Empire (i.e. Germany) as a consequence of the devastating war. The extreme loss in population was accompanied by the loss of most of the infrastructure, bridges, mills, cattle, even learning. After the long Swedish occupation, Brandenburg's once extensive network of canals connecting its many lakes and rivers totally disappeared. Farms had been deserted. Land had fallen fallow. After the Peace, the elector proceeded to have the canals re-dug.

With little access to international trade, poorly endowed territories of differing nature and differing legal systems, an exhausted population, far-flung borders and territories, and precarious military positions, the many rulers had to become inventive in their ways of governing. Those who did not would not survive.

CAMERALISM

Oddly enough, as the hard-pressed princes searched for innovative methods of government, they turned to the scholars who developed the administrative doctrine of cameralism. The Cameralists were those advisors (Schumpeter calls them consultant administrators) who had immediate access to the princes. Most were university teachers, often in chairs created for the purpose, typically at freshly founded universities. Indeed, the post-1648 period saw the foundation of a large number of universities, in spite of the poverty that had befallen the nations. The expansion was eventually reversed when the Napoleonic occupation resulted in the closure of half of Germany's universities.

The Cameralists, using their own multiplier analysis of public expenditure programs, pointed out with regularity that a university provided an export industry. Students who would otherwise have had to study abroad might stay home and spend their money. Other students could be expected to migrate to the university bringing their spendable funds. The higher the quality of the university, the more local students would be retained and the more foreign students would be attracted. Hence, Princes were advised to found universities, which required a charter from the Emperor. The charters were typically granted upon the Emperor's election, when a proclamation as the first imperial act would essentially grant all the privileges that had been promised in order to secure the election. This first declaration was called, fittingly enough, the *pragmatic act*.

The example of the universities shows the basic reasoning of the Cameralist advisors. In Europe after 1648 we can assume that borders were hard to protect, natural resources rarely were available, and the most important resource was an educated population in good health. Able citizens could easily migrate elsewhere; therefore, taxes were hard to levy. Further, the prince could not exploit tariffs beyond reasonable limits for fear of losing traffic on roads. In the face of these constraints, an economic doctrine had to be designed that emphasized development, the education of a well-maintained population, attractive conditions for immigration, law and order, good rules for commerce, a credible but not-too-expensive army, and a stable currency.

Cameralism, basically an economic doctrine, was typically taught in three parts. At the core, there were the principles of public policy, teachings about the operation of markets and the pre-conditions of their functioning. Second, the cameralists discussed issues in technology from mining to forestry, farming, husbandry and the like in great detail. And third, they dwelt on so-called police science, discussing the public-law aspects of an orderly commonwealth, including an interconnected treatment of jurisdiction, taxation, sanitation, poor laws, and the like.

The starting point for the Cameralist consultant administrator was the territory that had been inherited through rules of succession. He had to take the endowment of natural resources as given and seek ways to improve upon that endowment by introducing legislation that made industry and commerce attractive. One means of achieving this goal was the granting of religious freedoms, civil liberties and economic freedoms. Brandenburg, one of the most hard pressed but also major winners of the 30 Years War, repeatedly invited religious refugees to settle there. With few natural resources, mostly infertile soil (sand) and wetlands, Brandenburg brought in Dutch refugees to settle the Oderbruch, Austrian refugees to settle Eastern Prussia, and French Huguenots with either capital or marketable skills. Earlier than any other country of its size, Prussia became a safe haven for Jews, who were granted traders' licenses upon offering the proper credentials. After the emancipation of the Jews, Prussia (and notably its major cities) served as a magnet for Jewish immigration.

The Cameralist literature argued further that this carefully groomed population needed proper maintenance, health care, food, stable prices in basic necessities, and drinking water or fresh beer. They argued for the organization of fairs to promote commerce, the establishment of savings and loans associations to provide for capital accumulation, and the development of policies that gave people a positive outlook of the future in order to found families. The Cameralists developed basic administrative rules based on these precepts.

Faced with precarious borders, the Cameralists pointed out the necessity of a vigilant army. They discussed military issues in astonishing detail, dealing with how to maintain an army in good state so as to make it small; how to avoid campaigns that would inflict unnecessary injuries or lead to exposure to infectious disease; how to conduct a campaign with a minimum of human loss. The notion that humans were the most important resource these rulers could command can be found throughout their writings. Tolerance towards religions of different denominations was *de rigueur* under such a doctrine with an equal focus on intolerance against intolerant religions, which might have disrupted the entire carefully constructed edifice. The elector of Brandenburg and second King of Prussia went so far as to once-and-for-all end all disputes between Protestant clergy by forcing Lutherans, Calvinists, and other Protestants into one unified church under his own guidance as the supreme bishop. It is clear that his purpose was to reduce religious conflict because, although a pious man, the elector had no religious ambitions of his own.

The Cameralist doctrines extended to demands for a stable currency. When currencies compete, debasement of a currency implies that taxes are being paid in the debased currency and the better coins are being held out of circulation. If a country was able to maintain a stable currency (which also at the time required substantial craftsmanship in minting), it could reap substantial profit from seignorage through exporting the stable currency and taking advantage of debasement of neighboring currencies. Interestingly, this policy, combined with commercial liberties, solves the problem Adam

Smith thought was the Mercantilists' prime objective: obtaining and retaining as much gold as possible. The mint of the country with the stable currency will receive gold for the purpose of minting coins from countries with unstable currencies and thus retain seignorage from minting coins for other countries, as well.

It is useful to contrast the basic precepts of Cameralism with the major competing doctrine of Mercantilism. Mercantilism is an economic doctrine for sea-bound large and contiguous territories that can control their population. Typically, mercantilist policies toward commerce, taxation, agriculture, education, and trade are directed at maximizing the state revenue (preferably as mintable specie). In addition to revenues from military campaigns mercantilists sought substantial income from colonial expansion, while treating the local economy mostly (but not explicitly) as a given. As described earlier, France needed substantial revenues in mintable specie to expend in its various lobbying efforts in German capitals so as to fully profit from the terms of the Peace Treaty of Münster. It can be argued that France's reliance on income from colonies and military campaigns led to relative neglect of the productive forces at home. Unlike the Cameralist doctrine of Wolff (described below), no French or British philosophical system I have so far encountered emphasizes the duty to be industrious and the duty to invent. The Cameralist theory of productive forces, later to be reformulated by Friedrich List, falls into the same intellectual tradition.

CONSTITUTIONAL PRINCIPLES

What appeared to be a deliberately organized chaos created by the Peace Treaties of Münster and Osnabrück still turned out to be a system of which we can make sense. However, it could require substantial intellectual endeavor to accomplish this feat. On this point I should like to emphasize only one aspect. Each of the territories thus created under one particular ruler, was composed of entities of very different legal status. The ruler might be King of one part, Prince of another, Margrave of yet another. Within the same Kingdom he might enjoy certain rights of jurisdiction in one place and not in the other, be the bishop of one place but not the neighboring one, be the elder of an Abby with the concomitant resources yet face a chapter by virtue of faith opposed to his very existence. The ruler might be the protector of a Protestant university and accountable to defend its privileges and its faith while himself being a devout Catholic. He could hold several votes on the Knights Bench in one circuit and oppose those very knights in his capacity as a Count, Prince, or Duke in the same circuit. The potential for conflict was immense, yet so was the potential for designing rules governing those complicated matters.

In the context of these conflicting roles, the work of Christian Wolff takes on new meaning. Wolff is probably the first scholar who had ever received an imperial knighthood only on account of his scholarship and not on account of particular services he might have rendered. His work is important as it laid the groundwork that allowed this complicated system to run and produce technological leadership, which was the only conceivable resource that could be relied upon, because other resources were no longer available. Christian Wolff developed a complex system of natural philosophy that dealt with the doctrine of competing princes with its complex set of rules of cooperation. Wolff refers to the basic doctrine of Cameralism in his system of natural law. This interconnection is important in helping us understand how the Cameralists as the economic advisors could prevail when foreign and dynastic policy considerations seem to have had a supreme status. As it turned out, the country and the dynasty were best served by following Cameralist principles within the context of the natural law doctrines as set out by Wolff.

The Foundation of Economics as Practical Political Economy

In 1727 Frederick William I of Prussia, who was otherwise not particularly interested in the sciences, became so upset with the quality of instruction at the universities that he decided to take action. In particular, he was angered by the inability of the university educators to instill principles of economical behavior in the future administrators of the country. The university graduates, he wrote, are "poor economists" and therefore can be said to "starve the country." The king founded the very first chair in political economy at the University of Halle. During the same year, a second chair was created in Frankfurt (Oder). Soon other princes followed suit. These royal activities provided a program for political economy that married theory and practice with extra emphasis on the practice. The king was not aiming at highbrowed economic policies, but economic activities on all political levels, high and low.

Ironically, the same king had committed a serious blunder at the same university in 1723 when he gave in to the petitions of a group of jealous theologians and fired his own professor Christian Wolff, who in several ways can be considered the first influential German political economist. Christian Freiherr von Wolff (1679–1754) was trained as a philosopher and mathematician. His numerous writings contributed to virtually every aspect of knowledge, political economy included. Frederick William's successor, Frederick II (the Great) in 1740 succeeded in re-appointing a by now fairly disgruntled Wolff in Halle as the professor of International Law and "Senior" in the university. An imperial knighthood followed in 1745.[8] This peculiar episode and the even more unusual final outcome clearly indicate the importance Wolff enjoyed in his time.

Wolff was the first prominent university teacher in economics who stubbornly insisted on publishing his work in German as well as in the traditional Latin. He enjoyed a very wide following, and the Wolff School dominated university appointments in Germany for quite some time.[9] Wolff approached economics by way of the doctrines of natural law as did Adam Smith, and he established economics as the science of the modern welfare state. This was done in the context of his general theory of the state. In applying his strictly logical deductive approach, which he owed largely to Leipniz, he succeeded in adding an ethics or practical wing to the philosophy of natural law as a basis for a further development of a rough theory of economic policy. The first step to be taken in this endeavor was his demonstration that the theory of the state (political economy or "Staatswissenschaft") with practical applications was possible at all. I do not want to bore the reader with this "proof" and shall immediately turn to the tasks he defined for the practical political economists. To this very day, practical political economy can be defined in the same terms:[10]

> Now that we have established that a theory of public policy is not impossible, we have to indicate its contours a little more precisely. Whenever advice in political economy is needed, two questions arise: the first is the question of the policy options available. Is a particular measure of economic policy possible, or does it interfere with somebody's rights? The second question concerns the effect or usefulness of a proposed measure: is there a clear advantage in pursuing the policy measure?

Wolff foreshadowed problems with modern economic policy analysis, in which issues of distributive justice or equity play an important role after discussions of allocative efficiency. However, these economic discussions of equity issues typically do not even refer to the legal framework in which they ultimately have to find their application. This creates the possibility that the results of an analysis of welfare economics can be in direct conflict with legal realities. Ultimately, the legal realities prevail, and the ignorance of the legal framework leads to the impossibility of applying the results of economic theoretical work in practice. Wolff identifies this problem, which plagues modern economics to the extremes, and he insisted on the need to do the legal and economic analysis *in tandem*:[11]

> The practical political economist has to have above all two character traits: prudence and a sense of justice. A sense of justice is needed in order to ensure that the politicians do not overstep their legal boundaries. Prudence is required in order to prevent those who try to make improvements from actually bringing about damage.

Thus, early in the eighteenth century, Wolff identified the importance of the economic analysis of law or the new institutional economics, which both emphasize the legal and institutional constraints of economic policies in order to better assess their likely impact.

Wolff who was an indefatigable author of textbooks, nevertheless argued for their critical use in studying political economy. His ultimate purpose for academic instruction in political economy was the training of better political economists (Staatswirte) who could make use of their academic instruction in their daily practical work:[12]

> Our teaching the art of public office has no other purpose than to make the students aware of what is in the interest of the state and what they can usefully apply in their prudent management of public affairs. Although the teaching at many schools is irrelevant for this purpose, no one will deny that there are some authors whose books contain much that is relevant for a systematic teaching (Lehrbegriff) of political economy.

Wolff further explained that application of the theory was as important as the theory itself (p. 10); a theory could hardly be applied if the specific circumstances of this application were not adequately taken into account.

The principles of political economy that Wolff taught to his students can be found in six chapters of his book on public law, which itself is part III of his *Treatise on International Law* in six volumes. The central and very modern point is Wolff's definition of the state as a welfare state. In a nutshell, he already describes what we teach in our principles of economics courses today:[13]

> It is readily apparent that individual households cannot provide for themselves everything that is necessary in order to satisfy their basic needs, comfort and enjoyments, *i.e.* wealth. They cannot by themselves be sure to be able to enjoy the fruits of their property and to enforce their property rights. Nor can they defend themselves against aggression from outside. Therefore, we need a common social effort, *i.e.* a society through which the individual households can attain the maximum of their welfare.

Although Wolff clearly has the germs of the theory of market failure, he is not a modern economist in the sense that he definitely does not subscribe to methodological individualism. For him, the unit of analysis is not the individual but the household. What the individual households cannot provide for themselves is residually defined as the purpose of the state. Yet, Wolff at the same time cautions against overburdening the state. He clearly outlines the limits of state activity:[14]

> Since any measure of public policy has to be derived from and judged by a purpose (pp. 976, 972), it can only support those activities of the citizens which are conducive to the common welfare. Consequently, and since the liberty of the households can only be constrained in the interest of the common welfare, public policy can in no other way interfere with the affairs of the household.

Public policy is exclusively defined in terms of social welfare, and it is limited by the ability of the households to take care of their own affairs. The primary task of the welfare state is to support the households in such a way that they can take care of their own matters in finding the means for their existence. Wolff considers a fairly broad array of different policy measures to meet this criterion, including the modern economic policies of full employment,[15] the stability of the currency,[16] and even environmental policy. Wolff's interest in environmental policy was driven by the overexploitation of the forests, which in Wolff's time had resulted in a dramatic scarcity of wood, which in turn led to the first systematic policies of reforestation in central Europe. In the area of social policy, Wolff's program was similarly extensive. Again, from the simple principle of enabling the households to take care of their own affairs, he was able to derive a whole spectrum of social policy, including the assistance of the poor, orphanages, employment policies, schooling for reemployment, and even free schooling for the children of the poor.[17]

Such a broad program for a fairly extensive welfare state immediately raised the question of how to finance it. Again, Wolff is thorough in presenting the whole catalogue of traditional state revenues as a source of funds, although he warns against using customs duties and taxes. Taxes, he argues, only reduce the value of the object of taxation, a position today argued by Barro. Customs duties would only lead to increases in the prices of necessities and should therefore also be avoided. He makes no mention of excise taxes, and income taxes of course would come later.

Wolff's position contains the major elements of what was going to become the peculiar contribution of German political economy. Political economy emerged as the science needed for the administration and management of an enterprising welfare state, a science that is inseparably married to its application and the institutions in which it was to be applied. It is no surprise that the German word for political economy talks about the science of the state (Staatswissenschaften), and that the German word for economics (Volkswirtschaftslehre) also has the derivative of a 'Volkswirt', a term not quite correctly translated as economist. A "Wirt" is in modern English a manager, and in German the term applies to the managers of farms, forests, inns and those of the public economy alike.[18] This emphasis on management is not just a pure linguistic aberration. It is not a co-incidence that Wolff continuously uses the word prudence in order to emphasize that the political economist has to weigh alternatives. He also talks about the art of political economy, not the science. However, he wants to systematically teach this art, and that is what the Cameralists, the first professors in political economy, indeed set out to do.

The Subsidiarity Principle: From Wolff's Formulation to the Treaty of Maastricht

In an extended article in the *Wall Street Journal Europe*, David Howell summarized the subsidiarity principle in the context of ongoing political discussions in Europe as "the undertaking that the Community institutions should only exercise those tasks that they can carry out more effectively than the member states acting separately."[19] But he continued "Yet the more that is heard about the concept of subsidiarity the less protective of the roots of democracy it sounds. Even the word itself seems wrong. It is not actually in the Oxford English Dictionary but the nearest word, subsidiary, means secondary, or subordinate."[20] What appears to be an arcane principle to the observer from across the sea in fact has been a mainstay of European continental thought for several centuries.

Perhaps one of the earliest formulations of the principle of subsidiarity, which is also one of the first formulations of a full-scale state welfare program, can be found in Christian Wolff's *Principles of Natural Law*, published in 1754. There (p. 1022), he states the following:[21]

> In order for all subjects to lead a decent life, it is also necessary that the needy and the beggars receive what they require for their basic needs and, in order not to burden the subjects too much with requests for gifts and donations, one has to pay heed to what the natural law indicates on the subject of gifts and donations (section 488 ff.). Hence it is necessary to build houses of re-education where those who can work, but rather prefer the life of a beggar, learn how to work. Similarly, houses for the poor and destitute are necessary to provide for those who cannot earn their living with their own work and who have no relatives or friends who could support them. Further, it is necessary to have hospitals where the sick can be nourished and healed. Similarly, orphanages are necessary where the poor orphans will be educated as schools for the destitute need to be available in order to teach the children of poor parents, without asking for a fee, all those subjects which for them to know is either necessary or useful.[22]

Several elements of this exposition are particularly noteworthy. First, Wolff calls for a welfare state with a broad scope, including measures to alleviate the consequences of sickness, unemployment, poor health, orphanhood and poverty, as well as to provide schooling for the poor. Yet the rationale for this government welfare program, as Wolff explicitly states, is to keep the burden of the welfare taxes to be borne by citizens at a minimum. The welfare state intervenes if and because this is the least expensive way to alleviate the problem. Equally noteworthy is the precise circumscription of the instance under which the welfare state has to intervene, *i.e.*, if the person in need has no "relatives or friends who can take on the satisfaction of his needs." The welfare state, therefore, is only subsidiary to the traditional bonds of family and friendship. Thus, Wolff considers the extensive family, and not the individual, to be the nuclear entity of which the larger economy is composed:[23]

> § 972. We realize easily that there will be single households which are unable to sufficiently provide for themselves what they require for their basic needs, their comfort, pleasure and happiness. It is furthermore quite conceivable that single households may not be able to protect with certainty what is theirs and from which they may profit in peace, to demand what they have a right to receive from others and to protect their rightful property against the use of force. It is therefore necessary to maintain with a collective effort what a single household cannot maintain itself. It is with this purpose in mind that societies need to be formed. (§ 836).[24]

We realize then, that in Wolff's conception the principle supporting the unit of the welfare state was the house, *i.e.*, the classical household or micro-economy. Only when the household failed, was the larger politico-economic unit to intervene.

The interesting question then is what form this intervention was supposed to take. The answer is already implicit in Wolff; yet note that Schmoller, who was a most careful reader, chided his interventionism. A more explicit statement can be found in the writings of von Mohl, another authority on political thought in continental Europe writing about a hundred years after Wolff.[25]

> Of course, from the need to provide sufficiently for the basic necessities of life it does not follow that it is the state that has to make these provisions. On the contrary, the state will deal with this need as it does with any other demand of its citizens. The state has to provide with its administrative means only if there is an undeniable basic need coupled with the impossibility to satisfy this need with private means. As a rule, this condition will not be met, if the state follows a general policy encouraging the formation of wealth by its citizens.[26]

We can conclude that the structures created by the Peace of Westphalia, unworkable as they may seem at first sight, gave rise to an intellectual response that not only led to doctrines guiding economic development (Cameralism) but also tenets guiding complex organizational design and, in particular, an allocation of competencies according to what basically are concepts of economic efficiency in organizational design. An example is the subsidiarity principle which has now re-appeared in the Treaty of Maastricht. It was totally unknown in the Anglo-Saxon context, and subsidiarity was only known in the Roman countries through the version promulgated by the Catholic Church. In the German language countries, it had for long been a main stay of public law, being a necessary response to the multifarious relations of competitiveness and complementarity among different public bodies as created by the Treaties of Westphalia.

CONCLUSION: A REASSESSMENT OF THE TULLOCK HYPOTHESIS

Gordon Tullock hypothesizes that seven broad factors were conducive to Europe leaping forward at a much faster pace than Asia during the nineteenth century. This chapter has focused on Professor Tullock's emphasis on the role played by cameralism and the seemingly chaotic nature of competition among nation states. The seeds of this competition and the doctrines of political economy developed by the Cameralists can be found in the Treaty System of Westphalia at the end of thirty years of war in 1648. The Treaty System left a large area within Central Europe without a unitary state. Instead, there were ever-changing interconnections as well as rivalries between states. This competition among states and the poverty at the end of the war led many states to compete for human capital by offering religious and economic freedoms, while establishing great universities. The universities became the sources of new knowledge, particularly in the areas of political economy, where Christian Wolff and others developed the doctrines of cameralism, a pragmatic set of tenets by which to govern nation states that has much to teach modern economic policy analysts. The cameralists developed political-economic theories of the welfare state, directly advised their nations' leaders in putting these theories in practice, and taught the next generation of leaders. Ironically, the peculiar construction of the Wesphalian system of treaties that ended thirty years of war and the chaos and poverty in Europe at that time established fertile ground for the development of the wealth of nations for the following centuries.

Paper prepared for a conference in honor of Gordon Tullock, Hacienda del Sol, May 22, 1999.

[1] Durham: Duke University Press, 1966.

[2] By way of perspective, one should note that Tullock's treatment and the treatment offered here go further but are by no means incompatible with North (1981). North takes a universal approach based on the property- rights theory and has the question posed by Tullock only implicitly as a side line. The constitutional approach embedded in Tullock's treatment is compatible with the property-rights approach.

[3] The titles have been reproduced so carefully as they concern a point to be discussed further in the fourth section. Further titles include Duke of Brabant, Styria, Carinthia, Carniola, Marquiss of Moravia, Duke of Luxembourg, of Higher and Lower Silesia, of Wirtemburg and Teck, Prince of Suabia, Count of Habsburg, Tirol, Kyburg, and Goritia, Marquiss of the Sacred Roman Empire, Lord of Burgovia, of the Higher and Lower Lusace, of the Marquisate of Slavonia, of Port Naon and Salines.

[4] Ironically, probably due to a movie starring Greta Garbo, Queen Christina is today often pictured as an angel of peace. Her instructions to the Swedish negotiation team under the guidance of Oxenstierna fail to corroborate that view.

[5] The types of collective bodies might include a bench of knights, a synod of a bisdom or the chapter of an Abby, when two religions are present.

[6] As explained above, this essay addresses only the first aspect of the question as to the possible advantages that Europe had; it is silent on the situation in China.

[7] The constituents were not completely sovereign, but they could enter into alliances with foreign parties as long as those were not directed against the unity of the Empire or the Emperor, nor could the constituents, for instance, leave the Empire.

[8] Beginning in 1707 Wolff taught mathematics, philosophy, and natural sciences in Halle. Between 1723 and his return in 1740 he continued his work in Marburg.

[9] Schumpeter (1954, p. 117) also mentions Christian Thomasius (1654–1728) who also taught at the University of Halle since 1694, published in German and made contributions to public finance. In general, he is considered the founder of German journalism. Schumpeter, however, ranks him more highly than Wolff as an economist, not because he disagrees with Wolff's work, but because Wolff's great interest in the economic events and policies of his day (p. 117) was the interest of a polyhistor. In Roscher's terms, of course, Wolff was undoubtedly an economist.

[10] Christian Freiherr von Wolff (1740), S. 372–73. Nachdem es nun bekannt ist, daß die Erwegung der Staatsgeschäfte nichts unmögliches sey (. . .): so gebühret es sich nun dieselbige in etwas genauer zu betrachten. So offt man wegen der Staatsgeschäfte zu Rath gehet, so kommen zweyerley Fragen vor. Die eine Art derselbigen betrifft das Recht, ob man nehmlich eine Befugniss zu etwas habe, und es ohne dem Rechte eines anderen zu nahe zu treten thun könne oder nicht; die andere betrifft den Nuzen ob es nehmlich einen Vortheil bringe, dergleichen zu thun oder nicht."

[11] Es müssen demnach diejenigen, welchen die Sorge für die Staatsgeschäffte aufgetragen ist, zwey Tugenden vor anderen besizen; nehmlich die Gerechtigkeit und Klugheit. Jene haben sie nöthig damit sie nichts so thun verlangen noch dazu rathen dass man etwas thue, wenn es nicht gerecht ist, und damit sie vor der Ungerechtigkeit einen Abscheu haben: Diese aber wird dazu erfordert, damit sie keinen Schaden anrichten, indem sie Nuzen schaffen wollen. (Ibidem)

[12] Wolff (1947) p. 409.

"Mann lehret ja die Staatskunst in keiner andern Absicht, als damit mann lerne, was dem Staat zuträglich seye, und demnach dazu nüzlich seye, den Staatsgeschäfften klüglich vorzustehen. Ohnerachtet nun diejenige Staatskunst, welche gemeiniglich in den Schulen gelehret wird, solchen gar wenig nüzlich ist, welche mit einer Staatsklugheit versehen seyn müssen: so kan man jedoch nicht in Abrede seyn, dass in den Büchern verschiedener Schriftsteller, welchen man ihr Lob nicht nehmen kan, manches vorkommet, was dabei nüzlich ist, wenn man einen Lehrbegriff aufsezen will."

[13] Wolff (1754) III, 2.1. "Wir erkennen sehr leicht, daß eintzele Häuser sich selbst dasjenige nicht hinreichend verschaffen können, was zur Nothdurft, Bequemlichkeit und dem Vergnügen, ja zur Glückseligkeit erfordert wird, noch auch ihre Rechte ruhig geniessen, und was sie von andern zu fordern haben, sicher erhalten, noch auch sich und das ihrige wider anderer Gewaltthätigkeit schützen können. Es ist also nötig, dasjenige durch gemeinschaftliche Kräfte zu erhalten, was eintzele Häuser vor sich nicht erhalten können. Und zu dem Ende müssen Gesellschaften errichtet werden."

[14] Wolff (1754) III, 2.1. "Da die Herrschaft in einem Staate aus seiner Absicht ermessen werden muss (pp. 976, 972.); so erstreckt sie sich nicht weiter als auf die Handlungen der Bürger, welche zur Beförderung der gemeinen Wohlfahrt gehören; folglich da nur bloss in Absicht dieser Handlungen die natürliche Freyheit der einzelen Glieder eingeschränckt wird (pp. 975,77.); so bleibt sie in Ansehung der übrigen Handlungen ungekränckt."

[15] "Dass es denen nicht an Arbeit fehle, die Arbeiten wollen" (Paragraph 1021).

[16] "Muss man nicht gestatten, dass Theuerung gemachet werde" (Wolff [1754], Paragraph 1021).

[17] See Wolff (1754), Paragraph 1022.

[18] The German terms are "Landwirt," "Forstwirt," "Gastwirt," and "Volkswirt." The manager of a business enterprise is called a "Betriebswirt."

[19] David Howell was then the chairman of the House of Commons Select Committee on Foreign Affairs.

[20] See Howell (1990), p. 6, cols. 4–6.

[21] "Das Leben gehörig hinzubringen, wird auch erfordert, dass man vor die Dürftige und Bettler besorge, was zur Nothdurft des Lebens nöthig ist, und, damit die Unterthanen nicht gar zu sehr mit Allmosengeben beschwehret werden, ist in sorgfältige Betrachtung zu ziehen, was das Naturgesetz von den Allmosen feste setzt (488.sequ.). Daher sind Zuchthäuser aufzubauen, worinn diejenigen zur Arbeit angehalten werden müssen, welche, ob sie gleich Arbeiten könnten, doch lieber betteln wollen; ingleichen Armenhäuser, worinn man die dürftigen ernähret, die sich durch Arbeiten das nicht zu erwerben im Stande sind, was sie zur Lebensnothdurft gebrauchen, und keine Anverwandten oder Freunde haben, welche sich ihrer Bedürfnisse annehmen könnten; noch ferner Kranckenhäuser, worinn krancke Arme theils ernähret, theils geheilet werden; So auch Waysenhäuser, worinn man arme Waysen erziehet; endlich Armenschulen, in welchen man

die Kinder armer Eltern umsonst in demjenigen unterrichtet, was ihnen zu wissen nöthig und nützlich ist."

[22] Wolff (1754), III, 2.1.

[23] § 972. "Wir erkennen sehr leicht, dass eintzele Häuser sich selbst dasjenige nicht hinreichend verschaffen können, was zur Nothdurft, Bequemlichkeit und dem Vergnügen, ja zur Glückseligkeit erfordert wird, noch auch ihre Rechte ruhig geniessen, und was sie von andern zu fordern haben, sicher erhalten, noch auch sich und das ihrige wider anderer Gewaltthätigkeit schützen können. Es ist also nötig, dasjenige durch gemeinschaftliche Kräfte zu erhalten, was eintzele Häuser vor sich nicht erhalten können. Und zu dem Ende müssen Gesellschaften errichtet werden" (§ 836).?

[24] Wolff (1754) III, 2.1.

[25] "Natürlich folgt aus dieser Notwendigkeit des Besitzes genügender Lebensbedürfnisse noch keineswegs, daß sie gerade der Staat zu liefern habe. Im Gegenteil wird er sich zu diesem Bedürfnis wie zu jedem anderen Verlangen seiner Bürger verhalten. Er hat also namentlich polizeiliche Hilfe nur dann zu gewähren, wenn bei der grösseren Allgemeinheit eines Bedürfnisses auch die Unmöglichkeit vorliegt, daßelbe mittels Privatanstrengung zu befriedigen. Und in der Regel wird Letzteres nicht der Fall sein, wenn die allgemeinen Massregeln zur Erwerbung von Vermögen gehörig getroffen sind und benützt werden."

[26] Mohl (1844), (2), pp. 265–66.

REFERENCES

Howell, D. (1990). "Ridley and Europe's Power Balance." *The Wall Street Journal Europe*, July 16.

Jakob, Ludwig Heinrich von (1806). "Grundsätze der national-Ökonomie, oder Theorie des National-Reichtums," Halle, 3rd edition, 2 vols., Halle: im Kommission bei Friedrich Ruff., 1825, 322; XIV, p. 632.

Mohl, R. von (1844). *Die Polizeiwissenschaft nach den Grundsätzen des Rechtsstaates*, Tübingen, (2).

North, D. (1981). *Structure and Change in Economic History*. New York: Norton.

Schumpeter, J. (1954). *History of Economic Analysis*. New York: Oxford University Press.

Tullock, G. (1966). *Organization of Inquiry*. Durham: Duke University Press.

Wolff, Christian Freiherr von (1740). "Von einer Erwegung der Staatsgeschäfte". In: *Gesammlete kleine philosophische Schriften*. Halle: Renger.

______ (1754). *Grundsätze des Natur- und Völckerrechts*. Halle: Renger.

VARIATIONS ON TULLOCK'S ROAD MODEL

James M. Buchanan and Yong J. Yoon
Center for Study of Public Choice
George Mason University
Fairfax, Virginia 22030
U.S.A.

INTRODUCTION

Four decades past, Gordon Tullock published a short paper, "Problems of Majority Voting" (1959), that proved to be seminal in the subsequent development of public choice theory. The central argument of the paper was incorporated as an element in *The Calculus of Consent* (Buchanan and Tullock, 1962), and, separately, the discussion of logrolling stimulated a large body of literature.[1]

Our purpose in this chapter is limited. We propose to take the particular example that Tullock used in his paper, that of identical farmers who benefit separately from tax-financed supply-maintenance of local roads and to subject this example to critical analytical scrutiny. Our ultimate purpose is, of course, the same as that which motivated Tullock's early effort: To understand more fully the implications of the institution of majority voting in politics. However, our focus is quite different from Tullock's. Whereas he was primarily interested in the formation of majority coalitions, as facilitated by logrolling or vote trading, and in the stability properties of predicted outcomes, we concentrate attention on properties of the equilibrium solutions generated under differing institutional settings, all of which embody majority voting.

Our results confirm Tullock's generalized hypothesis that the institutional structure of majority voting, under the conditions that he postulated, will generate allocative inefficiency in the form of excessive investment in the collectively financed partitionable good, along with the more specific hypothesis that *all* persons in the polity will consume or use quantities of the good beyond the efficient level. Our analysis does not, however, fully support Tullock's apparent suggestion to the effect that all persons will share symmetrically in the net surplus, positive or negative, and/or will use equal quantities of the good, even in the model where persons are identical in capacities and in preferences.

SIMPLIFYING ASSUMPTIONS

Analysis is facilitated through the use of the following simplifying assumptions, which are designed to capture fully and to isolate the basic features of the Tullock model:

(1) All persons are identical, both in capacities and preferences;
(2) Each person secures measurable benefits from use of a partitionable (private) good (local roads in Tullock's example) that is produced-supplied-financed only by the collectivity. The benefits increase with increasing quantities, over some range, but at a decreasing rate;
(3) The collectivity, as such, supplies-finances no other good, whether partitionable (separately provided and privately valued) or nonpartitionable (Samuelsonian "public");
(4) There are no spillover benefits to persons other than the direct user;
(5) The good, as made available to any user, involves outlay on behalf of the collectivity that increases proportionately with quantity. That is, marginal cost is constant;
(6) All outlay on the good, to whomever provided, is financed exclusively from a general tax, imposed equally on all members of the community;
(7) Each person is interested only in maximizing net measurable benefits from collective action. There are no utility interdependencies;
(8) Authoritative decisive coalitions may be formed costlessly;
(9) In reaching decisions within existent coalitions, persons do not consider prospects for subsequent actions that may be taken by alternative coalitions.

In sum, these assumptions restrict the analysis to the bare-bones model implicit in the initial Tullock presentation. We do not extend analysis beyond Tullockian limits in any of the several directions that offer interest.

SINGLE MAJORITY

The solution is straightforward in a model in which only a single majority coalition is authorized to undertake collective-fiscal action. In a large polity with n members, a minimal-sized coalition ($n / 2 + 1$) will be formed, and this coalition will authorize collectively financed outlay on the provision of the partitionable good *only* to its own members. The quantity of good per person will be set at the level at which the marginal benefit (product or utility), which is equal among all recipients, approaches one-half of the per person tax cost (levied on all persons in the polity).

Figure 1 illustrates. On the abscissa we measure the physical quantity of good made available to a person, as defined in units of the *numéraire*. The cost of a unit is, by definition, one unit of the *numéraire*. On the ordinate, we measure benefits and costs. If the use of the good should be privatized, the equilibrium of a person (any person) is the position shown at E, where marginal evaluation equals price-cost. This position, of course, meets the criteria for allocative efficiency under the conditions postulated. If the provision of the good is collectivized under single majority rule, members of the majority will each pay only $1 / n$ shares in total outlay, while each will

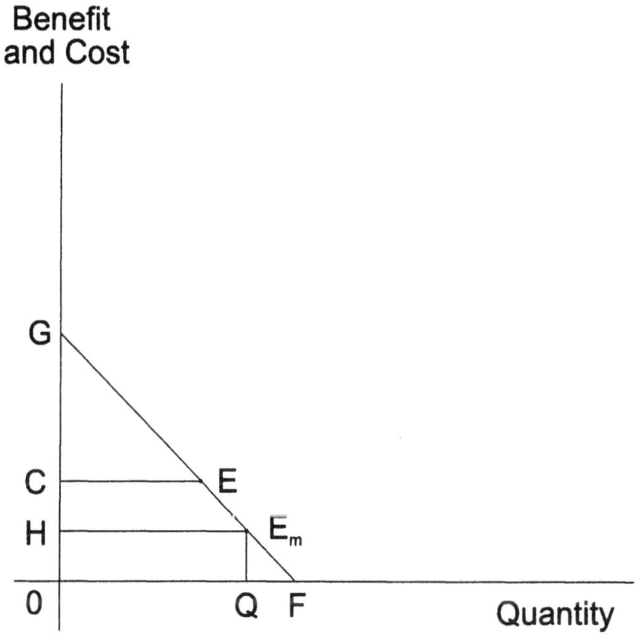

Figure 1. Majoritarian Equilibrium

secure 2 / n of the total benefits. The majoritarian equilibrium, preferred by each member of the successful coalition, is shown at E_m. Each member of the majority gets a net surplus measured as the triangle GE_mH in Figure 1, and each member of the excluded minority suffers a net loss in tax payments, measured by the rectangle OQE_mH, with no offsetting benefits.

MULTIPLE MAJORITY COALITIONS—SEQUENTIAL FORMATION

The majoritarian solution is Pareto inferior. Conceptually, members of the majority coalition could be provided with more value at a lower cost to members of the minority if side payments in money were institutionally feasible—in which case there need be no inefficiently large quantities of good available to members of the majority coalition. Under the constraints postulated, however, direct side payments are not possible. Members of the majority coalition cannot be compensated to refrain from implementing their own utility-maximizing solution as defined, which does involve inefficiently large quantities of the good.

Let us now assume, however, that this initial majoritarian choice need not exhaust the set of possible collective actions during the projected budgetary period. *Any* majority coalition may authorize collective action, and, subsequent to the initial coalition's choice, there may remain prospects for further action by alternative majorities. Members of the polity who are left out in the first stage of collective action may seek improvement in their own positions by dealing with some members of the initial majority through the "coin" of extensions in provision of the designated partitionable good.

Consider, then, the prospect for a mutually advantageous agreement between members of the minority and a member of the initial majority, who already has a guarantee of attaining the position shown at E_m.[2] At this position, for each member of the majority, there remains a positive evaluation of extensions in the quantity of the good. Any person in the majority would, therefore, agree to some extension in outlay, with a corresponding tax increment, provided that there is some addition to net surplus, which allows for some range of budgetary extension through the formation of subsequent majority coalitions that introduce discrimination in the allocation of outlay, within the coalitions themselves. As a second stage move, for example, a person in the initial majority agrees to join a new majority, thereby extending her own usage of the good, provided that she secures more than a $2 / n$ share of the goods financed from the aggregate budgetary extension, in exchange for a willingness on the part of each of those excluded initially to accept less than a $2/n$ share in the goods that are incrementally supplied.

As the sequence proceeds, more and more members of the initial majority coalition are separately engaged, so to speak, attracted by the promise of differentially larger quantities of the partitionable good. This process comes to completion only when the evaluation of additional quantities of the good is fully offset by the differential in the effective cost to members of the initial minority. Members of the initial majority coalition may secure benefits of goods quantities beyond their first-stage exploitation equilibrium, while members of the initially disadvantaged minority can secure benefits of goods quantities only below those defined for members of the majority in the initial round, but in excess of the efficient quantities that would be secured under market provision.

The asymmetry in the distribution of surplus and/or usage of the good is a different result from that suggested in Tullock's early paper. He implies, correctly, that each person (or group) will finally become a party to a separate majority coalition and that each coalition will take similar action in the form of providing tax-financed benefits to its own members. But he also seems to suggest that, in the final position, all persons will be symmetrical with respect to their final positions. The relevant passages from Tullock's paper are:

> The outcome is clear. Each farmer would enter into bilateral agreements with enough farmers on other roads to insure that his own was repaired. He would then be forced to count as part of the cost of getting his road repaired the cost (to him) of repairing the roads of 50 other farmers. These bilateral agreements, however, would overlap .... The natural result would be that each road would be maintained at a level considerably higher and at greater expense than is rational from the standpoint of the farmers living along it (p. 575).

Tullock does not seem to recognize that there is some necessary differential, however slight, between the position secured by those who are members of the initial majority coalition that is formed and those left out of the coalition, and that the action of all subsequent majorities must involve net extensions in goods provision to at least some members of the initial majority, extensions that must at least, when taken one at a time, leave them no worse off than in the first stage solution.[3] At the same time, for those persons left out of the initial majority coalition, any successful effort to form new coalitions must involve some willingness to reduce their own shares in benefits below those that might be available to members of the initial majority. On the other hand, Tullock's more general claim that each person in the whole polity may be provided with a quantity of the good that is larger than that quantity that would be "rational" under private market supply seems correct.

Note that, although differing majority coalitions emerge sequentially to make collective decisions, the model does not involve majoritarian cycling in the conventional sense. As specified, each majority coalition implements a collective result. And, as the sequence plays itself out, a final result is achieved when all majoritarian prospects have been exhausted. At this point, there is no majority that can be organized that can promise net gains to all its members,[4] despite the fact that, for all persons in the polity, there will be an institutionally generated inefficiency in the collective provision of the private good.

A SPECIFIC NUMERICAL EXAMPLE

We illustrate the analysis by introducing a specific numerical example. We assume that the politically organized community includes 99 identical persons, thereby making 50 the size of the minimal majority coalition. The geometrical representation in Figure 2 builds on the like construction in Figure 1. The abscissa measures physical quantities of the partitionable good defined in dollars' worth (valued at cost). The units measured on the ordinate are cents; the cost per unit is, therefore, fixed at 100.

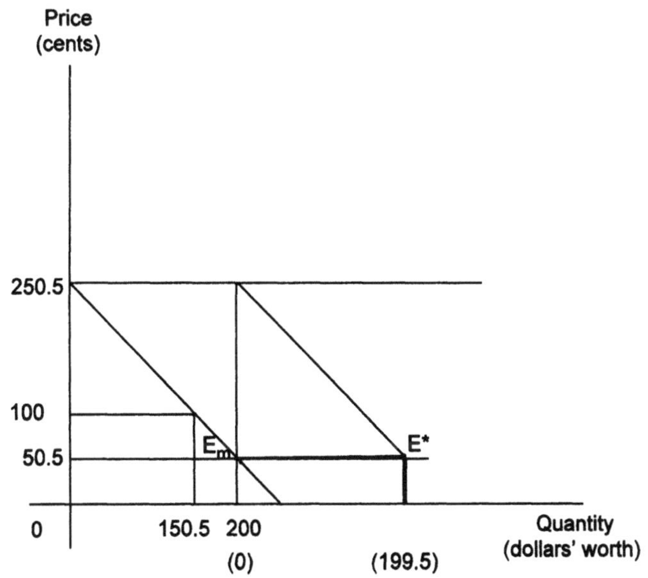

Figure 2. Numerical Extension

We specify that the demand or marginal evaluation schedule for a single person is defined by

$$T = 250.5 - Q. \tag{1}$$

Where T is effective tax price, in cents, and Q is quantity of good for private use by the person. We assume away income effect feedbacks; this allows us to treat equation 1 as both a demand and a marginal evaluation schedule.

In the polity with 99 members, the effective tax price to any member of a minimal majority coalition is constant at 50.5 cents per unit

$$T = 50.5. \tag{2}$$

An initial or first-round equilibrium is reached (E_m) with 200 units (dollars' worth) of the privately valued good provided to each person in the coalition. This total exceeds the quantity of 150.5 units, which would be demanded at the full cost price of 100 cents, the solution under market arrangements.

At this first-stage position, no member of the majority would agree to any extension in the quantity of the good supplied for her own use unless this quantity might somehow be offered on terms more favorable than those indicated by the equality between effective tax price and marginal evaluation, both set at 50.5 cents. How much, then, would the initially excluded minority have to give up to compensate a single member of the initial majority coalition to secure agreement to some extension in the budget, with benefits to be shared with this recruit and the previously excluded minority? What is the effective minimal marginal supply price faced by the minority coalition, as it bargains with a single potential recruit from the initial majority?

We know that, at the position E_m, any potential recruit places a marginal value of 50.5 cents on units of the good. Any extension is valued at less than this amount, and the difference between the marginal evaluation and the effective tax price that confronts members of any majority measures the minimal supply price.[5] As a potential "supplier," the relevant marginal evaluation schedule for a member of the initial majority is limited to that range beyond the first-round equilibrium. Hence, this schedule is

$$T = 50.5 - Q^* \tag{3}$$

where Q^* measures quantities beyond the initial equilibrium for a member of the initial majority and also quantities made available to members of newly formed majorities subsequent to the first stage. Note that this schedule must reflect the source of any supply that members of the minority may expect, since at least one person from the initial majority must join any new coalition.

For any member of a majority coalition, the effective tax price is 50.5 cents; the remaining 49.5 cents of the cost of a unit are imposed on those persons who remain outside the coalition as net taxpayers. The minimal supply price asked by any member of the initial majority is the difference between the effective tax price paid and the "price" that will equal marginal evaluation. Numerically in our example, this Marshallian supply price, S, becomes

$$S = 50.5 - (50.5 - Q^*), \text{ or,} \qquad (4)$$
$$S = Q^*$$

which indicates that, beyond E_m, the first-round equilibrium, the minority must compensate the single recruit from the initial majority in order to secure agreement to extend the provision of the good, to the recruit and other members of the new majority coalition, and that the marginal supply price (in cents) increases proportionately with quantity (in dollars' worth).[6]

There are 49 minority members, each one of whom shares in the benefits from the agreement by a single recruit to accept budgetary extension. The required compensation to the recruit assessed (symmetrically) against each member of the initial minority is, therefore, $Q^*/49$. A single member of this minority faces a schedule of marginal supply price

$$S = 50.5 + Q^* / 49 \,. \qquad (5)$$

The 50.5 cents here is the pro rata tax share that each member of any majority coalition must effectively pay, and the $Q^* / 49$ is the share of the single member in the compensation required to secure the recruit's agreement.

For each person in the initially excluded minority, equation 5 becomes the schedule of minimal marginal supply price for units of the good, which takes the form of agreements on the part of a single person, any one member of the initial majority coalition, to join a newly formed majority that proposes to finance-supply units of the good to the 49 members of the initially excluded group, along with some units to the new recruit, units that extend this person's usage beyond the first-stage equilibrium, E_m.

The minority need not, however, seek to "purchase" agreement from only one person. Each of the 50 persons in the initial majority coalition can be similarly confronted, and each can be separately recruited into differing majority coalitions, one for each initial member. In a sense, each member of the initial majority is, through these sequentially formed majorities that are organized with members of the initial minority, exploiting her fellow initial majority members.[7] But for the single member of the initial minority, as the 50 members of the initial majority are separately recruited and organized into new majorities, the schedule of minimal marginal supply price becomes

$$S = 50.5 + Q^* / (49)(50), \text{ or,} \qquad (6)$$
$$S = 50.5 + 0.000408\, Q^* \,.$$

Note that, by the assumed absence of income effect feedbacks, the demand or marginal evaluation schedule for a member of the initial minority remains identical to that defined in equation 1 for a member of the initial majority. Hence, we may solve equations 1 and 6 simultaneously to obtain

$$Q^* = 199.92, \text{ and} \qquad (7)$$
$$T^* = 50.58$$

where T^* denotes the effective marginal tax price to a single member of the initial minority. See E^* in Figure 2. For a member of the initial majority, comparable values become

$$Q_{maj} = 204 \qquad (8)$$
$$T_{maj} = 46.5$$

where the subscripts designate the quantity and effective marginal price to a single member of the initial majority.

This numerical example embodies the assumption that all of the surplus, the "gains from trade" apparently achieved by the extension of outlay beyond the first-stage equilibrium accrues to members of the initially excluded minority. Recruits who are separately attracted into newly-formed majority coalitions remain at the same level of utility, plus only the epsilon of value required to attain their acquiescence. This result represents, of course, the extreme or limiting case for the distribution of the apparent net gains from the separately organized bargains between single recruits and the initial minority. Alternative distributional assumptions might, of course, be made, but the general properties of the solution would remain unchanged. Distributions at or near the limit noted seem plausible, however, when we recognize that all members of the initial majority are competitors for what will seem to be differentially favorable treatment that may be offered by the initial minority.

The example demonstrates that, in the final political equilibrium, under the conditions postulated, each member of the initial minority receives almost as many units of the good (199.92) as the quantity received by each member of the initial majority in the first-round result (200), and before any subsequent formation of differing majority coalitions. This result seems counter-intuitive (and it did to us) until it is recognized that each incremental unit of the good offered to a single recruit is part of a budgetary package that simultaneously provides an increment to each member of the initial minority, all of whom join the recruit in making up the new majority. And, because there are 50 potential recruits to 50 new majorities, the required per unit compensation faced by a single member of the initial minority remains extremely small.

Note that the example tends to corroborate Tullock's basic hypothesis that all persons in the polity secure quantities of the privately valued and partitionable good well in excess of those quantities that would be secured under market institutions. A Pareto-superior "constitutional" shift from collective to market organization is clearly feasible, given the conditions as postulated.

IS SYMMETRY POSSIBLE?

As suggested, the solution that emerges in the model examined does not fully correspond to Tullock's plausible intuition that full symmetry would describe the distribution of surplus, positive or negative, and/or the quantities available for private use. He seems to have had in mind a result analogous to an *n*-person symmetric prisoners' dilemma, where each person in the whole community would be provided with an inefficiently large quantity of the collectively financed good (local roads), but where it would not be advantageous for any person, or coalition, to modify behavior. Can we construct an institutional setting such that the operation of a majority decision rule will generate the strictly-defined Tullock outcome?

First, let us neglect majority rule and assume a "constitution" that allows each person, separately, to authorize outlay on the privately used partitionable good, but at the expense of the whole community that is subjected to the general tax. In this setting, each person will secure the full benefits from each unit provided for her exclusive usage, but will, at the same time, be subjected to only $1/n$ share in the cost. Outlay, for each person, will be extended far beyond efficiency levels, but no person would, independently, find it advantageous to modify his behavior. The result suggested by Tullock for the operation of majority rule holds under this single-person rule.[8]

The same result will hold in all cases in which the number of persons authorized to implement collective action remains evenly divisible into the total number of members in the whole community. Hence, in our numerical example in the preceding section, in the polity with 99 members, decision rules that allow 1, 3, 9, 11, or 99 persons to authorize collective action, within the constraints postulated, may generate results that reflect full symmetry among all persons. If, however, such even divisibility is not present, persons cannot attain symmetry in the distribution of surplus in the ultimate political equilibrium.

Consider, within the 99 person community illustration, a rule that authorizes, say, any coalition of four persons to implement collective action in the form of general taxation to finance-supply privately valued goods to members of the authorizing coalition. Twenty-four separate four-person coalitions may be organized and each may extend on its own members' privately valued goods to the point at which the marginal evaluation per unit is equated with 4/99 of the per person cost. In each of the coalitions, the included members, 96 in all, may be symmetrically treated. But consider the plight of the three persons who are left outside any coalition. In a manner similar to that traced out in the numerical illustration above, these three persons may combine to bargain with single members of existing coalitions and, in this way, get some goods financed for their own use. But as the earlier illustration showed, these initially excluded persons must have access to a lower quantity of good and/or remain with a relatively smaller share in the potential surplus than those persons who were successful in becoming members in one of the first four-person sets.

Our primary concern here, however, is with majority rather than with any less-than-majority rule for collective action. Consider, then, a setting in which any majority may authorize tax-financed outlay on the provision of privately valued goods to its own members . For one majority coalition, the solution has already been examined. But is a model in which separate majority coalitions emerge simultaneously rather than sequentially internally coherent?

Suppose that a single majority coalition is formed, as analyzed. Each member attains a position such as that depicted at E_m. The formation of a different majority coalition is not possible without including some members of the same coalition already formed. The only means available to those persons who are left out of the initial coalition is that outlined in the sequential process carefully examined earlier. And this process insures that the final political equilibrium is characterized by asymmetry in the distribution of surplus and/or the quantities of goods available for use, no matter how slight this asymmetry might be. We may note, however, that symmetry is approached as a limit when the number of members in a polity becomes large. As the numerical example suggests, the marginal supply price confronted by members of the initial minority depends initially on the size of the polity's membership.[9]

THE ANALOGY WITH THE COMMONS

There are aspects of the basic Tullock model that are similar to the classic commons, and his overall results evoke comparisons with the conventional overusage tragedy (Buchanan and Yoon, 1998). The analogy is not so direct as it may seem, however, because we have assumed that the good is fully partitionable in use and, further, that taxes involve no excess burden. What, then, is the Tullockian analogue to the common resource that is overused, thereby dissipating its value potential?

The answer is that each person's own evaluation of the good in question is subjected to exploitation by her own behavior, as she responds to the incentives that are created by the collectivization of provision under general tax financing, along with decision rules that are less inclusive than unanimity. It is as if each person, as both a user of the good and as a participant in the collective decision process, ignores the external effects on others that are introduced by the decision rule itself. In this fundamental sense, the problem is fully analogous to the classic commons setting.

The limiting case, traced out earlier, in which each person may be authorized, separately, to act on behalf of the collectivity in making tax-financed outlay on her own goods is relatively straightforward. If the polity is large, persons will act as if the good is free; provision will be extended to satiety for all persons; and the total surplus, which the resources devoted to provision of the good might have generated, is dissipated.

The results become more complex in all settings where the decision rule requires assent by more than one person but less than all members of the polity. If a single choice is authorized, the relevant decision-making coalition will approve the outlay indicated to be maximally exploitative, given the size of the coalition relative to the whole community membership. The degree of inefficiency in resource use will be inversely related to the relative size of the decision-making coalition.

If more than a single collective choice within a budgetary period is permissible under the effective constitution—that is, if more than one decision-making unit or coalition is authorized to dictate tax-financed outlay, with the differing instructions to be implemented separately but simultaneously—commons-like overextension of outlay on collective provision of privately valued goods is assured, and asymmetry in the distribution of the goods and/or the potential surplus tends to emerge in all except special cases.

In all settings along some imaginary decision-rule spectrum, Tullock's basic hypothesis concerning excessive outlay seems to hold, although his implied symmetry is not fully descriptive except as a limit in large-number electorates. In any non-unanimity setting, it is difficult to construct a model that will not generate some wastage of potential value, effectuated through the provision of excessive quantities of the good to users. There is, indeed, a "tragedy of the commons" present in all cases in which essentially private and partitionable goods are collectivized under less-than-unanimity rules, along with generalized taxation. How much overusage inefficiency will exist, and what will be the degree of asymmetry in the distribution of the net surplus, negative or positive? These questions depend on particular features of the institutional structure, on the expectations of participants, and, importantly of course, on the empirical relevance of the behavioral model that informs the whole analysis.

[1] The analysis was followed up by a discussion between Anthony Downs (1961) and Tullock (1961). Downs's criticism was based largely on alleged institutional and informational deficiencies in Tullock's stylized model of majority voting. Our analysis, and Tullock's, incorporates the presumption that participants possess full knowledge.

[2] Conceptually, Pareto-superior bargains might be struck between the initial majority coalition, as a unit, and the initial minority, as a unit—bargains that would involve agreement to supply-finance some quantities of the good to minority members. We do not examine such possible bargains here since we concentrate on the effects of majority decision rules that do not embody any Pareto constraint.

[3] For the initial majority, as a group, of course, the piecemeal "defection" of members to new majorities that then generate exploitation of their original "fellows" can only reduce aggregate utility.

[4] We assume here that binding agreements among members of any majority that prevent membership in alternative coalitions are not permissible.

[5] The analysis here is analogous to, but not equivalent with, that of Marshallian joint supply. (Marshall, 1920, pp. 388–93.)

[6] Aside from our assumption that direct side payments are not possible, we need not specify here the precise form that the required compensation takes. If all taxation must remain strictly general, any discrimination must involve differentiation among shares in budgeted outlay (recruits get more dollars spent on their roads than others in the newly organized majorities). Or, as an alternative, special exception may be made so as to allow departure from strict tax uniformity.

[7] Note that the exploitation occurs here, not by defection to join another replacement coalition as in the conventional majoritarian cycle, but rather by joining another coalition that will add to or supplement the actions of the coalition that is organized first.

[8] The construction in *The Calculus of Consent,* which relates external costs to the inclusiveness of the decision rule, is essentially the same as that sketched out here for the one-person case.

[9] This relationship may be illustrated with reference to equation (6) in the numerical example. If we define the size of membership in the inclusive polity as N, the coefficient of Q^* becomes $1/(N/2 - 1)(N/2 + 1)$. This value moves toward zero as N becomes large.

Note also that this value falls rapidly as N increases for small-number ranges.

REFERENCES

Buchanan, James M., and Gordon Tullock (1962). *The Calculus of Consent: Logical Foundations of Constitutional Democracy.* Ann Arbor: University of Michigan Press.

Buchanan, James M., and Yong J. Yoon (1998). "Majoritarian Management of the Commons." Center for Study of Public Choice, George Mason University, Fairfax, Virginia, working paper.

Downs, Anthony (1961). "In Defense of Majority Voting." *Journal of Political Economy* 69 (April): 192–99.

Marshall, Alfred (1920). *Principles of Economics.* 8th ed. London: Macmillan.

Samuelson, Paul A. (1954). "A Pure Theory of Public Expenditure." *Review of Economics and Statistics* 36 (November): 387–89.

Tullock, Gordon (1959). "Problems of Majority Voting." *Journal of Political Economy* 67 (December): 571–79.

______ (1961). "Reply to a Traditionalist." *Journal of Political Economy* 69 (April): 200–03.

INSTABILITY OF VOTING OUTCOMES, LOGROLLING, ARROW, COASE, AND ALL THAT: A DIFFERENT INTERPRETATION

Peter Bernholz
WWZ, Center for Economics and Business
Universitaet Basel
CH-4003 Basel
SWITZERLAND

INTRODUCTION

For decades Gordon Tullock has been one of the pioneering Public Choice theorists studying the phenomena of voting and logrolling. The flagrant contradiction between the instability of outcomes predicted by theory for a whole class of widely used voting procedures and the empirical observations of rather stable political outcomes has led him to ask: *Why so much stability*? Tullock has recently re-addressed this question in his book *On Voting* (1998). Why this repetition? Is it because he wants to communicate his results to a wider audience? Or is there a lingering insecurity about whether the answers presented were the right ones?

Given Gordon's renewed interest, it seems fitting to pursue this subject that has given rise to friendly disputes between us since, I believe, 1974. In doing so, I will prove seven propositions with the help of examples and by reference to earlier work. The first proposition relates "cyclical social preferences" to negative externalities:

1. *Negative externalities are a necessary condition for the existence of cycles* (Bernholz [1982]). Here negative externalities are defined broadly. They include not only externalities brought about by individuals and organizations for outsiders, but also "political" externalities within organizations for "outvoted minorities" (Buchanan [1962], and Buchanan and Tullock [1962] 60–62). We may thus speak of *external* and *internal negative externalities.*

The next five propositions refer to the case of two or more issues and assume that no "social preference cycles" exist for alternatives that are different in only a single issue.

The following results hold:

2. *The existence of contracts between different subsets of society (individuals or organizations), which have the right to decide different issues, is a necessary condition for cycles.* Logrolling is just a special case of such contracts (Bernholz [1981], and Schwartz [1981, 1986]). In the case of logrolling, identical subsets of society have the right to decide several issues, usually by majority voting. But different majorities may be decisive for different issues. Thus a logrolling contract between them may be beneficial for their members.
3. *The Arrow theorem* (Arrow, [1963]) *covers all cases of decentralized decision making (including logrolling) in which subsets of society make contracts (beneficial to their members) regarding a specific use of their decision rights.* In fact, they are the only cases included by the theorem if two or more issues are considered.
4. *The paradox of voting is identical with the cycles implied by explicit or implicit logrolling* (as defined by Tullock [1967] 59).
5. *With complete information and no transaction costs, a stable, Pareto-optimal outcome can always be reached either by a reassignment of the rights to decide issues* (Bernholz [1986]), *or by an exchange of rights, or by binding external (between different individuals and/or organizations) and internal (among decisive members of an organization) contracts.* The latter possibility corresponds to a generalized Coase Theorem (Bernholz [1997, 1998]). For the limited case of a perfect vote market this result was first derived by James Coleman (1966, 1967).
6. *Sen's* (1970) *paradox of a Paretian Liberal is also a special case of external negative externalities created by individuals for other individuals* (Bernholz [1976]), *and thus of Arrow's Theorem. The paradox can thus be solved as indicated in proposition5.*

The seventh proposition refers to the misconception that "cyclical social preferences" arise only out of transitive individual preferences. It states:

7. *Cyclical social preferences can arise even if individuals have identical preferences provided that they are faced by different restrictions.* This implies, however, that in the "normal case" in which individual preferences are different and in which individuals are confronted with different restrictions (such as incomes, prices, available time, and legal and social rules), "cyclical social preferences" are caused by both preferences and restrictions. The name of the concept is thus misleading. This proposition has been well known for a long time (Breyer [1980]), but has not been given adequate attention in the social-choice literature. Perhaps this can be explained by the fact that scholars in this field began with the idea of constructing a "social welfare function" out of individual preferences.

In the following sections I will illustrate these propositions and refer to the formal general proofs. Before doing so, however, I would like to state my interpretation of "cyclical social preferences" and thus the Arrow Theorem. In my view, the respective phenomena have nothing to do with a Social Welfare Function or a Social Decision Function, which are constructs without correspondence in reality, unless one is considering a centrally planned economy, which might pursue the aims implied by such a function. But then cycles mean nothing but the fact that decisions taken by different subsets of society—having the right to do so for different issues—may be inconsistent. Depending on the procedures used, outcomes may thus be unstable, not Pareto-optimal or even determined by chance.

SOME DEFINITIONS AND ASSUMPTIONS

In any non-anarchical decentralized system there must exist at least two sets of rules:

(1) Rules assigning the right to decide different issues (property rights, political rights, etc.) to subsets of society;

(2) Rules for decision-making that are valid for the members of the different subsets of society having the right to decide issues. If an issue has, for instance, been assigned to a certain subset of society (which we call an *organization* if it contains more than one member), there must be rules about which subset of the members can make a valid decision for the organization. Such rules can be simple or qualified majority voting, or a majority of the shares held by the members, or even unanimity.

Note that the second set of rules would be unnecessary only in a decentralized society in which the right to decide each issue was assigned to a different individual (which we may call *extreme liberalism*). Note, also, that a case opposite to extreme liberalism would be *total democracy*—a system in which the rights to decide all issues were assigned to all (sane and adult) members of society, who in all cases decide by simple majority voting. Total democracy, however, should not be confused with a system applying the rule of unanimity to all issues assigned in the same way. Though the latter system would also be extremely collectivized, each individual would still have veto power over all issues.

Let us now assume that set V contains all (adult and sane) members of society and that $M = \{M_1, M_2, \ldots, M_n\}$ is the set of n issues present. Each issue comprises two or more alternatives. Further, let $V_i \subseteq V$ denote the n subsets of society to which the rights to decide these issues have been assigned. In the examples used subsequently we will confine ourselves to a society consisting of at most three people and to not more than three issues. But this is only a device to make life easier. The propositions stated above are valid for any society with any finite number of people and issues. And for each issue different decision rules can be used as long as they are "rational" (for the postulates concerning the decision rules see Bernholz [1997]). Note, finally, that the problems discussed would not exist if only one person and/or one issue were present. We thus assume $|V| \geq 2$, $|M_i| \geq 2$. If $|V_i| \geq 2$, we are speaking of an organization.

THE PARADOX OF VOTING AND LOGROLLING BY MAJORITIES ARE IDENTICAL

After these definitions and assumptions let us prove the validity of the propositions stated above. In Sections 3 and 4, we demonstrate the validity of Theorems 1–5 for two examples. The first example, to which we turn now, is well known. In working through it, we will prove the identity of the paradox of voting and of majority logrolling, when two or more issues are present. For this purpose let us turn to the graphical representation in Figure 1. In the example, two issues, M_1 and M_2, with infinitely many alternatives are assumed. Society comprises only three members as voters. Also let $V_1 \equiv V_2 \equiv V \equiv \{1, 2, 3\}$, i.e. all members of society have the right to decide the two issues. As a decision rule, simple majority rule is assumed for both issues. The most preferred outcomes for voters 1, 2, and 3 are x_1, x_2, x_3 respectively. The circles or ellipses around these points combine all outcomes for which the voter in question is indifferent. The space within each circle or ellipse includes outcomes acceptable to the voter, with those closer to the center preferred to those farther away.

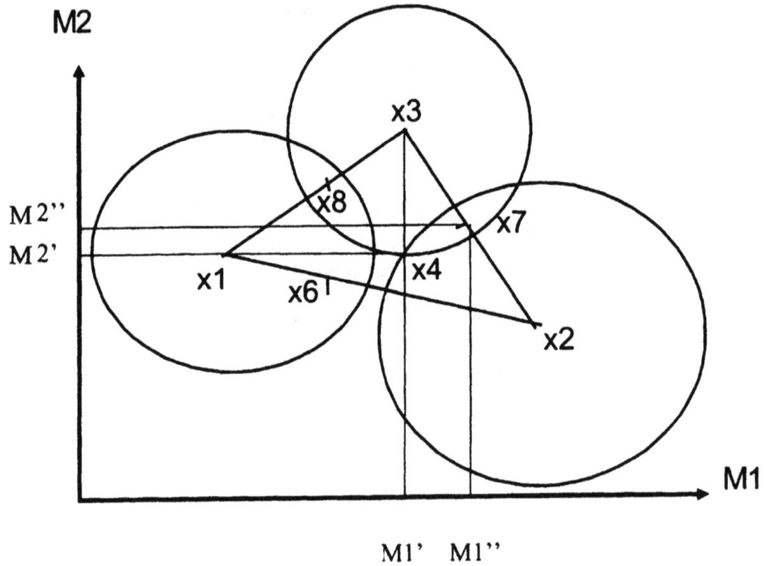

Figure 1. The Paradox of Voting and Logrolling

This implies that the three voters have single-peaked preferences. But it is well known that this is not a condition sufficient to secure a stable outcome if simple (and in this case even two-thirds) majority voting is used. True, if voting were to take place independently on the two issues, $x_4 = \{M_1', M_2'\}$, which combines the two most preferred positions of the two different median voters, would be selected. But voters 2 and 3 prefer $x_7$to this outcome, so that it will receive a majority if put to a vote against x_4. But the former is itself dominated by x_8, which is preferred by voters 1 and 3. Similarly, x_8 is dominated by x_6, itself dominated by x_4. Thus a cycle exists and no outcome is stable. We know that this is just one of infinitely many possible cycles and also, that the conditions for a stable outcome are very restrictive (Plott [1967], and Kramer [1973]).

We note next that by moving from one outcome to another, the respective majority is creating in each case an internal negative externality to the outvoted voter (minority). Thus, as was stated in Theorem 1, negative externalities are a precondition for a cycle in our example. Moreover, the majorities in question have to reach an agreement as to their voting behaviour. This can be done in either of two ways. The first possibility is an explicit logrolling contract between two parties, for instance between voters 2 and 3, that would result in x_7 being chosen instead of x_4. Both agree to vote for M_1'' and then for M_2''. This type of contract works when voting on the two issues takes place separately. If the two issues are bundled together (e.g., in one bill), so that only one vote takes place, voters 2 and 3 agree to choose $x_7 = \{M_1'', M_2''\}$. This is a contract that Gordon Tullock has named implicit logrolling. Explicit logrolling is problematic because voter 2 would prefer not to keep his part of the bargain in the second vote and therefore might break the agreement and vote for M_2'. But even if x_7 is brought about (as will certainly be the case if implicit logrolling is used), it will still be unstable. For other contracts are better for other majorities, thus implying further logrolling agreements, which lead to cyclical social preferences. Thus Theorem 2 is valid: contracts are a precondition for cyclical preferences. Moreover, it has been shown that the paradox of voting for two or more issues is identical to the fact that majority logrolling is possible (Theorem 4).

With many voters present it may not be possible for them to conclude logrolling agreements. But in this case parties may exist which propose packages in their election platforms containing alternatives of several issues. If such a package is beneficial to a majority of voters, we have another case of implicit logrolling, but with the contract now proposed by outsiders, the parties. As a consequence, cyclical social preferences are present again. And this means that any program proposed by one party can be defeated by that of another party, as already recognized by Anthony Downs (1957, pp. 55–60). Note that in this and only this case the outcome may wander anywhere in the issue space, for instance of Figure 1 (McKelvey [1976]).

Let us finally see whether Theorem 5 holds for our example. We note first that voters 2 and 3 conclude an *internal contract* to use their voting rights for the two issues such that alternatives M_1'', M_2'' will be selected, and therefore outcome x_7 will result. Now to move in a similar way from this outcome to x_8 would require another internal contract between voters 1 and 3, in which 3 would promise to vote differently on the two issues than he is obliged by his contract with 2. However, if internal contracts are binding, x_7 would be a stable outcome. It is Pareto-optimal because it is located on the straight line connecting the outcomes most preferred by 2 and 3.

The remaining open question is, then, how contracts can be made binding. This problem is especially obvious for the case mentioned above, in which parties compete with their platforms. For no party is bound by the program of the other, since it has not concluded a contract with it. It has only provided an implicit contract for the voters it hopes to attract. But in spite of this, Theorem 5 remains true. For if the implicit contract were binding for the voters who benefit, the outcome would be stable and Pareto-optimal.

Also, it is not difficult to see that the second part of Theorem 5 holds. If 2 and 3 could exchange their voting rights on issues M_1 and M_2, x_7 would again be a stable and Pareto-optimal outcome. For then voter 2 (3) would have two votes for issue M_2 (M_1) and would use them to vote for M_2'' (M_1''), since this means a better outcome for him, quite independently of what 3 (2) will be doing. The same result is obviously obtained, if corresponding voting rights were assigned to both from the very beginning.

The example discussed in this section is characterized by the fact that the same subset of society has been assigned the right to decide all issues. Since no outsiders were taken into account, no external, but only internal negative externalities were thus present. This is typical of all the models in which only political decision-making inside an organization is taken into account. In the next section we turn to a more general example in which decision rights are not assigned to only one subset of society and which thus contains internal and external negative externalities.

INTERNAL AND EXTERNAL NEGATIVE EXTERNALITIES

In the following example we assume *strong* individual preference orderings, three issues, each with only two alternatives, and a society consisting again of three individuals, i.e. $V = \{1, 2, 3\}$. Individual preference orderings over the outcomes $x_1, x_2, \ldots, x_8$, are given in Table 1. Note that the further up an outcome is positioned in a column, the more it is valued by member i ($i = 1, 2, 3$) of society.

Table 1. Preference Orderings for the Members of Society

	1	2	3
Strong Individual Preference Orderings over Outcomes	x_3	x_2	x_6
	x_1	x_1	x_8
	x_4	x_6	x_2
	x_7	x_4	x_4
	x_8	x_8	x_5
	x_5	x_5	x_1
	x_6	x_7	x_7
	x_2	x_3	x_3

Each of the three issues comprises exactly two alternatives, yielding eight possible combinations of choices across the three issues. The three issues M_1, M_2, and M_3 are represented by the three dimensions of Figure 2, where each issue contains only two alternatives. Thus, for example, outcome x_8 is different from x_1 in the alternatives of all three issues, x_3 only in those of the first issue.

All rights refer to issues and are assigned to subsets of society. In our example the right to decide the first issue is assigned to individual 1, and the right to decide the third issue is assigned to individual 3. All individuals together have the right to decide M_2. Thus we have $V_1 = \{1\} \subset V$, $V_2 = \{1, 2, 3\} = V$, and $V_3 = \{3\} \subset V$. V_2 is thus an organization comprising the whole society. We assume further that M_2 is decided by simple majority vote.

It is obvious that, in contrast to the last section, not only internal, but also external negative externalities are present in the example. For example, a decision by 1 to move from x_5 to x_7 implies negative external externalities for 2 and 3. But 1 has the right to do so, since the first issue has been assigned to it. And it can do so, if x_5 happens to be the status quo. Similarly externalities are present in other cases. For example, if a majority $\{2, 3\}$ decides concerning issue 2 to move from x_5 to x_6, it implies an internal negative externality to the outvoted minority, voter 1. Note further that there are inseparabilities present in individual preference orderings. For instance, 2 prefers x_1 to x_5, but at the same time x_7 to x_3.

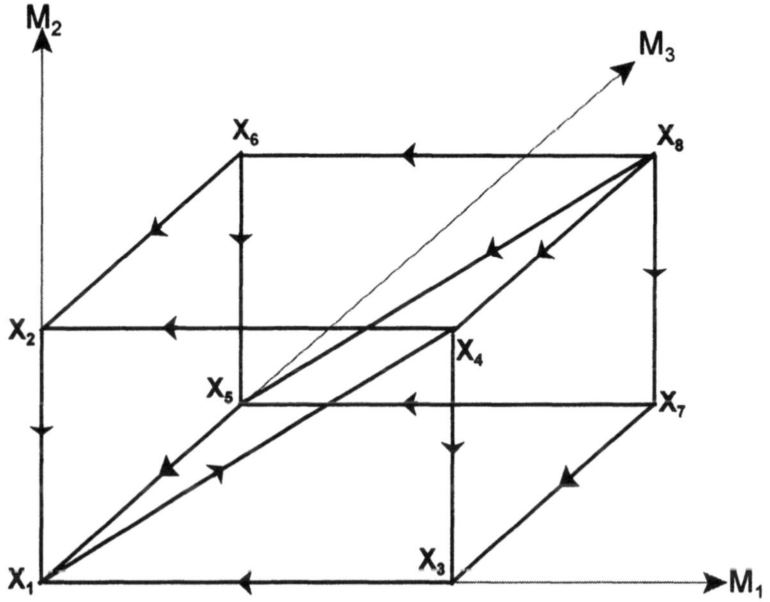

Figure 2. Negative External Externalities

The arrows in Figure 2 point from the dominating to the dominated outcome. Thus, since 1 has the right to decide M_1, the arrows in that dimension correspond to his preference ordering. The right to decide M_2, however has been assigned to $V_2 = \{1, 2, 3\}$ who decide by simple majority. Now 2 and 3 form such a majority, e.g., for the decision between x_4 and x_3. As a consequence the arrow points to the latter, since it is worse for both of them. Finally, we have to mention that a move, let's say, from x_5 to x_8 or x_4 can only be accomplished with the help of a contract between V_1 and V_2 or among V_1, V_2, and V_3, respectively, since rights refer only to issues.

Now let us first assume that only the first two dimensions exist and thus only the first four outcomes. Then, without any contract, x_4 would be the outcome. But this is dominated by x_1, which is preferred by both 1 and 2. And since 1 has the right to decide the first issue and they both together as a majority the second issue, they can agree on a contract between 1 and the organization represented by them, to move to x_1. But this outcome is itself dominated by x_2, since it is preferred by 2 and 3, who as a majority could bring it about. x_2 is again dominated by x_4, which is preferred by 1 and can be brought about by it. As a consequence, a cycle is present.

But note that the cycle is stabilized if contracts are *binding*. Note also that there is first an *external contract* between 1 controlling $M_1$and the organization having the right to decide M_2. Second, there exists an *internal contract* between 1 and 2 to decide the latter issue in a way that $x_4$can result. Both contracts would have to be broken to bring about

x_2. This is obvious for the external contract which obliged the organization to bring about the first alternative of M_2, a decision which would now have to be reversed. But it is at the same time a violation of the internal contract between 1 and 2 to bring about this first alternative. For 2 would now combine with 3 to form a majority to reverse this decision. Thus if either *external* or *internal contracts are binding*, x_1 remains as a stable outcome. This outcome is also (in this example trivially) Pareto-optimal.

Finally, we realize that the same result could also be obtained, if 2 exchanges his right to vote on M_2 with 1's right to decide M_1, or if this assignment of rights is present from the very beginning. 1 would then be able to cast two votes and could prevent a move from x_1 to x_2. Note that these two solutions remove the externality which would follow from 2's voting behaviour for 1.

We thus conclude that:

1. Only the existence of a contract brings about the cycle;
2. The contract is concluded between a private person and an organization applying majority voting for its decisions. This is thus not a case of logrolling in which votes are exchanged.
3. Both external and internal externalities are present;
4. With binding external and internal contracts we get a stable and Pareto-optimal outcome.
5. The same result is obtained if rights can be exchanged or are appropriately assigned in the beginning.

Unfortunately the Pareto-optimality of the result is trivial, since all four outcomes are Pareto-optimal. We thus extend the example now by adding issue M_3. Then not all eight outcomes are Pareto-optimal, for x_5 and x_7 are not. But 3 prefers the former to x_1 and has the right to decide M_3. He will thus bring about this outcome, since he has not been a partner to a contract concerning the third issue. True, he is bound by the external contract of the organization obliging it to decide in favour of the first alternative of M_2. But this contract refers only to selecting an alternative of issue M_2 and is thus not violated by his decision to select the second alternative of M_3. But finally, since 1 and 2 prefer x_8 to x_5 they will agree on a contract to move to the former, which is a stable and a non-trivial Pareto-optimal outcome.

It is, moreover, easy to see that no outcome can be stable if it is not Pareto-optimal. For then there exists an outcome better for all members of society, who together control all issues. They can thus always bring about a Pareto-better outcome by an appropriate contract. This establishes the Generalized Coase Theorem for our example, since the result is not dependent on the initial assignment of rights to decide issues. We have thus proved for our example Theorems 1–3 and 5.

EXTERNAL NEGATIVE EXTERNALITIES AMONG INDIVIDUALS (SEN'S THEOREM)

We next turn to Sen's (1970) well-known theorem that Minimal Liberalism may imply non-Pareto-optimal outcomes. Minimal Liberalism here postulates the right of different individuals to decide the issues assigned to them according to their preferences. Sen's theorem has been considered to be important because it shows that in a purely liberal (in the European sense) society individuals may end up worse than they could if everybody decides independently of others according to his preferences.

Sen's theorem will be illustrated and critically discussed by using his example concerning the conflict between mother and daughter whether they should read *Lady Chatterley's Lover* or not. In this example no organizations are present. Decision rights for the two issues are only assigned to individuals, namely mother and daughter. As a consequence only external negative externalities are present and only external contracts can be concluded. In this sense it is an example of pure (though in my view incomplete) liberalism, quite the opposite of the case of total direct democracy considered in the first example.

More formally, assume $V_1 = \{1\}$, $V_2 = \{2\}$, and $V = \{1, 2\}$ where 1 denotes the mother and 2 the daughter. The two issues M_1 and M_2 refer to the reading of the book by mother and daughter, respectively. The two alternatives of each issue are "reading" and "not reading" by mother and daughter. Table 2 describes the strong preference orderings of mother and daughter over the four outcomes. The arrows in Figure 3 have the same meaning as those in Figure 2.

Table 2. Preference Orderings of Members of Society

	Mother 1	Daughter 2
Strong,	x_1	x_4
Separable, Individual	x_2	x_2
Preference	x_3	x_3
Orderings	x_4	x_1

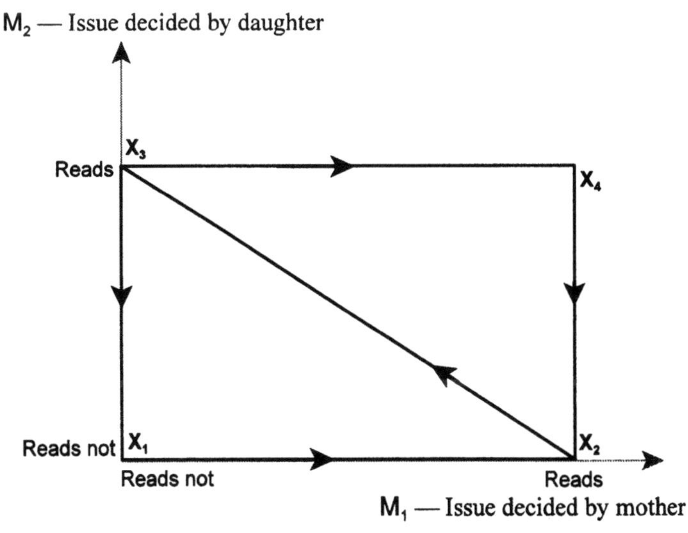

Figure 3. An Illustration of Sen's Theorem

The stable outcome without contract, x_3, is Pareto-inferior. It illustrates Sen's theorem. If both mother and daughter decide independently according to the rights assigned to them, namely each of them determines whether she reads *Lady Chatterley's Lover* or not, we get this Pareto-inferior outcome. The mother does not read the book, but the daughter does. But this is worse for both of them than the outcome x_2.

But this is not the end of the story. For if we allow a contract between mother and daughter, Pareto-optimal outcome x_2, where the mother, but not the daughter reads the book, will be agreed on, since both prefer x_2 to x_3. But again, outcome x_2 is only stable if this time the *external* contract is *binding*. If contracts are not binding we have a cycle, another confirmation of the fact that only contracts lead to cyclical social preferences. But it is also clear that there exists no paradox of a Paretian Liberal if *binding external* contracts can be concluded. But the right to conclude contracts beneficial to the partners, which can be enforced legally is—at least in my view—an essential trait of liberalism. Sen's definition of *minimal liberalism* is just too narrow.

Let us finally note that the stable Pareto-optimal outcome can also be reached if mother and daughter exchange their rights to decide issues, so that the daughter has now the right to decide M_1 and the mother to decide M_2, or if these issues are assigned to them from the beginning. It follows that besides Theorem 6, Theorems 1–3 and 5 are again confirmed for this example of pure liberalism.

CYCLICAL SOCIAL PREFERENCES GIVEN IDENTICAL INDIVIDUAL PREFERENCES

We turn now to the proof of Theorem 7. Let us consider three individuals with identical utility functions and thus preferences. The utility function $U = \ln(x) + \ln(y)$ has the usual characteristics, namely

$$\frac{\partial U}{\partial x}, \frac{\partial U}{\partial y} > 0, \frac{\partial^2 U}{\partial x^2}, \frac{\partial^2 U}{\partial y^2} < 0.$$

x is the amount of a private good, y of a public good. The individuals have different incomes u, v and w. Individual 1 has the lowest and 3 the highest income: $u < v < w$. To provide the public good individuals are taxed. Three different types of tax regimes A, B, and C are proposed, on which the three individuals have to vote. The first regime is a proportional tax $t(A)$ on incomes. The second is also a proportional income tax $t(B)$, but an amount z is deductible to secure a minimal standard of living. The third tax regime C employs a progressive income tax, such that $t_1(C) = au^2$, $t_2(C) = av^2$, and $t_3(C) = aw^2$. The sum of the taxes on the incomes of the three individuals is used to cover the expenses for the proposed amount y of the public good, which is assumed to be the same in all cases. The three proposals on which the individuals have to vote are thus $\{t(A), y\}$, $\{t(B), z, y]\}$, and $\{t_1(C), t_2(C), t_3(C), y\}$. Finally, the prices of the two goods are $p_x = 1/4$, $p_y = 1$.

It should be noted that we confine ourselves to one issue in this example. For the tax rates are determined by the fixed amount y of the public good and the fixed deduction z, once the tax regime is determined. Voters have thus only to decide on the tax regime.

In the following example we assume $u = 1$, $v = 7$, $w = 12$, $z = 1$, and $y = 10$. The values for individual utilities derived for this example (see Appendix 1) are presented in Table 3:

Table 3. Individual Utilities, Given Identical Preferences for Individuals

Tax Regimes (Outcomes)	1	2	3
A	2.996	4.942	5.481
B	3.689	4.933	5.399
C	3.684	5.365	4.986

Thus in Table 4 we see the following ranking of the three outcomes by the three individuals:

Table 4. Ranking of Outcomes by Individuals

	Individuals		
	1	2	3
Tax	B	C	A
Regimes	C	A	B
(Outcomes)	A	B	C

Since this a well-known arrangement, we see at once that cyclical social preferences result from voting. Thus we have proved Theorem 8, namely that such social preferences can arise with identical individual preference orderings if restrictions for individuals are different.

CONCLUSION

Gordon Tullock (1998, Chapter 8) put forward the hypothesis that, besides setting the agenda, logrolling is another means to remove the paradox of voting, since the alternatives put to the vote are narrowed down in advance by vote trading. Our analysis has shown that this is not the case since the paradox of voting and logrolling are inextricably linked. Indeed, we have seen that contracts including logrolling are a precondition for cyclical social preferences if there are several issues and no one-issue cycles are present.

But then why so much stability? A first possibility refers to the absence of contracts. If no contracts were concluded, say, since transaction costs—which have been neglected in the foregoing analysis—are too high, then cycles are prevented. But this leaves two problems: First, there may still be many cases in which transaction costs are not high enough to prevent contracts. And worse, even if a stable outcome results because of high transaction costs it may not be Pareto-optimal. Against this latter kind of reasoning one could argue that the outcome would be Pareto-optimal if transaction costs were included, as they should. But even this argument is not conclusive. For a Pareto-better result may still be reached—as we have seen—if an exchange takes place or if there were another initial assignment of rights, (i.e. another institutional and organizational setting would be introduced). Of course, in reality this would require that the transaction costs for exchanging rights or for institutional reforms were lower than for concluding contracts on how to use decision rights; and/or that the information needed to assign decision rights correctly was available. This may or may not be the case. Anyhow, it is obvious that many unresolved questions relating to law and economics and to institutional economics emerge if these problems are faced.

Our remarks point to a second solution to instability: the exchange of rights or the reassignment of rights to decide issues. For we have seen that in the absence of transaction and information costs this would always lead to a stable Pareto-optimal solution. But as just pointed out, transaction costs may not be negligible and the information necessary about the preferences of all members of society is certainly not available. Also, in politics, the exchange of voting rights is not allowed. Thus cycles may remain or stable outcomes may not be Pareto-optimal. Finally, reassignments of rights may also erode the safety of property rights and thus lead to less effort by individuals, with obnoxious economic consequences.

This leaves us, apart from the possibility that elites or oligarchies are privileged to set and to narrow down agendas, with binding external and internal contracts as a solution. This seems indeed, besides exchanging property rights, to be a widely used device in the private and market spheres. Most of such contracts are legally enforceable and their violation is costly or will be punished with the help of legal authorities. One has to realize, however, that this is much less true for internal contracts within organizations than with external contracts. And it is especially less true in the political sphere, in which logrolling contracts like vote selling are not legally enforceable or are even forbidden. Even worse, if parties propose platforms to voters containing implicit logrolling bargains they are certainly not bound legally to keep their promises. And, as we have seen, even if they were legally bound, the voters and the other parties are not a party to any contract, which implies that cycles are possible.

Given these facts, what stabilizing forces remain in the political sphere? One is the well-known possibility that an iterative game is played by a limited number of participants (e.g., in Parliamentary committees), which ends with only a low probability after each play. Then a stable Pareto-optimal outcome will result under certain conditions (Bernholz [1978]). Another stabilizing factor for the case of competing parties may be that their ideological positions are arranged on left-right scales to save information costs for voters. As a consequence, they are not allowed to jump with their platforms over the positions of other parties, since this would lead to a loss of credibility and thus of voters.

APPENDIX: DERIVATION OF THE RESULTS IN TABLE 3

Given is the utility function $U = \ln(x_i) + \ln(y)$ which is identical for the three individuals composing society. Their incomes are 1, 7, and 12, respectively. x_i and y are the amounts of the private and the public good consumed by individual i ($i = 1, 2, 3$). The price of the private and the public goods are $p_x = 1/4, p_y = 1$. A fixed amount of the public good, $y = 10$, is provided in the three platforms on which the three individuals have to vote. These platforms are different only in the tax regimes, which are called *A*, *B*, and *C*, and which imply different outcomes for them. Next we present the first tax regime and its results.

A) In this case a proportional income tax t is used to finance the supply of the public good. The tax revenue covers the outlays for this good:

$$t(1 + 7 + 12) = 1*10, \tag{1}$$

$$t = 1/2. \tag{2}$$

1. We turn now to the first individual who has to pay an income tax of ½. Thus his disposable income is also ½, which he can use to buy ½*4=2 units of the private good. Since he would also receive the 10 units of the public good, his utility amounts to:

$$U(A) = \ln(2) + \ln(10) = 2.996. \tag{3}$$

2. The second individual pays an income tax of 1/2*7 = 7/2 and has a disposable income of 7 - 7/2 = 7/2, which can be spent on 4*7/2 = 14 units of the private good. His utility is given by

$$U(A) = \ln(14) + \ln(10) = 4.942. \tag{4}$$

3. The third individual can spend his disposable income of 6 on 24 units of the private good and has a utility of

$$U(A) = \ln(24) + \ln(10) = 5.481. \tag{5}$$

B) The second tax regime proposed is also characterized by a proportional income tax t, but this time with a deduction of $z = 1$. t can thus be calculated as follows

$$10 = t(1 - 1) + t(7 - 1) + t(12 - 1) = 17t \tag{6}$$

$$t = 10/17. \tag{7}$$

1. The first individual pays no income tax and can spend it on 1*4 = 4 units of the private good. His utility would thus be

$$U(B) = \ln(4) + \ln(10) = 3.689. \tag{8}$$

2. Individual 2 pays (7-1)*t = 60/17 in income tax. His disposable income 7 - 60/17 = 59/17 can buy 236/17 of the private good, so that he would enjoy a utility of

$$U(B) = \ln(236/17) + \ln(10) = 4.933. \tag{9}$$

3. The 3rd individual pays an income tax of 11*10/17 = 110/17, so that his disposable income is 12 - 110/17 = 94/17. Thus he can buy 376/17 of the private good and his utility amounts to

$$U(B) = \ln(376/17) + \ln(19) = 5.399. \tag{10}$$

C) In the third tax regime a progressive tax on income has to be paid. The tax rate t grows with income I:

$$t = aI^2 \tag{11}$$

a and thus t can be calculated as follows, given the incomes of the three individuals:

$$10 + a{*}1^3 + a{*}7^3 + a{*}12^3 = a(1 + 343 + 1{,}728) = 2{,}072a, \tag{12}$$

$$a = 10/2{,}072 = 5/1{,}036. \tag{13}$$

1. Individual 1 has to pay an income tax of $1{*}t = 1{*}5/1{,}036$. Thus his disposable income amounts to 1 - 5/1036 = 1031/1036, which can be spent on 1031/259 units of the private good. This would give a utility of

$$U(C) = \ln(1{,}031/259) + \ln(10) = 3.684. \tag{14}$$

2. The income tax of individual 2 amounts to (5/1,036)*7*7*7 = 1,715/1,036, so that a disposable income 7 - 1,715/1,036 = 5,537/1,036 results. For this 5,537/259 units of the private good can be bought, so that utility would amount to

$$U(C) = \ln(5{,}537/259) + \ln(10) = 5.365. \tag{15}$$

3. Individual 3 pays an income tax in the amount of (5/1,036)*12*12*12 = 8,640/1,036 = 2,160/259, so that he would enjoy a disposable income of 12 - 2,160/259 = 948/259. For this he can get 3,792/259 units of the private good, so that his utility would amount to

$$U(C) = \ln(3{,}792/259) + \ln(10) = 4.986. \tag{16}$$

This concludes the calculation of the utility numbers contained in Table 3.

REFERENCES

Arrow, Kenneth J. (1963/51). *Social Choice and Individual Values*. New York: John Wiley & Sons.

Bernholz, Peter (1976). "Liberalism, Logrolling and Cyclical Group Preferences." *Kyklos* 29, 26–37.

______ (1978). "On the Stability of Logrolling Outcomes in Stochastic Games." *Public Choice* 33 (3) 65–82.

______(1981). "A General Social Dilemma: Profitable Exchange and Intransitive Group Preferences." *Zeitschrift fuer Nationaloekonomie* 40, 1–23. Reprinted in: J. M. Buchanan, and R. D Tollison, *Public Choice II*, 361–81. Ann Arbor: University of Michigan Press, 1984,

______(1982). "Externalities as A Necessary Condition for Cyclical Social Preferences." *Quarterly Journal of Economics* 47 (4) 699–705.

______(1986). "A General Constitutional Possibility Theorem." *Public Choice* 51, 249–65.

______(1997). "Property Rights, Contracts, Cyclical Social Preferences and the Coase Theorem: A Synthesis." *European Journal of Political Economy* 13 (3) 419–64.

______(1999). "The Generalized Coase Theorem and Separable Individual Preferences: An Extension." *European Journal of Political Economy* 15, 331–35.

Breyer, Friedrich (1980). "On the Relevance of Preference Similarities for the Paradox of Voting: Identical Utility Functions and Cyclical Majorities." *Kyklos* 33, 523–30.

Buchanan, James M. (1962). "Politics, Policy and the Pigovian Margins." *Economica*, N.S. 29, 17–28.

Buchanan, James M., and Gordon Tullock, (1962). *The Calculus of Consent*. Ann Arbor: University of Michigan Press.

Coleman, James (1966): "The Possibility of a Social Welfare Function." *American Economic Review* 56, 1105–22.

______ (1967). "Reply." *American Economic Review* 57, 1311–17.

Downs, Anthony (1957). *An Economic Theory of Democracy*. New York: Harper & Row.

Kramer, Gerald (1973). "On a Class of Equilibrium Conditions for Majority Rule. *Econometrica* 41, 285–97.

McKelvey, R. D. (1976). "Intransitivities in Multidimensional Voting Models and Some Implications for Agenda Control." *Journal of Economic Theory* 12, 472–82.

Plott, Charles R. (1967). "A Notion of Equilibrium and Its Possibility Under Majority Rule." *American Economic Review* 57, 787–806.

Schwartz, Thomas (1981). "The Universal Instability Theorem." *Public Choice* 37, 487–501.

______ (1986): *The Logic of Collective Choice*. New York: Columbia University Press.

Sen, Amartya (1970). "The Impossibility of a Paretian Liberal." *Journal of Political Economy* 78, 152–57.

Tullock, Gordon (1967). *Toward a Mathematics of Politics*. Ann Arbor: The University of Michigan Press.

______ (1998): *On Voting: A Public Choice Approach*. Cheltenham, and Northampton, MA: The Locke Institute. Edward Elgar.

REFLECTIONS ON THE OPTIMAL SIZE OF GOVERNMENT

Hans G. Monissen
University of Würzburg
Sanderring 2
97070 Würzburg
Germany

0. ON GORDON TULLOCK

"It is not always easy to see a common thread in Tullock's work: he is almost too fertile and throws off so many ideas in all directions that the connecting links between them threaten to disappear from view. Any simple summary of his 'system,' therefore, must wait on some future effort of his own. However, a common thread in his work, as in that of all public choice theorists, is the view that human behaviour must be viewed in all circumstances as a 'rational' response to the twin constraints of the physical environment and the prevailing social institutions; people will always strive to maximize their satisfactions in the face of these constraints, taking due account of the costs of alternative choices" (Blaug [1985] 252–53).

Gordon Tullock is the 1998 Distinguished Fellow of the American Economic Association. In the enclosed short appreciation of his work we read: "Tullock's scholarship and entrepreneurship have left an indelible imprint on economics. He is a pioneer who has worked almost exclusively at the frontiers of the discipline" (American Economic Review [1998]).

Inspecting Gordon Tullock's curriculum vitae, which contains 37 pages compiling his published work will indeed confirm the assertion that his scientific work is concentrated at the frontiers of our discipline. However, Tullock has not only extended the domain of economic inquiry, but also strengthened the core of our discipline. As opposed to Blaug's remark we should note that there exists a simple summary of his "system." It was in 1975 when Gordon Tullock with his co-author Richard McKenzie published one of the most fascinating introductory textbooks in economics which exposes the authors' view of the workings of the socio-economic process. In their standard model the basic unit of analysis used is *homo oeconomicus* as characterized above. The authors apply this role model consistently and successfully to a wide range of both market and non-market phenomena.[1]

This chapter, "Reflections on the Optimal Size of Government," should, at least subjectively, reflect Gordon Tullock's influence on our perspective. However, we have to admit our analytical shortcomings of not being able to simultaneously include such Tullockian topics as rent-seeking, demand-revealing, bureaucratic behavior (to name only some of his important insights) into an envisaged general-equilibrium model.

1. INTRODUCTION

Most economists in the classical liberal tradition associate with Adam Smith (1976, 208–09) by assigning only three duties to the government: "first, the duty of protecting the society from the violence and invasion of other independent societies; secondly, the duty of protecting, as far as possible, every member of the society from the injustice or oppression of every other member of it, or the duty of establishing an exact administration of justice; and thirdly, the duty of erecting and maintaining certain public works and certain public institutions, which it can never be for the interest of any individual, or small number of individuals, to erect and maintain; because the profit could never repay the expense to any individual or small number of individuals, though it may frequently do much more than repay it to a great society."[2] To provide the necessary financial funds for implementing these duties, Adam Smith's system of natural liberty has to be completed by a set of fiscal rules or a fiscal constitution. Since the publication of the seminal book by Brennan and Buchanan *The Power to Tax* with the programmatic subtitle *Analytical Foundations of a Fiscal Constitution* ([1980]; see also Brennan and Buchanan [1977]), the general conceptional ingredients for such a completion seem to be available. However, as known from the literature, applying operational criteria to limit government activities in a dynamic setting is not an easy task (see Inman [1982 and 1987]).

The fundamental constitutional approach by Brennan and Buchanan advocating several constraining principles for Leviathan remains somewhat controversial. Some economists subscribing to the theory of optimal taxation[3] argue that an implicit trade-off between overall efficiency and a smaller government sector size may be biased. Avoiding a general discussion of this issue, we take a more pragmatic stance and consider the theory of optimal taxation at least as a useful starting point describing a "what-could-be" position.[4]

This chapter is organized as follows: In Section 2, a simple choice-theoretic general equilibrium model describing government productive activity is presented.[5] The government supplies a public good that becomes effective as an infrastructure investment enhancing the productivity of the private sector. This type of government productive activity should be distinguished from the Keynesian view of the typical macroeconomic model in which the government activity remains not only unproductive but also welfare reducing if potential multiplier effects of government activity on employment are ignored. However, a government above a critical size will bring forth Leviathan who might appear in two quite different roles: he might materialize as a selfish dictator maximizing a surplus to be appropriated for personal uses or as an anonymous bureaucracy trying to maximize the size of the budget. In supplementing the standard public-choice perspective, the model could rationalize efforts of "organized labor" to redistribute income in the functional sense from capital to labor by fixing the real wage rate at too high a level for overall efficiency. These efforts may lead to an excessive size of government over time.

Section 3 discusses the economic problem for a benevolent dictator under the perspective of the modern theory of optimal taxation. In addition to the infrastructure effect of the public good the model includes two private goods and a pure public good for our representative consumer. For this extended model the second-best tax structure is derived. These more technical aspects should complete the discussion in Sections 2 and 4. In particular, Section 3 allows the formal computation of the Lindahl equilibrium included in Table 1.

In Section 4, relying on a numerical example, the pattern of production and employment under competing objectives is evaluated for a benevolent dictator. This "first-best" solution provides the reference situation against which other objectives such as maximizing aggregate consumer surplus, national product or national income (private production) are evaluated. Section 5 deals with the effects of a budget- or revenue-maximizing bureaucracy with some interesting results for efficiency. The simple model of Section 2 summarized in equations I and the one underlying the discussion in Sections 4 and 5 regard a basic problem from two different angles. The first emphasizes more the productivity aspects and the second focuses mainly on welfare issues. Section 6 briefly summarizes the main results. Two supplementary appendices to Sections 2 and 3 are included at the end of the chapter.

2. A SIMPLE CHOICE-THEORETIC MODEL DESCRIBING GOVERNMENT PRODUCTIVE ACTIVITIES

The point of departure is a simple choice-theoretic model incorporating a representative private consumer and a complementary private firm. The role of government derives from the fact that a public good is included. This public good operates as an efficiency parameter in the production function for private output but, for the present, remains excluded from the utility function. In Section 3, the model will be extended to cover such a utility effect. The wage bill of the public sector has to be financed by taxes. The funds will be raised by imposing a proportional income tax. In deriving the structure of the model, special care is necessary to demarcate the functional role of the representative agent. As in all market systems the private agents are characterized by partial ignorance which allows to treat specific prices as parameters.[6] In socio-political models the representative agent frequently plays the dual role of a typical consumer in the market arena and a median voter driving the political process and controlling government activities.[7] It should be noted that a representative agent in a comprehensive sense does not need a government because he controls all resources and all instruments to maximize his private utility or, for that matter, the welfare of the economy with identical individuals.

We postulate a simple utility function with standard properties:[8]

$$U = u(x^p, R - y^w), \qquad u_1 \text{ and } u_2 > 0. \tag{2.1}$$

x^p denotes the output disposable for the private consumption, R identifies the total time endowment available for work time, y^w, and leisure, y.

The private budget constraint is defined as follows:

$$x^p = (1-t)wy^w + (1-t)\pi \tag{2.2}$$

Gross wages, wy^w, plus gross profits, π, minus the tax burden define the disposable income for the economy which is large enough to buy the whole product if the government abstains from engaging in transactions that reduce this consumption potential. The first-order conditions are familiar:

$$\frac{\partial u / \partial y}{\partial u / \partial x^p} = (1-t)w = \left(-\frac{dx^p}{dy}\right). \tag{2.3}$$

The consumer treats the real wage rate, w, and real profits, π, as parameters, thereby ignoring the fact that both magnitudes depend on his employment decision.

Because working hours supplied both to the private and the public sector, y^p and y^g, command the same real net wage rate, the allocation of the working time is, to begin with, indeterminate. Output produced in the private sector is not only a function of the employment level and the capital stock in the private sector, y^p and $\overline{K}^p$, but also of the employment level in the public sector, y^g. The latter variable determines a public good or an infrastructure component, z, which multiplies a private output component f:

$$\begin{aligned} &x = z(y^g)f^*(y^p;\overline{K}^p) \equiv z(y^g)f(y^p), \\ &z' > 0, \quad z'' < 0, \quad f' > 0, \quad f'' < 0. \end{aligned} \tag{2.4}$$

The right side of the equation suppresses the term for the capital stock in the private sector which will be kept constant. The signs of the stated derivatives follow *a priori*-reasoning where the signs of the public component could be switched to allow for a more pessimistic view of the economic role of government. Different from the procedure in Section 4, the effect of z on x is simply proportional.

Overall efficiency requires that a marginal shift of employment between the two sectors should produce the same effect on the private production level:

$$z'(y^g)f(y^p) = z(y^g)f'(y^p). \tag{2.5}$$

How is the efficiency requirement brought about? Without evoking a benevolent social planner the actions of the government have to be constrained by appropriate budgetary rules. Sufficient rules, as will be seen in a moment, are the imposition of an optimal tax rate and the requirement of a balanced budget to be defined below. Before the attention is directed to the government budget constraint the model has to be solved for w and π. These solutions are derived from the private business sector:

$$w = z(y^g)f'(y^p), \tag{2.6}$$

$$\pi = z(y^g)f(y^p) - wy^p. \tag{2.7}$$

The government uses the tax receipts for paying off the government employees and financing a possible extra absorption of the private output, x. This discretionary expenditure component will be referred to as Keynesian government expenditures, x^g. As in most macroeconomic models these expenditures constitute economic waste or a welfare loss.

$$tx \equiv tz(y^g)f(y^p) = (1-t)wy^g + x^g. \tag{2.8}$$

If we set x^g equal to zero, all requirements are fulfilled to solve for the optimal tax rate, t^0:

$$t^0 = \frac{wy^g}{x + wy^g}. \tag{2.9}$$

The denominator, $x + wy^g$, identifies national product as conventionally measured by national income and product accounting and the numerator indicates the output of the public sector, wy^g. If all leisure effects are ignored, it should be private production, x, rather than national product defining the appropriate welfare indicator (cf. Section 4).

In order to derive solutions for y^g, y^p and x^p which could be easily incorporated into the government budget constraint, it is necessary to work with specific functional forms of the representative actor's utility function. A frequently implicit assumption followed in standard macroeconomics is to rely on a so-called no-wealth effects utility function[9] or, more concrete, on a utility function which is quasi-linear in consumption:[10]

$$U = x^p + \frac{(R - y^w)^{1-\theta}}{1-\theta}, \qquad 0 < \theta < 1. \tag{2.1a}$$

The strictly concave term in leisure specifies constant relative risk aversion, a property which might be useful under an extended analysis covering uncertainty. The specific functional form has no essential bearing on our results, except that the profit term remains excluded from the labor market, which simplifies the analysis. Because the main objective of this section is to analyze a regime with an institutionally fixed real wage rate, the utility function remains incidental. Of course, the profit or wealth term could be removed from the model by restricting the private production function. This would, however, destroy the thread of the basic hypothesis of this section: It is "organized labor" which gains from a wage rate fixed at an excessively high level, thereby redistributing income from capital to labor.[11]

The implied solutions for the central variables are:

$$y^w(\equiv y^g + y^p) = R - [(1-t)w]^{-\frac{1}{\theta}}, \tag{2.10}$$

$$x^p = (1-t)w\{R - [(1-t)w]^{-\frac{1}{\theta}}\} + (1-t)\pi. \tag{2.11}$$

Equation 2.10 reflects our no-wealth effects labor supply function.

The decomposition of y^w from the demand side is brought about by the government employment decision given profit maximization by the private firms. However, the labor market reflects the trade-off between real consumption and leisure. If this relation remains excluded, the government budget constraint becomes

$$t^0 z(y^g) f(y^p) = (1-t^0) z(y^g) f'(y^p) y^g \tag{2.12}$$

and the employment level is restricted by

$$R = y^g + y^p. \tag{2.13a}$$

The following implicit relation specifies the more general case:

$$\frac{(R - y^g - y^p)^{-\theta}}{1-t^0} = z(y^g) f'(y^p). \tag{2.13b}$$

This leads to an interesting paper published by Ronald Findlay and John D. Wilson (1987) some years ago on "The Political Economy of Leviathan," to which we owe some important insights. Findlay and Wilson exclude a leisure-income trade-off in their simple model which amounts to maximizing the production of private output.

If the employment level is exogenously fixed, $y^w = \bar{y}^w$, a slightly more general form of the Findlay-Wilson model could start from

$$U = u(x^p, R - \bar{y}^w).$$

Overall efficiency requires maximizing x^p. Relying on the efficient allocation of the given working hours, the government budget constraint simplifies to

$$tx = (1-t)wy^g. \tag{2.8a}$$

Equation 2.6 shows that the wage rate is equal to the marginal product of labor in the private sector. Because the labor supply, y^w, is fixed, equation 2.8a can be rewritten as follows:

$$t^0 z(y^g) f(\bar{y}^w - y^g) = (1-t^0) z(y^w) f'(\bar{y}^w - y^g) y^g. \tag{2.8b}$$

In equation 2.8b the tax rate is introduced as a parameter and, as a matter of expediency, t^0 identifies the welfare maximizing rate. The left-hand side of equation 2.8a has a definite maximum which may be intuitively evident from the fact that the size of the government may be either too small or too large for maximizing private production. This maximum will be reached, if equation 2.5 is met. The public component, z, may be restricted in such a way that a minimum private production is forthcoming even if the employment level in the public sector is nil. The right-hand side of equation 2.8b has a positive slope throughout. We assume that this slope is increasing over the positive domain of y^g. A difference between the left- and the right-hand side terms identifies government discretionary expenditures or the budget surplus. A negative difference, denoting a deficit, remains excluded under the structure of the model. A government materializing in a selfish dictator will maximize the surplus x^g to be appropriated for personal uses.

As compared to a budget maximizing bureaucracy, the selfish dictator creates serious, uncontrollable welfare problems. At least in principle, Leviathan in the form of a budget maximizing bureaucracy could be tamed by appropriate fiscal rules (i.e., assigning the optimal tax rate). In this case the self-interested bureaucracy is guided by an invisible hand to support the welfare of society. This information is compiled in Figure 1.[12]

There is an important difference between our more general model and the special one discussed by Findlay and Wilson. If a consumption-leisure effect remains excluded, the government could set $t = 1$ and confiscate the whole of the private production. In the general case, there is a well defined tax rate $0 < t < 1$ which maximizes government appropriation, i.e. Keynesian government expenditures or the budget surplus. We refer to our numerical illustrations in Section 4 and state without proof that the general case can be pictured in a qualitative similar way as in their model, which is condensed in Figure 1.

Some interesting results can be derived from a partial structure of our model. These results have immediate bearing on the interpretation of macroeconomic processes and provide possible interpretations both on the size and the growth of the public sector. The assumption is that the real wage rate is fixed at a level too high to support a welfare-maximizing equilibrium. There is no need to work with specific production functions. For the results to be derived only the usual assumption about the signs of the first and second derivatives are sufficient. Essential for the analysis is the fact that the profit share in the functional income distribution is a variable.

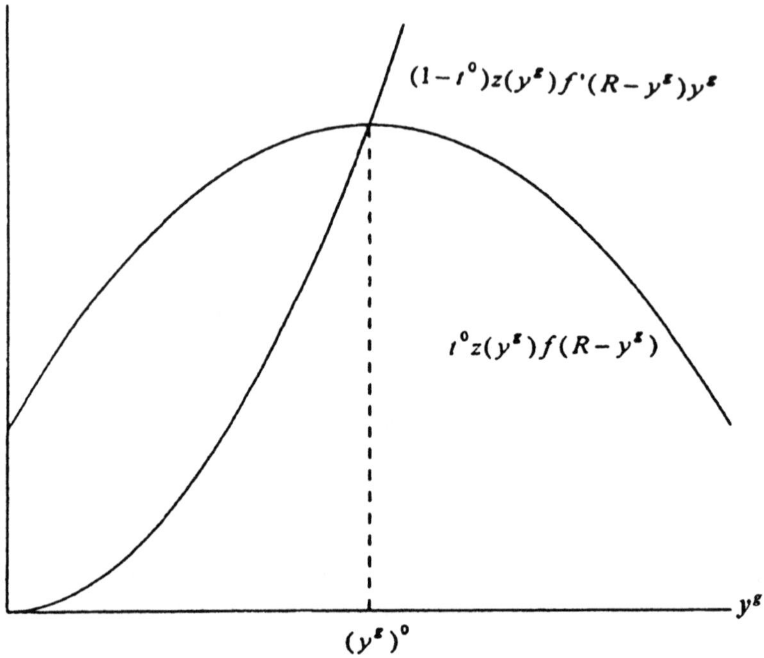

Figure 1. The Government Budget Constraint in General Equilibrium

$$\begin{aligned} z(y^g)f'(y^p) &= w, \\ y^g + y^p &= R, \\ x - z(y^g)f(y^p) &= 0, \\ tx - (1-t)wy^g &= x^g. \end{aligned} \tag{I}$$

A linear approximation of the system yields:

$$\begin{pmatrix} z'(y^g)f'(y^p) & z(y^g)f''(y^p) & 0 & 0 \\ 1 & 1 & 0 & 0 \\ -z'(y^g)f(y^p) & -z(y^g)f'(y^p) & 1 & 0 \\ -(1-t)w & 0 & t & x+wy^g \end{pmatrix} \begin{pmatrix} dy^g \\ dy^p \\ dx \\ dt \end{pmatrix} = \begin{pmatrix} dw \\ dR \\ 0 \\ dx^g + (1-t)y^g dw \end{pmatrix}. \tag{Ia}$$

Let us assume that the changes in the time endowment, dR, and in discretionary expenditure, dx^g, are zero. The resulting response pattern for a change in the wage rate, w, reads as:

$$\frac{dy^g}{dw} = \frac{(x + wy^g)}{\Delta} > 0, \tag{2.14}$$

$$\frac{dy^p}{dw} = \frac{-(x + wy^g)}{\Delta} < 0, \tag{2.15}$$

$$\frac{dx}{dw} = \frac{(x + wy^g)}{\Delta}[z'(y^g)f(y^p) - z(y^g)f'(y^p)] < 0, \tag{2.16}$$

$$\Delta = (x + wy^g)[z'(y^g)f'(y^p) - z(y^g)f''(y^p)] > 0. \tag{2.17}$$

If the wage rate is set above the efficiency level, the marginal product of labor in the private sector is higher than the corresponding marginal product in the public sector:

$$zf' > z'f.$$

In this range an increase in w will reduce private production, x.[13] Because the model prevents the government from running a deficit and x^g remains constant, the marginal tax ratc, t, will adjust. Equation 2.18 shows that this ratc will increase:

$$\frac{dt}{dw} = \frac{1}{\Delta}\{(1-t)y^g[z'(y^g)f'(y^p) - z(y^g)f''(y^p)] + \\ t[z(y^g)f'(y^p) - z'(y^g)f(y^p)] + (1-t)w\} > 0. \tag{2.18}$$

The change in disposable labor income can be calculated from a change in the net wage rate, w^n, because the government guarantees "full" employment by hiring any excess supply of labor at the prevailing wage rate.

$$w^n = (1-t)w. \tag{2.19}$$

Using equation 2.18 we may write

$$\frac{dw^n}{dw} = (1-t)\frac{dw}{dw} - w\frac{dt}{dw}. \tag{2.20}$$

Equation 2.20 yields a rather complex expression. We follow our intuition and state without proof that for a range of wage rates above the efficiency level an increase in the gross wage rate will lead to a corresponding increase in the net wage rate, too. This is indeed an elaborate argument for collective wage bargaining. A weaker argument, however, may be sufficient: Similar to the familiar wage-push theory of inflation, organized labor might initiate a wage-tax spiral over time. The argument will be reinforced if the government is allowed to run deficits and to shift the relative tax rate from labor to capital. These results and the thrust of the general discussion could provide evidence for the hypothesis that even if the median voter or an anonymous group of bureaucrats does not exercise power to affect the budget, organized labor, possibly in tacit or implicit agreement with the incumbent bureaucracy, may be the decisive group, determining the size of the budget over time.

Let us conclude this section by adding some remarks on the effects of changes in the other parameters of the model. An increase in R will produce higher employment levels in both sectors. These effects are neither equal nor proportional. The increase in private employment will produce an increase in private production. To finance the increased public employment level taxes must be increased. The qualitative information provided by the production functions, however, is not sufficient to decide in what direction the tax rate will change, given the endogenous increase of tax revenues provided by the higher tax base, x.

Changes in discretionary government expenditures constitute pure economic waste because the level of private production, x, remains unaffected. Inspection of our system demonstrates that a change of x^g has no effect on the employment levels y^g and y^p. The crowding-out of private expenditures by public expenditures will be brought about by an increase in taxes induced by a higher marginal tax rate.

The above stated results are the main implications of our simple model. An appendix included at the end of the paper describes alternative socio-economic arrangements derived from the basic model and focuses on Leviathan's activities introduced in two variants.

3. THE ECONOMIC POLICY PROBLEM FOR A BENEVOLENT DICTATOR

Section 3 solves the problem of the optimal size of government from the perspective of the theory of optimal taxation. The more technical discussion extends the decision set for the representative agent to two private goods and one public good. The utility function is now quasi-linear in leisure, a functional form which is more convenient for deriving the technical aspects and more useful for the simple numerical simulation in the remaining sections:

$$U = u(x_1, x_2, z) + (R - y^w). \tag{3.1}$$

Utility is a function of two goods produced by the private sector, x_1 and x_2, and a pure public good, z, produced by the government. The component u is a strictly concave function. Leisure, y, as in the above model is the difference between the total time endowment and the time supplied for work. The budget constraint for the consumer reads as

$$wy^w + \pi = p_1 x_1 + p_2 x_2. \tag{3.2}$$

The private goods are produced by a representative firm and are available at competitive gross prices, p_1 and p_2. Nominal profits, π, plus nominal wages, wy^w, define the income of the representative consumer. In our first model a proportional income tax specified the second-best tax arrangement. Given the fact that it is not possible to tax the time endowment, charging commodity taxes is the efficient second-best solution here.

The consumptive optimum is described by two equations:

$$\frac{p_1}{w} = \frac{\partial u}{\partial x_1}, \qquad \frac{p_2}{w} = \frac{\partial u}{\partial x_2}. \tag{3.3), (3.4}$$

Equation 3.5 specifies the productive possibilities open to the private firm. The variable y^p indicates the labor input used to produce the private goods. To keep the model as general as possible, we continue to include z as an efficiency parameter in the private production function. To facilitate the reconstruction of the model, the supply quantities are identified by asterisks:

$$y^p = y^p(x_1^*, x_2^*, z). \tag{3.5}$$

Equation 3.6 defines profits whereby the net sales revenue is the product of the net prices and the quantities sold. The specific tax rates t_1 and t_2 are stated in terms of the number of *numéraire* units per unit of product sold.

$$\pi = (p_1 - t_1)x_1^* + (p_2 - t_2)x_2^* - wy^p(x_1^*, x_2^*, z). \tag{3.6}$$

The productive optimum is described by two equations:

$$\frac{p_1}{w} = \frac{t_1}{w} + \frac{\partial y^p}{\partial x_1^*}, \qquad \frac{p_2}{w} = \frac{t_2}{w} + \frac{\partial y^p}{\partial x_2^*}. \tag{3.7), (3.8}$$

The input requirement for the production of the public good which is under the control of the government is stated in equation 3.9:

$$y^g = y^g(z). \tag{3.9}$$

The tax revenues are used to finance the production of the public good. The government budget has to be balanced, a fact which prevents the government from generating a surplus:

$$t_1 x_1^* + t_2 x_2^* = wy^g(z) \equiv C(z). \tag{3.10}$$

Market equilibrium is described by three equations, although by referring to Walras's law, only two are independent:

$$x_1 = x_1^*, \qquad x_2 = x_2^*, \qquad y^w = y^p + y^g. \qquad (3.11)-(3.13)$$

The model specifies twelve independent equations to determine twelve independent variables, if the nominal wage rate, w, is set equal to one and the tax rates are treated as policy parameters.

Given the utility function, the solutions for x_1 and x_2 have a simple form:

$$x_1 = x_1(\frac{t_1}{w}, \frac{t_2}{w}, z), \qquad x_2 = x_2(\frac{t_1}{w}, \frac{t_2}{w}, z). \qquad (3.14), (3.15)$$

A benevolent dictator or an enlightened social planner will maximize social welfare subject to the government budget constraint:[14]

$$\text{Max} U = u[x_1(.), x_2(.), z] + \left\{R - \frac{t_1}{w} x_1(.) - \frac{t_2}{w} x_2(.) - y^p[x_1(.), x_2(.), z]\right\} \quad (3.16)$$

subject to $$t_1 x_1(.) + t_2 x_2(.) = C(z).$$

We recall that x_1 and x_2 are determined by a first stage maximization process which allows to interpret the utility function in 3.16 as an indirect utility function. We also notice that the quantities in the budget restraint are replaced by using equations 3.14 and 3.15.

If λ is introduced as an undetermined multiplier, the necessary conditions for the solution of the policy problem can be derived. Needless to say, the solution describes only a second-best optimum:

$$\frac{\partial u}{\partial z} - \frac{t_1}{w}\frac{\partial x_1}{\partial z} - \frac{t_2}{w}\frac{\partial x_2}{\partial z} - \frac{\partial y^p}{\partial z} = \lambda(\frac{\partial C}{\partial z} - t_1\frac{\partial x_1}{\partial z} - t_2\frac{\partial x_2}{\partial z}), \qquad (3.17)$$

$$t_1\frac{\partial x_1}{\partial t_1} + t_2\frac{\partial x_2}{\partial t_1} = \frac{1 - w\lambda}{w\lambda} x_1, \qquad (3.18)$$

$$t_1\frac{\partial x_1}{\partial t_2} + t_2\frac{\partial x_2}{\partial t_2} = \frac{1 - w\lambda}{w\lambda} x_2. \qquad (3.19)$$

Equation 3.17 reads as a modified variant of the familiar Samuelson condition for the optimal supply of public goods. Including z in 3.14 and 3.15 will effect the tax bases, which carry over to the last two terms in brackets. The multiplier λ identifies the shadow price of the costs of producing the public good reduced by the above mentioned revenue effects. As illustrated by the numerical example in Section 4, this shadow price is greater than one. The net marginal willingness to pay is measured by the expression on the left side of the equation. The term in brackets on the right side adjusts the cost of producing the public good by the marginal net revenue induced by the increase in the quantities of the private goods caused by the larger quantity of the public good. The two other equations, 3.18 and 3.19, depict the so-called Ramsey-Boiteux conditions. Because an income effect is not operating in the standard demand functions for x_1 and x_2, the cross effects are symmetrical. This yields the following formulation:

$$t_1 \frac{\partial x_1}{\partial t_1} + t_2 \frac{\partial x_1}{\partial t_2} = \frac{1 - w\lambda}{w\lambda} x_1, \tag{3.18a}$$

$$t_1 \frac{\partial x_2}{\partial t_1} + t_2 \frac{\partial x_2}{\partial t_2} = \frac{1 - w\lambda}{w\lambda} x_2. \tag{3.19a}$$

Only if the two goods are unrelated, both in demand and supply, the simpler form of the inverse elasticity rule can be derived.

To relate the analysis directly to Section 2 and illustrate the argument by a concrete numerical example, some simplifications are appropriate. Because working with two private goods does not provide further insights, the analysis can be simplified here, too.

4. THE SIZE OF GOVERNMENT UNDER COMPETING POLICY OBJECTIVES: SOME NUMERICAL ILLUSTRATIONS

By restricting the structure of the model to only one private good which remains earmarked for taxation, the Ramsey-Boiteux conditions are reduced to the following equation:

$$t \frac{\partial x}{\partial t} = \frac{1 - \lambda w}{\lambda w} x.$$

The simplified functional forms allow us to illustrate the qualitative analysis by working with a concrete numerical example. Given the structure of the model, the proportional (or flat rate) income-tax regime is equivalent to a value-added tax regime. The latter in turn can be derived from our commodity tax on x.[15]

Our model will now be adjusted in such a way to allow for a direct computation of the reduced forms without starting in a possibly intractable way from the first-order conditions and transform the problem to a second-stage maximization problem. Because the functional form of the utility function is maintained, the profit variable materializes as an additive term in an otherwise log-linear system. In the following equation, 3.5a, β_1 will be set equal to one to keep marginal costs constant. In extension of the previous model the effect of z on the employment level in the private sector, y^p is subject to decreasing returns, i.e. β_2 is larger than -1. It should be noted that the loss of generality caused by the following specification is acceptable because the qualitative characteristics are maintained:

$$U = \ln x + \ln z + (R - y^w), \quad \text{with} \quad R = 3, \tag{3.1a}$$

$$wy^w + 0 = px, \tag{3.2a}$$

$$\frac{p}{w} = \frac{1}{x}, \tag{3.3a}$$

$$y^p = Ax^{\beta_1} z^{\beta_2}, \quad \text{with} \quad A = 0.08, \quad \beta_1 = 1, \quad \text{and} \quad \beta_2 = -0.25, \tag{3.5a}$$

$$[\pi = 0], \tag{3.6a}$$

$$\frac{p}{w} = \frac{Az^{\beta_2}}{1-t}, \tag{3.7a}$$

$$y^g = Bz^\gamma, \quad \text{with} \quad B = 0.2, \quad \text{and} \quad \gamma = 5, \tag{3.9a}$$

$$ptx = wBz^\gamma. \tag{3.10a}$$

p_1, the price of x, will be set equal to one. The wage rate, w, will be endogenously determined. As mentioned above, t denotes a marginal commodity tax rate (resp. a value-added tax rate). The equations 3.2a to 3.10a, excluding equation 3.6a, can be written as a log-linear system and then solved in a routine way. The endogenous variables are y^w (resp. $R - y^w$), y^p, y^g, x, z, and w. The tax rate, t, operates as a parameter (policy instrument) to be determined by assigning alternative roles to the government. The following equations denote the solutions for the variables entering the private agent's utility function:

$$x = \left(\frac{1-t}{A}\right)\left(\frac{B}{t}\right)^{\frac{\beta_2}{\gamma}} = \left(\frac{1-t}{0.08}\right)\left(\frac{0.2}{t}\right)^{-0.05}, \tag{4.1}$$

$$z = \left(\frac{t}{B}\right)^{\frac{1}{\gamma}} = \left(\frac{t}{0.2}\right)^{0.2}, \tag{4.2}$$

$$y^w = \frac{p}{w} x = 1. \tag{4.3}$$

The remaining solutions can be derived by direct substitution into the equations of the system. Information and transaction costs may impose restrictions on the benevolent dictator, thus preventing him from pursuing a first-best optimum. Similar cost barriers will prevent the arrangement of a Lindahl-tax system. Financing the production of the public good by levying value-added taxes restrict the optimum to a second-best utility level, U^{sb}. It might be the case that the benevolent dictator must content himself with more conventional goals such as national product (*NP*), defined as $x + wy^g$, or national income (*NI*), recorded here as x.

The above stated reduced-form equations apply only to cases of so-called non-first-best solutions, where the representative consumer and producer are not charged the correct "price" for the public goods. A first-best solution or a utility maximum can be derived by maximizing utility subject to the resource constraints. The formal computation of a Lindahl equilibrium could follow the rules derived in the Appendix to Section 3. However, given the specification of the model, this equilibrium creates problems of interpretation: Introducing a competitive market for the public good will turn the private production function into one with increasing returns. This implies losses for the private firms. The public sector will earn profits. The sum of these two items which is positive should be included in the private sector's budget constraint.

To derive the second-best solutions, we proceed as follows: Given the definition of the policy goal under discussion, the reduced-form solutions in terms of the tax rate are substituted for the respective variables. Setting the first derivative equal to zero allows solving for the respective tax rate and the policy variables involved.

Table 1. Efficient Size of Government under Competing Goals

Goal	U	$R - y^w$	y^p	y^g	$x = w$	z	t
U^{sb}	4.302	2	0.8	0.2	10.0	1.0	0.2
	(4.296)	(2)	(0.84)	(0.16)	(10.35)	(0.96)	(0.16)
NP	4.292	2	0.84	0.16	10.42	0.95	0.16
	(4.015)	(2)	(0.5)	(0.5)	(6.25)	1.2	0.5
NI	4.114	2	0.95	0.05	11.04	0.75	0.05
	not def.	(2)	(1.0)	(0)	(12.5)	(0)	(0)
U	4.340	1.75	1.0	0.25		1.05	
Lindahl	4.340	1.75	1.0	0.21	12.7	1.05	$t_{=}^{f} = 3.34$ $t_{=}^{c} = 12.10$

The first three second-best policy alternatives should be evaluated against the ideal norm of the first-best solution or the Lindahl equilibrium. The solution values for these competing arrangements are stated in Table 1. The numbers in brackets describe the case in which the productive effect of the public good remains excluded and only the utility effect is operating. The results of the simulations confirm what should be expected from *a priori*-reasoning: Social welfare or utility, U, is highest under the first-best or Lindahl solution. Maximizing *NI* instead of focusing on *NP* will reduce welfare. It may be surprising and may run counter to intuition that the level of employment distributed over the two sectors remains constant under all three second-best solutions. This result is the consequence of the specific form of the utility function and the fact that a profit term in the private sector budget constraint does not become operative. The employment level will be higher in the Lindahl equilibrium, which is equivalent to the first-best utility solution, because the privatization of the market for public goods generates profits as described above. Under the first-best utility solution the scarcity prices of the public good both for the consumers and the firms are implicitly included. Given the constant level of employment under second-best solutions, the interesting aspect of the numbers in Table 1 is the distribution of employment and production over the two sectors. The higher welfare under the *NP*-goal as compared to the *NI*-goal is associated with a larger public sector, measured either by tax revenues, public good production or public sector employment. Maximizing national income directs production from the public good to the private good. Maximizing second-best utility, U^{sb}, will reinforce this mechanism if compared to the *NP*-goal. Finally, a very important result should be noted: If the policies of the benevolent dictator approach the first-best solution, the optimal and efficient size of the government will increase.[16] However, to assess the consequences of the model appropriately, it should be made clear that the government materializes here in the role of a benevolent dictator and not in a Leviathan who will be analyzed in Section 5.

Once more, our model incorporating a productive government should be contrasted with the standard macroeconomic model in which the government has no useful role to play. At least under full employment, the welfare-maximizing size of the government is simply zero.

The reduced-form equation 4.1 specifies a Laffer-type curve for x. As shown in Table 1, this curve has a regular maximum at the tax rate $t = 0.05$ (see the row for *NI* in Table 1). A government maximizing tax revenues will operate on the Laffer curve—in the usual denotation—and thereby, as a typical monopolist, fix a tax rate in the falling range of the reduced-form equation for x. Under the specified parameter constellation, tax revenues are:

$$\ln(tx) = \ln t + \ln(1-t) - \ln A - \frac{\beta_2}{\gamma}\ln t + \frac{\beta_2}{\gamma}\ln B. \tag{4.4}$$

The first-order condition,

$$\frac{d\ln(tx)}{dt} = \frac{1}{t} - \frac{1}{1-t} - \frac{\beta_2}{\gamma}\frac{1}{t} = 0,$$

yields a tax rate $t \approx 0.51$ for $\frac{d^2 / \ln(tx)}{dt^2} < 0.$

5. GOVERNMENT AS LEVIATHAN

The benevolent (and efficient) dictator is the implicit role model of the more orthodox public finance literature. The results derived from such a model are not different from an extreme variant of a public choice model in which an enlightened median voter is able to fully constrain the political process from the demand side. As in Section 2, it makes sense to contrast this case with a Leviathan government. Leviathan may either materialize as a surplus-maximizing dictator or a budget-maximizing anonymous bureaucracy. In this final section we concentrate only on this second variant.

It should be noted that the typical model of the literature, incorporating a revenue-maximizing politician-bureaucrat with standard reference to Niskanen (1968 and 1971)[17], remains incomplete as long as it ignores the productive activities provided by the government. In order to prevent a so-called worst-case scenario leading to a complete confiscation of private production, the familiar consumption-leisure trade-off will be retained. Including a production function for the public good in connection with the revenue-maximizing hypothesis reveals some surprising results for efficiency. The politician-bureaucrat, at least in a technical sense, is forced to be efficient in order to maximize tax revenues.

To illustrate the results, the standard microeconomic technique contrasting indifference relations with underlying restrictions can be used. A graphic analysis allows us to separate the behavior of a Leviathan bureaucracy from that of the benevolent dictator.

For the consumer-voter both the tax rate and the quantity of the public good are given parameters. A benevolent dictator will strive to maximize the private agent's utility function:

$$U = xze^{(R-y^w)}. \qquad (5.1), [(3.1a)]$$

Substituting from equations 4.1 and 4.2 and applying equation 4.3 to simplify the expressions yields

$$U = \frac{1-t}{A} z^{(1-\beta_2)} e^{(R-1)} = \frac{1-t}{0.08} z^{1.25} e^2.$$

The marginal rate of substitution in *t*-*z*-space has a positive slope because the tax rate operates as an economic bad. The rate of change of the slope of an indifference curve is negative:

$$\left.\frac{dt}{dz}\right|_U > 0, \qquad \frac{d^2t}{dz^2} < 0.$$

In both Figures 2 and 3 three typical indifference curves are presented. For the moment the set of indifference curves, U_0^g, U_1^g, and U_2^g, which will be discussed in a moment, should be ignored.

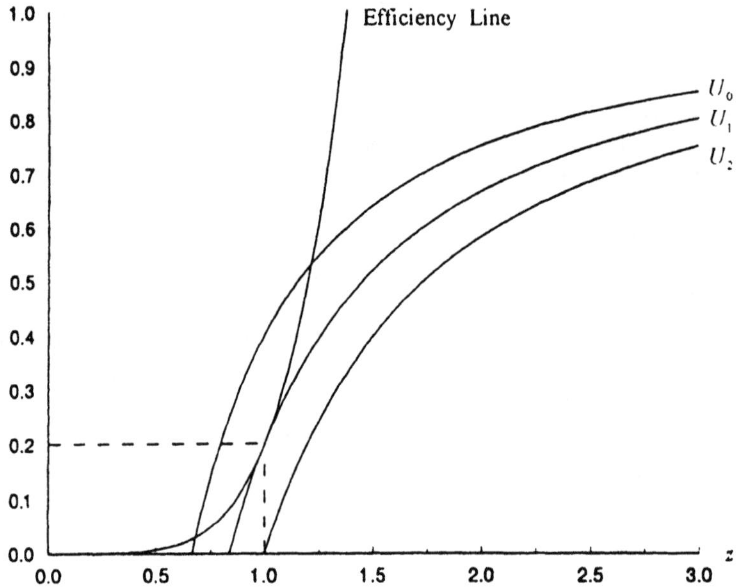

Figure 2. The Second-Best Optimum

The efficiency line or restriction depicting the maximum level of the public good for any given tax rate is identical with the reduced-form equation 4.2 for z. The efficiency line has a positive slope throughout, due to the fact that the demand function for x has unitary elasticity:

$$t = 0.2z^5, \qquad \left.\frac{dt}{dz}\right|_E > 0, \qquad \frac{d^2t}{dz^2} > 0. \qquad (5.2), [(4.2)]$$

The efficiency line is depicted both in Figures 2 and 3. The standard microeconomic problem can be solved in a routine way. Figure 2 illustrates the optimization problem for a benevolent dictator with the implicit second-best solution for utility. The solution values, $z = 1$ and $t = 0.2$, reproduce the second-best solution for utility, U^{sb}, shown in Table 1.

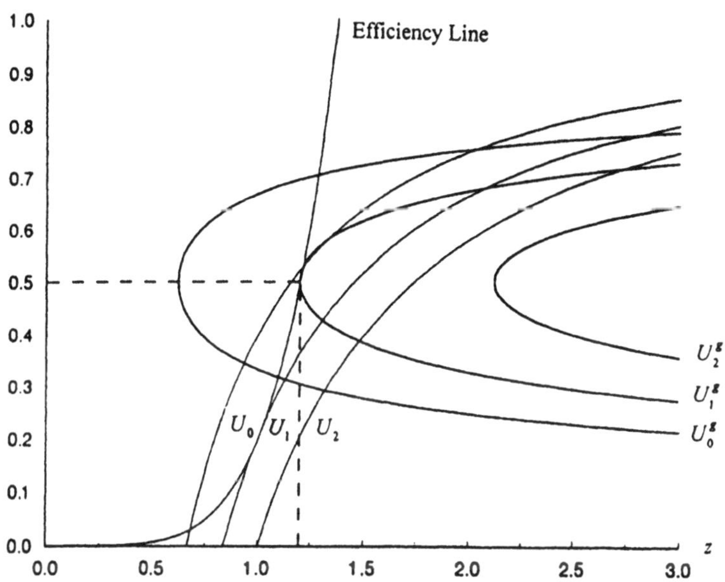

Figure 3. The Budget-Maximizing Bureaucrat.

Our simple hypothesis for the politician-bureaucrat is that he strives to maximize tax revenues:

$$U^g = tx. \tag{5.3}$$

Substituting the reduced form for z yields:

$$U^g = t(\frac{1-t}{0.08})(\frac{t}{0.2})^{0.05}$$

As shown in the last section—see equation 4.4—maximizing tax revenues results in a tax rate that is much higher than the one maximizing x. The quantity of the public good, z, associated with the revenue-maximizing tax rate of $t = 0.51$ is 1.21.

This solution could, of course, be derived by using standard indifference curves to be derived from the following utility function:

$$U^g = t\frac{1-t}{0.08}z^{0.25}.$$

The substitution procedure parallels the one described above. Without further discussion we graph the government's indifference curves shown in Figure 3. It certainly does not come as a surprise that the size of government under this hypothesis will be more excessive, thereby reducing utility or welfare.

6. SUMMARY

In the preceding discussion we have tried to reconcile the neoclassical approach of optimal tax theory with a simple public choice model. The analytical basis for this attempt was provided by a general equilibrium model with a public good produced by the government which enhances utility and increases the productivity of the private sector. The public good is financed by levying optimal second-best taxes given the fact that the prevailing institutional arrangement prevents a first-best solution.

In Section 2, a simple choice-theoretical model was presented in which the public good operates only as a productive factor via the infrastructure thereby enhancing the productivity of the private sector. The income tax system operates as a flat income tax. Given the optimal tax rate, the appropriate rule for a welfare maximizing dictator is to balance the budget. The same unintended social consequences are brought about by a budget-maximizing bureaucracy constrained by the same optimal income tax rate. The basic model proved especially useful in the modeling of alternative social arrangements: e.g., if organized labor succeeds in fixing the real wage rate over the efficiency level, the marginal productivity in the private sector will increase both because the level of private employment will decrease and the level of public employment will increase. As the government is forced to pay competitive wages, this collective action leads to a redistribution of income from capital to labor, thereby increasing the size of the government. It should be emphasized that the model of a productive government could be reformulated without analytical difficulties to extend or to replace the typical Keynesian perspective of the standard macroeconomic models. Leviathan played either the role of a budget-maximizing bureaucrat or a surplus-maximizing selfish dictator.

In Section 3, the economic problem for a benevolent dictator was discussed from the perspective of the theory of optimal taxation. Because several private goods were included, the second-best tax system is one of distinct commodity taxes. If only one private good is available, a commodity-tax system can be easily transformed into a value-added tax system which under the structure of the model is equivalent to a proportional income tax system. This more technical discussion was used to derive some useful first-best conditions which are important for the institutionalization of a demand-revealing process or possible Lindahl-tax prices.

The main part of Section 3 was the analysis of alternative government arrangements based on a concrete numerical example where the public good operated both through the utility function of the representative agent and the production function of the private sector. The pattern of production and employment under alternative governmental goals was derived for a benevolent dictator. The "first-best" or Lindahl solution thereby supplied the reference situation against which competing goals such as aggregate consumer surplus, national product or national income could be evaluated. Rather surprisingly, the size of the government increased with government efforts to maximize welfare by establishing a more efficient tax rate. Subsequently, the behavior of an optimizing politician-bureaucrat was modeled according to a Leviathan perspective, whereby the relevant structural restrictions were consistently derived and not postulated in an *ad hoc* fashion. The excessive size of government in this case did not come as a surprise. A graphic illustration helped to elucidate the analysis and summarize the major results.

The deplorable fact of excessive (inefficient measured against optimal "social welfare") government size along an explosive growth path for almost all Western countries would certainly suggest the need for fiscal reforms on a constitutional level. Constitutional limitations upon government taxing activities as proposed by Buchanan and Brennan are without doubt a most effective recipe for taming Leviathan. A serious objection, of course, remains because pulling away the government from the Leviathan equilibrium is no guarantee that the new equilibrium is preferable from an overall welfare point of view. Further understanding of the welfare reducing effects of a Leviathan government presupposes opening the "black box" called government and analyzing its internal structure and organization.[18] This procedure, however, remains basically a partial one with the difficulties holding the strings together under a general equilibrium perspective. The main theoretical avenue seems to be clear: Fiscal reforms should start from an economic model of the behavior of the politician-bureaucrat, whereby modern microeconomics could provide the technical details for an efficiently designed contract mechanism. Such a mechanism, together with the specification of the proper role of the government in a market economy, could provide efficient incentives for the political actor to redirect his behavior toward a "first-best" solution.

Appendix to Section 2: Some Variations of the Basic Model

Model II restates a second-best utility solution excluding the consumption-leisure trade-off of the general model:

$$\begin{aligned} &z(y^g)f'(y^p) - w = 0, \\ &y^g + y^p = R, \\ &z(y^g)f'(y^p) - z'(y^g)f(y^p) = 0, \\ &x - z(y^g)f(y^p) = 0, \\ &tx - (1-t)wy^g = x^g. \end{aligned} \tag{II}$$

The endogenous variables are y^g, y^p, x, w, and t.

If a consumption-leisure trade-off is included, the economic process is described by model III:

$$
\begin{aligned}
&z(y^g)f'(y^p) - w = 0, \\
&y^g + y^p + [(1-t)w]^{-\frac{1}{\theta}} = R, \\
&x - z(y^g)f(y^p) = 0, \\
&tx - (1-t)wy^g = x^g.
\end{aligned}
\tag{III}
$$

The endogenous variables are y^g, y^p, x, and w. Including our efficiency condition will endogenize t. It is possible to include the utility function as a second-best welfare function, too. This procedure constitutes the subject matter of Sections 4 and 5.

Model IV and model V could be used to analyze Leviathan in either of two roles: A specific dictator will maximize x^g[19], and an anonymous group of bureaucrats aims at maximizing the size of the budget. If the Leviathan of model V uses the tax rate as an instrument the government, as a monopolist, will operate in the declining range of a curve relating x to t (see Section 4). Model IV reads as:

$$
\begin{aligned}
&z(y^g)f'(y^p) - w = 0, \\
&y^g + y^p + [(1-t)w]^{-\frac{1}{\theta}} = R, \\
&x - z(y^g)f(y^p) = 0, \\
&tx - (1-t)wy^g - x^g = 0.
\end{aligned}
\tag{IV}
$$

The endogenous variables are y^p, x, w, and x^p. Including the efficiency condition from equation 2.5, once more, will endogenize t.

$$
\begin{aligned}
&z(y^g)f'(y^p) - w = 0, \\
&y^g + y^p = R, \\
&x - z(y^g)f(y^p) = 0, \\
&tx - (1-t)wy^g = 0, \\
&T - tx = 0.
\end{aligned}
\tag{V}
$$

The endogenous variables are y^g, y^p, x, w, , and T.

Appendix to Section 3: Some General Welfare Remarks

Given the case of one private good, x, and one public good, z, an omniscient benevolent dictator would maximize social welfare or aggregate consumer surplus which is much simplified by the fact that only one representative consumer is included:

$$\mathrm{Max}\,U = u(x,z) + [R - y^p(x,z) - y^g(z)].$$

The first order conditions are as follows:

$$\frac{\partial U}{\partial x} = \frac{\partial y^p}{\partial x}, \quad \text{and} \quad \frac{\partial U}{\partial z} - \frac{\partial y^p}{\partial z} = \frac{\partial y^p}{\partial z}.$$

From these equations the conditions for an equivalent Lindahl equilibrium may be reconstructed:

$$\frac{\partial U}{\partial x} = \frac{\partial y^p}{\partial x}, \qquad p_z^c = w\frac{\partial u}{\partial z}, \qquad \text{and} \qquad p_z^f = -w\frac{\partial y^p}{\partial z}.$$

The personalized prices p_z^c and p_z^f denote the marginal willingness to pay of consumers and firms respectively. These equations can be rearranged to yield the familiar Lindahl conditions which are nothing more than another expression for the general Samuelson conditions:

$$p_z^c + p_z^f = w\frac{\partial y^g}{\partial z} \equiv \frac{\partial C}{\partial z} = (t_z^c + t_z^f).$$

The Lindahl equilibrium thus selects the first-best optimum.

Our abstract analysis has direct bearing on a number of interesting policy applications among which the demand-revealing scheme seems to be the most important. Demand-revelation could overcome the incentive problem inherent in the Lindahl-tax scheme. Tullock (together with Nicolas Tidemann) not only coined the term "rent-seeking" but he himself contributed to the theoretical development of this theory (e.g. Tidemann and Tullock [1976]).

The author gratefully acknowledges helpful comments and suggestions by Price Fishback, Günter Krause, Stephan Monissen, and the participants of the conference. Of course, any remaining errors and omissions are those of the author.

[1] The 5th Edition from 1989 was revised 1994 and retitled. The 5th Edition was reissued 1994 as *The New World of Economics*. Gordon Tullock's public choice perspective is included in a later book which unfortunately did not receive the commercial influence it deserved: Gordon Tullock and Richard B. McKenzie (1978). "On the Trail of Homo Economicus" is the apt title of a collection of Gordon Tullock's previously unpublished papers edited by Gordon L. Brady and Robert D. Tollison (1994).

[2] In a recent paper James Gwartney, Randall Holcombe and Robert Lawson present an empirical assessment of Adam Smith's core functions of government (1998).

[3] As a general reference to the modern theory of optimal taxation see Alan J. Auerbach (1985).

[4] This analytical variant is a useful extension of the standard positive-normative spectrum, cf. here James M. Buchanan (1998).

[5] The structure of the model builds on Hans G. Monissen (1985). His model incorporates a monetary sector, an extension which has no consequence for the problems under discussion here.

[6] See John S. Chipman for a detailed discussion of this point (1965).

[7] The specific circumstances under which a voting process with heterogeneous actors will generate a Pareto-optimal provision of a public good are no more restrictive than those under which the representative actor operates in modern economic theory. A standard reference in this context is an early paper by Howard R. Bowen from 1943.

[8] The model is set up in such a way that it allows approximately a sequential solution.

[9] For a lucid discussion in the context of macroeconomic theory see Stephen McCafferty (1990).

[10] A more general treatment is given by Hans G. Monissen (1996).

[11] Theories trying to explain the size of government and its development over time are mushrooming. A recent popular thesis is that the openness of an economy is a critical factor. An open economy is exposed to external risk necessitating the insurance role of the government; cf. here Dani Rodrik (1998) or Alberto Alesina and Romain Wacziarg (1997).

[12] Our figure corresponds to their Figure 8.2 on page 294.

[13] The marginal product in the private sector which determines gross compensation of labor in the public sector is higher than the marginal product of *z*. If the efficiency condition is fulfilled, the change in *x* is zero depicting the maximum value for *x*.

[14] The general argument presented here is based on the technical analysis in Claude Henry (1989).

[15] Value-added taxes are levied *ad valorem* which changes the Ramsey-Boiteux condition. Tax revenues are now *tpx*, where *t* is the value-added tax rate. The Ramsey-Boiteux condition has now to be extracted from the following equation:

$$\frac{\partial p}{\partial t}\frac{tx}{w}+\frac{px}{w}=\lambda\left(\frac{\partial p}{\partial t}tx+px+pt\frac{\partial x}{\partial t}\right).$$

[16] This interesting observation should be related to the empirical findings published in a recent paper by Gary S. Becker and Casey B. Mulligan (1998). But we should note that Becker and Mulligan start from a somewhat different perspective.

[17] It should be noted that Niskanen explicitly acknowledges here the "powerful insight" provided by Gordon Tullock (1968, p. 294).

[18] In this context it is impossible to summarize Tullock's guiding contributions to this problem over several decades. A representative reference is here Gordon Tullock (1992). The same problems are at present on the agenda of modern contract theorists, see for instance Jean Tirole (1982).

[19] It is here where Tullock's work on rent-seeking could be usefully integrated. The seminal contribution is Tullock's paper from 1967. For an effort to integrate rent-seeking into a general equilibrium frame see Hans G. Monissen (1991).

REFERENCES

Alesina, Alberto, and Romain Wacziarg (1997). "Openness, Country Size and the Government." *NBER*, Working Paper No. 6024.

American Economic Review, September 1998, 88 (4).

Auerbach, Alan J. (1985). "The Theory of Excess Burden and Optimal Taxation." In Alan J. Auerbach and Martin Feldstein, eds., *Handbook of Public Economics*. Vol. I, pp. 61–127. North Holland: Elsevier Science Publishers.

Becker, Garry S. and Casey B. Mulligan (1998). "Deadweight Costs and the Size of the Government." *NBER*, Working Paper No 6789.

Blaug, Mark. (1985). *Great Economists since Keynes: An Introduction to the Lives and Works of One Hundred Modern Economists*. Cambridge: Cambridge University Press, pp. 252–53.

Bowen, Howard R. (1943). "The Interpretation of Voting in the Allocation of Economic Resources." *Quarterly Journal of Economics* 58 (1) pp. 27–48.

Brady, Gordon L., and Robert D. Tollison, eds. (1994). *On the Trail of Homo Economicus: Essays by Gordon Tullock*. Fairfax, VA: George Mason University Press.

Brennan, Geoffrey, and James M. Buchanan (1977). "Towards a Tax Constitution for Leviathan." *Journal of Public Economics* 8 (3) pp. 255–73.

______ (1980) *The Power to Tax: Analytical Foundations of a Fiscal Constitution*. Cambridge: Cambridge University Press.

Buchanan, James M. (1998). "Has Economics Lost Its Way? Reflections on the Economists' Enterprise at Century's End." In James M. Buchanan and Bettina Monissen, eds., *The Economists' Vision: Essays in Modern Economic Perspectives*. Frankfurt: Campus Verlag, pp. 17–29.

Chipman, John S. (1965). "The Nature and Meaning of Equilibrium in Economic Theory." In Don Martindale, ed., *Functionalism in the Social Sciences: The Strength and Limits of Functionalism in Anthropology, Economics, Political Sciences and Sociology*. Philadelphia: American Economic Academy of Political and Social Science, pp. 35–64; reprinted in Harry Townsend, ed., (1971) *Price Theory, Selected Readings*, Harmondsworth, Middlesex, England: Penguin Books Ltd., pp. 341–71.

Findlay, Ronald, and John D. Wilson. (1987). "The Political Economy of Leviathan." In Assaf Razin and Efraim Sadka, eds., *Economic Policy in Theory and Practice*. Houndsmill, Basingstroke, Hampshire and London: The McMillan Press Ltd., pp. 289–304.

Gwartney, James, Randall Holcombe, and Robert Lawson (1998). "The Scope of Government and the Wealth of Nations." *Cato Journal* 18 (2) pp. 163–90.

Henry, Claude (1989). *Macroeconomics for Public Policy: Helping the Invisible Hand.* Oxford: Clarendon Press.

Inman, Robert P. (1982). "The Economic Case for Limits to Government." *American Economic Review* 72 (2) pp. 176–83.

______(1987). "Markets, Governments, and the 'New' Political Economy." In Alan J. Auerbach and Martin Feldstein, eds, *Handbook of Public Economics,* Vol. 2, pp. 647–777. North Holland: Elsevier Science Publishers.

McCafferty, Stephen (1990). *Macroeconomics.* New York: Harper & Row.

Monissen, Hans G. (1985). "Optimale Staatsgröße in einem Einkommensteuerregime." In Hellmuth Milde and Hans G. Monissen, eds, *Rationale Wirtschaftspolitik in komplexen Gesellschaften.* pp. 195–205. Stuttgart: Verlag W. Kohlhammer.

______ (1991). "Rent-Seeking in General Equilibrium: A Didactic Illustration." *Public Choice* 72, pp. 111–29.

______ (1996). "Verallgemeinerungen einfacher quasi-linearer Nutzenfunktionen." *Jahrbücher für Nationalökonomie und Statistik* 215 (1) pp. 1–13.

Niskanen, William A. (1968). "The Peculiar Economics of Bureaucracy." *American Economic Review* 58 (2) pp. 293–305.

______(1971) *Bureaucracy and Representative Government.* Chicago: Aldine-Atterton..

Rodrik, Dani (1998). "Why Do More Open Economics Have Bigger Governments?" *Journal of Political Economy* 106 (5) pp. 997–1032.

Smith, Adam. *An Inquiry into the Nature and Causes of the Wealth of Nations.* Edited by Edwin Cannan. (1976). Chicago: The University of Chicago Press, Volume Two, Book IV, Chap IX.

Tidemann, Nicolas T., and Gordon Tullock (1976). "A New and Superior Process for Making Social Choices." *Journal of Political Economy* 84 (6) pp. 1145–59.

Tirole, Jean (1982). "The Internal Organization of Government." *Oxford Economic Papers* 46, pp. 1–29.

Tullock, Gordon (1967). "The Welfare Costs of Tariffs, Monopolies and Theft." *Western Economic Journal* 5, pp. 224–32.

______(1992). *Economic Hierarchies, Organization and the Structure of Production: Studies in Public Choice.* Norwell, MA/Dordrecht: Kluwer Academic Publishers.

Tullock, Gordon, and Richard B. McKenzie (1975). *The New World of Economics: Explorations into the Human Experience.* Homewood, IL: Richard D. Irwin.

______(1978) *Modern Political Economy: An Introduction to Economics.* New York: McGraw-Hill.

MONOPOLY AS A COORDINATION PROBLEM

Dwight R. Lee
Economics Department
Terry College of Business
University of Georgia, Athens
Athens, GA 30602
U.S.A.

Richard B. McKenzie
Graduate School of Management
University of California, Irvine
Irvine, CA 92697
U.S.A.

INTRODUCTION

The contribution to the theory of monopoly that most people recall when considering Gordon Tullock's work concerns the rent-seeking cost of monopoly. After Tullock published his justly famous 1967 article "The Welfare Costs of Tariffs, Monopolies, and Theft" economists could no longer think of the social cost of monopolies solely in terms of the dead-weight losses of Harberger triangles. Monopolists devote resources to securing and maintaining their monopoly positions. The value of those resources, in their best alternative use, represents a social costs of monopoly that is generally larger than that represented by the area between the demand curve and marginal cost curve over the range from the monopoly output to the competitive output. Without downplaying the importance of Tullock's rent-seeking theory to understanding monopoly behavior, we want to emphasize another of his contributions that has important implications for the theory of monopoly, which has been largely ignored. There are two reasons for this oversight. First, the contribution we have in mind comes from his 1965 book *The Politics of Bureaucracy* and has been developed by, and primarily associated with the work of others, work that now goes by the name of principal-agent theory. Second, principal-agent theory has implications for monopolies that have not been recognized and which we develop in this chapter. So, as with so many other things we have written, this chapter is rooted in fundamental ways on the insights and contributions of Gordon Tullock.

We begin by considering the traditional theory of monopoly, which leads to a set of theoretical deductions widely accepted by economists. A monopolist, protected against competitors by external barriers to entry, will reduce output below the level expected under idealized perfectly competitive market conditions. The purpose of the output restriction is, of course, to raise the market price above the competitive level, thereby generating monopoly rents. The consequence is a dead-weight loss resulting from the failure to produce units worth more than they cost.[1] This traditional view of monopoly is typically devoid of any consideration of the institutional setting of a monopoly-organized market compared to that of a competitively organized market.

Following the insight of Tullock (1967), it is now commonly accepted that the social cost of a monopoly is greater than indicated by the traditional theory. Monopolies, and the rents they create, are typically the creations of government restrictions on entry. These monopoly rents are created and allocated in response to rent seeking, and the social cost of this rent seeking adds to the dead-weight loss associated with monopoly restrictions on output. A guiding presumption in discussions of monopoly is that the only meaningful barriers to achieving monopoly price and output levels are external to the monopoly.[2] This means that the only rent seeking relevant to the welfare costs of a monopoly position is unrelated to organizational or managerial problems within the monopoly firm.

In this chapter, we seek to challenge the conventional view of monopoly output and pricing behavior by taking account of the required institutional shift when a market is monopolized. Our point is simple one: *Aside from one-person firms, in which the residual claimant, principal, and agent are one and the same person, the achievement of monopoly rents is itself a coordination problem of bringing about restrictions on output through agents inside the firm whose incentives are imperfectly aligned with the interests of the principal(s).* That is to say, rather than viewing a monopoly as a single-minded entity within which everyone is driven exclusively by the goal of maximum firm profits, a monopoly is best viewed as a group of individuals who are pursuing their own advantage through internal rent seeking that induces monopoly profits.[3]

We posit that achieving monopoly results is limited by both external *and* internal constraints, a fact that makes monopoly output restrictions less likely, and less severe, than the conventional theories of monopoly and rent seeking would indicate. This perspective on monopolies leads to conclusions that stand in sharp contrast with conventional implications: Even if production technology remains the same, the monopolist's marginal and average cost curves will not be the same as the competitive supply curve. Indeed, contrary to what might be thought, the average cost faced by the monopolist will be higher than the average cost faced by independent competitors (again, assuming that production technology is the same), while the monopolist's marginal cost curve is lower than the competitors' marginal cost curves. The monopoly profits will necessarily be smaller than is conventionally assumed, regardless of the elasticity of demand. The reduced monopoly rents mean that there will be less political rent seeking to achieve monopoly ends and fewer monopolies than would be implied by conventional monopoly theory.

Our arguments lead to the conclusion that in seeking to achieve monopoly profits, the monopolist must not only be concerned by external entry barriers, but also internal constraints in the form of agency costs that can reduce the degree to which output can be restricted and profits generated and retained by the monopoly firm. High agency costs can, in other words, have the same impact on monopoly output decisions as low entry barriers. Improved systems of internal control of agents' behavior lead to several outcomes not fully appreciated in the literature: greater restrictions on output and higher prices and profits in monopolized markets, more political, or external, rent seeking, and more government-imposed restrictions on market entry

THE CONVENTIONAL VIEW OF MONOPOLY

Figure 1 shows the usual way the efficiency of monopoly and competitive markets are compared. The long-run marginal (and average) cost curve for the monopolist is assumed to be horizontal for simplicity of exposition. For purposes of making welfare comparisons between monopoly and competitive markets, the common assumption is that the MC curve is identical with the supply curve for a collection of competitors in

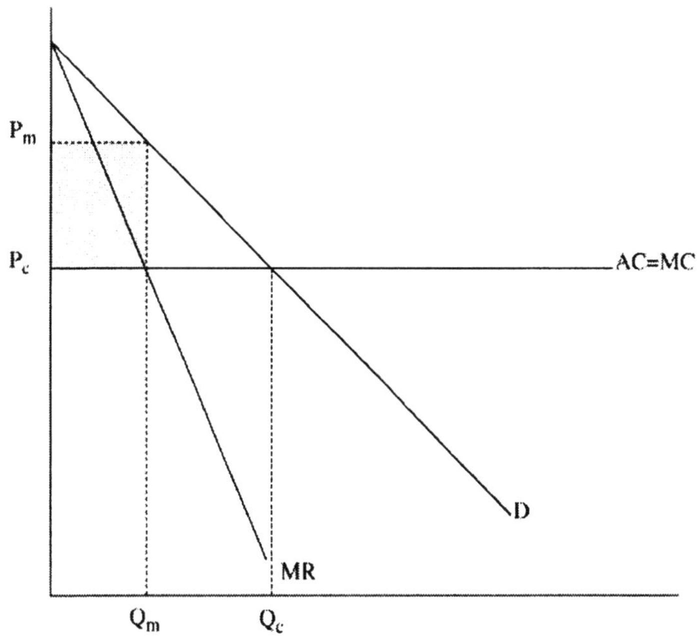

Figure 1. The Conventional View of Monopoly

a perfectly competitive market. The underlying presumptions are that the monopolistic firm has as much incentive to minimize its production costs as do competitors and that agency costs are unaffected by the market structure. After all, if the monopolist is intent on maximizing profits, then it has every incentive to hold costs down to the minimum. As is conventional, Michael Jensen and William Meckling (1976) have concluded that it is wrong to presume that monopolization of markets will lead to less "value maximization" than would be observed in competitive markets: "Since the owner of a monopoly has the *same wealth incentives* to minimize managerial costs as would the owner of a competitive firm, both will undertake that level of monitoring which equates the marginal cost of monitoring to the marginal wealth increment from reduced consumption of perquisites by the managers" (emphasis added).

As a consequence, a monopolist that takes over a once-competitive market will reduce output from Q_c to Q_m in order to raise the price from P_c to P_m and reap profits equal to the shaded rectangle. This sets an upper limit on the amount of rent seeking to achieve the monopoly profits. As is standard, the inefficiency of the monopoly takeover is represented by the area of the welfare-loss triangular plus some portion of the profit rectangle that is dissipated through political rent seeking.

Along much the same line, competitors are unable to achieve monopoly results through the creation of a cartel because the profit incentives that might lead them to consider curbing output will undermine the curbs that are agreed upon. Once the cartel agreement is in place, each competing firm can improve its individual profits by not restricting output. The openness of competitive markets further destabilizes cartels simply because openness increases the number of competitors, actual and potential, who will likely charge less than the cartel price.

AN UNCONVENTIONAL VIEW OF MONOPOLY THEORY

Clearly, there is an asymmetry in conventional theory in the way competitive and monopoly markets are conceived. The presumption is that free riding (or the threat of it) is rampant in competitive markets, so much so that those competitors in perfectly competitive markets need not even try to cartelize their market. On the other hand, it is implicitly assumed that once a monopoly firm has been established through barriers to entry, free riding is no longer a problem worth analytical consideration. All that the monopolist needs in order to achieve maximum monopoly rents is to be protected by barriers to entry. The extent to which the market is closed will determine the elasticity of demand, which will, in turn, determine the extent of the monopoly profits, given the minimum cost structure.

However, when tenets of principal-agency theory are applied to monopoly theory, the monopoly results are not likely to be achieved so costlessly as is conventionally posited. When a market is converted from being fully competitive to fully monopolistic, the market participants within the production units change their economic roles rather dramatically as they shift from being residual claimants of the individual competitive firms to being members of a much larger group of stockholders.[4] Accordingly, the residual claimants have less of an incentive to devote themselves to the objective of profit maximization in the monopoly than they had when they were independent competitors.

If the former competitive market is assumed to have been composed of idealized one-person firms, the principals and agents were one and the same, meaning there was no prospect of misalignment of incentives—and no incentive for uneconomical shirking or misuse of firm resources, given that the any costs incurred would have been fully internalized.[5] However, when the industry is monopolized, the principals become agents who have the prospect of externalizing a share of the costs of their own actions. Alternatively, the principals switch from being single proprietors to being shareholders with minor stakes in the new company, and, again, have impaired incentives to monitor firm costs.

If the former competitive market were made up of firms with separate groups of owners and agents, the problems of separation and control and agency costs would still be increased by the shift from a competitive to monopoly market. Many former principals will become agents within a much larger organization, and the actions of each principal and agent will become less consequential in the context of the total monopoly.[6] They have more of an incentive to engage in opportunistic behavior because the costs of such behaviors are spread over a larger number of stockholders.

Moreover, the pressure on both principals and agents to minimize agency costs will not be nearly so great in monopoly markets, simply because the monopolist's position is less threatened (because of the barriers to entry) than is the case in competitive markets. Perfectly competitive firms face eminent elimination when agency costs exceed minimum levels, monopoly firms do not. Agents who absorb a portion of the profits through internal rent seeking—for such rewards as excessive salaries, extra perks, and larger staffs—are more likely to survive within a monopolistic firm than in a competitive firm, if for no other reason than that these activities would make survival very unlikely under perfect competition.[7] Also, competitive market structures, through trial and error and experimentation, can generate information on low-cost procedures and arrangements, information that can be disseminated through the industry and which is far less likely to be generated at all in a monopoly situation.

The rent created by monopoly restrictions should be expected to give rise to efforts by the firm's employees to capture some of the rents—and the greater the monopoly rents, the greater the rent-seeking effort.[8] Clearly, firms devise policies and structures to reduce organizational rent seeking that reduces profits.[9] This implies that the more the monopoly firm restricts output back toward the idealized monopoly output level (Q_m), with greater rents being generated, the greater the attendant agency cost in the form of rent seeking and attempts to reduce rent seeking. This necessarily means that the average cost curve facing firms in a perfectly competitive market and the monopolist cannot be one and the same. If the average cost curve looks like AC_1 in Figure 2 when the market is competitive, it will look like AC_2-AC_1 under monopoly. The exact position and shape of the new average cost curve will depend on exactly how monopoly profits change as output is restricted, and how much those profits are drained off through internal rent seeking.

The marginal cost curve also changes in unsuspected ways. The marginal cost curve for the monopolist with agency costs associated with restricted output lies below the standard marginal costs curve, and is given by MC_1 in Figure 2 (the mathematics is relatively simple, but proof of the shape of the curve is relegated to the appendix). The agency cost and internal rent seeking reduce the marginal cost curve because they increase with the additional profits generated as output is *contracted* toward Q_m. This means that as output is *expanded* from, say, Q_m toward Q_c the marginal cost is lower than the old marginal cost under competitive conditions without (or with much lower) agency costs because the cost of one more unit of production is the old marginal cost *minus* the agency/rent-seeking costs that are no longer incurred. As the monopoly rents decrease, the marginal agency costs go down, which implies an upward-sloping marginal cost until production level Q_c is achieved, at which point MC_1 becomes identical to MC. As shown in Figure 2, the monopolist's profit maximizing output level is Q_1, not Q_m.

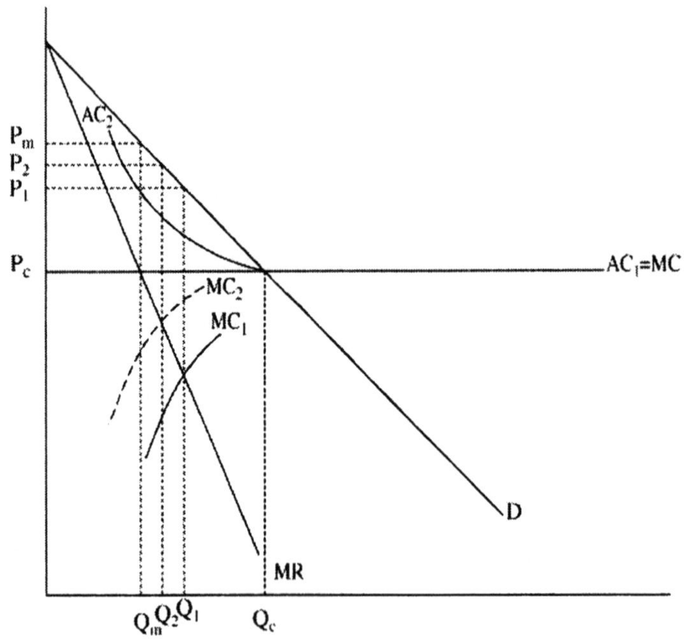

Figure 2. Monopoly with Agency Costs

Our discussion leads to the proposition that a monopolist who simply takes over a previously competitive market will necessarily face the problem of coordinating the activities of a number of previous competitors, which may differ in size and be scattered geographically. The previous owners/residual claimants of the previously individual firms will then be agents of the monopolist, with the new agents taking on decidedly different roles with dramatically different incentives. Each agent will want to use the discretion at her disposal to maximize her own welfare at the expense of the principal/monopolist. The central problem the monopolist confronts is similar—but, of course, not identical—in structure to the problem faced by a cartel: overcoming the tendency of individual producing units to free ride and sacrifice potential collective gain for local or individual profits. The lack of independence of individual producing units within a monopoly no doubt mutes somewhat the costs considered here, but the hierarchy itself superimposed over the various producing units within the monopoly necessarily creates costs of its own, mainly because the chain of command and control will be longer. The requisite incentive and monitoring systems will drain, to one extent or another, firm resources.

Admittedly, how costly the hierarchical system is cannot be determined conceptually and is actually irrelevant to the challenge to conventional theory mounted here. All we need to note is that an effective monopoly replacement for an otherwise competitive market structure implies some system of monitoring costs, or else the restriction on output cannot be coordinated with any better profit results than is expected under a truly competitive market made up of independent producers. The free riding within a cartel, if left unchecked, will cause the cartel to collapse; the free riding within the monopoly, if left unchecked, will drain the monopoly of all rents.

If a monopolist must incur coordinating costs, just to reduce agency costs, the monopolist's marginal cost curve cannot be the same as the competitive supply curve. As a consequence, the profit-maximizing output level of the monopolists will unlikely be the Q_m in Figure 1. It will surely be greater than Q_m but less than Q_c, depending on the exact relationship between coordination costs and the achievement of a lower output. If rent-seeking dissipation within the monopoly firm cannot be controlled at all, except at considerable cost, restriction on output through monopolization of the market would never be attempted. Hence, the extent of monopolization depends on more than external barriers to entry. It also depends on coordination or, what amounts to the same thing, agency costs.

Hence, the monopolist's profits will be something less than is conventionally believed for two reasons: First, the costs associated with excessive perks and with monitoring will soak up some of the profits, and divert production from Q_m. In this case, the waste of monopoly is larger than traditionally specified, the inefficiency triangle, by the amount of the real resources soaked up in coordination of the output restrictions. Second, to achieve cost-effective coordination in restricting output, the monopolist will likely have to share some of the potential rents with the agents in the various producing units. It should be acknowledged that any lax work on the part of the agents will fortify the firm's efforts to constrict output toward Q_m.

It is possible, of course, that the internal rent seeking takes place in such a way that it reduces monopoly profits by a fixed percentage, no matter what those profits are, and thus has no effect on marginal cost. In this case, the firm would still operate as a traditional monopolist would, with the same Harberger welfare lose. And if the agents who are in a position to capture the profits are also those who determine how much pre-monopoly political rent seeking takes place, they might be willing to spend as much on that political rent seeking as in the case in which internal rent seeking is not considered.[10] This might seem to be the worst of all worlds. But we believe that it is unlikely that internal rent seeking will take place without affecting marginal costs. Even if the same percentage of profits were siphoned off at each level of profit, the rent-seeking and monitoring costs would surely increase with profits. Also, to the extent that internal rent seekers are willing to spend the same amount on political rent seeking to establish the monopoly in the first place, it would be because they are able to capture the profits as pure transfers, with no costs to doing so. This situation is not any worse that the Tullock rent-seeking story, even if we assume that internal rent seeking does not affect marginal cost and that the traditional monopoly solution prevails. Of course, it is hard to imagine such pure, no-cost transfers. And anyway, it is unlikely that the internal agents who capture the profits are the ones who make the decisions on political rent seeking. Therefore, the existence of internal rent seeking means that the profits to be realized by those doing the political rent seeking for entry barriers will be less than conventionally thought. This implies that there should be less political rent seeking than in the standard Tullock situation. This also means that there should be fewer monopoly restrictions achieved through government policies. There will be less monopoly profits transferred to those who can provide monopoly privileges. Hence, the prospect of rent absorption within a monopoly, once fortified, should reduce the prevalence of monopolies, given the lower return on rent-seeking to secure and protect a monopoly position.

CHANGES IN AGENCY COSTS

A major tenet of principal-agency theory is that agency costs retard efficiency in markets and that reductions in agency costs spell improved efficiency. The unconventional view of monopoly presented previously leads to a significantly different, more complicated conclusion: *Agency costs can impair rent seeking and reduce the monopolization of markets.* They can also reduce the extent to which output is restricted and the price is raised by monopolization. This implies that, given our revised perspective, a *reduction* in agency costs and internal rent seeking—through, for example, technological development (in such fields as computers and communication systems)—that lead to more productive monitoring systems, can mean greater monopolization of markets, lower outputs, and higher prices.[11] This is because the monopolist can more cost effectively coordinate restrictions on output with more-cost-effective monitoring of agents and thereby curb the costs that agents impose on the firm.

In terms of Figure 2, a reduction in agency costs will lead to an upward shift in the monopolist marginal cost curve. With the shift in the marginal cost curve from the solid line to the dashed line (or from MC_1 to MC_2), the profit maximizing output level falls (from Q_1 to Q_2) while the price rises (from P_1 to P_2). At the same time, the average cost curve falls and monopoly rents grow, because of the greater curb in production and the elimination of coordination and agency costs, (which are not shown in the figure to keep the figure relatively simple.)

Whether the inefficiency loss goes up or down because of improved monitoring is uncertain, because output is further restricted, increasing the size of the Harberger triangle, but the real waste from excessive perks and monitoring goes down. Nevertheless, the expected greater monopoly rents garnered by the firm can increase entry-barrier rent seeking and result in more monopolized markets.

CONCLUDING COMMENTS

Conventional monopoly theory presumes that profit maximization of the monopoly firm is virtually automatic, that the mere existence of the "firm" implies that the agents will do what the stockholders tell them. Hence, it should be no surprise that discussions of incentives within the firm are totally absence in conventional analysis. This standard discussion needs to be brought up to date with the recent insights provided by rent-seeking and agency costs. If monopoly is seen as a problem in coordinating the work of agents who do not "naturally" follow the dictates of the principals, the monopolist's marginal cost curve cannot be equivalent to the industry supply curve under competitive markets conditions. And while it may be true that the monopoly firm can be expected to curb output to some level below that achieved under perfectly competitive conditions, other conclusions regarding the nature of the monopoly's cost structure and, therefore, its ability to extract monopoly rents are not warranted.

A central conclusion of this chapter is that more than external entry barriers count in the ability of monopolies to extract monopoly rents and, for that matter, for firms to seek monopoly positions. Agency costs, which necessarily arise because monopoly must be a coordination problem, also matter. Agency costs will impair the ability of a monopoly to restrict output precisely because agency considerations change the cost structure of the monopolist and, therefore, the profit-maximizing output level.

Our line of analysis leads also to the conclusion that the inefficiency of monopoly can be, though is not necessarily, less than conventionally thought. There are two consequences of market monopolization that affect the market efficiency of monopoly in opposite ways: On the one hand, the prospects of monopoly agency costs that involve the use of real resources will add to the inefficiency of the monopolization process. On the other hand, the agency costs associated with restrictions on the monopoly output level will cause output to be higher than is conventionally thought. That means that the rent available to shareholders will be lower than conventionally thought, and the amount of rent seeking is likely to be lowered because of the agency costs.

Conventional principal-agency theory suggests, without qualification, that any improvement in the ability of firms to monitor their agents will increase productivity and efficiency. Our analysis introduces a major qualification. While improvements in monitoring might reduce agency costs that are created in the process of monopolizing a market, the improvements also ease the coordinating/monitoring problems the monopolist faces in curbing the output level. Reductions in monitoring/agency costs, in other words, can be expected to lead to a reduction in the output of the monopolist, an increase in monopoly rents, an increase in the "inefficiency triangle," and an increase in rent seeking to obtain monopoly protection.

APPENDIX

The implications of agency costs for a cartel can be highlighted with a simple model. Let $P(Q)$ be the downward-sloping inverse demand curve facing the cartel, where Q is the quantity of cartel output. The cost the cartel incurs for each quantity of output is given by $C(Q, Q_C - Q)$, where Q_C is the competitive output—the quantity produced by the industry without cartel restrictions. We make the following plausible assumptions about this cost curve. Letting $C(Q)$ be the cost curve for the industry before formation of the cartel, $C(Q, Q_C - Q) > C(Q)$ for all $Q < Q_C$. The total costs, and therefore the average costs, are higher for the cartel than for the uncartelized industry at all output quantities less than Q_C. But at $Q_C = Q$, $C(Q, Q_C - Q) = C(Q, 0) = C(Q)$. Furthermore, as is standard, we impose the restrictions that $C_1 > 0$ and $C_{11} > 0$, along with the equally plausible restrictions that $C_2 > 0$ and $C_{22} > 0$. Increasing Q, everything else equal, increases costs at an increasing rate, and increasing the gap between Q_C and Q, everything else equal, also increases costs at an increasing rate.[12]

We can now express the cartel's objective as choosing the Q that maximizes the profit function

$$P = P(Q)Q - C(Q, Q_C - Q) \tag{1}$$

The maximizing Q, which we denote as Q^*, necessarily satisfies the condition

$$dP / dQ = P + (dP / dQ)Q - (c_1 - C_2) = 0 \tag{2}$$

or

$$P + (dP / dQ)Q = C_1 - C_2 \tag{2'}$$

Condition 2' yields to the standard interpretation of the requirement for monopoly profit maximization: that marginal revenue equal marginal cost. The only difference is that in the cartel case marginal cost is lower than in the standard case because of the agency costs of reducing output: $C_1 - C_2 < C_1$. Although the agency costs associated with cartel enforcement increase the average cost, they reduce the marginal cost. When output is less than Q_C, an increase in production reduces the agency costs and therefore generates a partial offset to the increase in the standard costs of production. In the absence of agency costs, with $C_2 = 0$ for all Q, condition 2' becomes the standard monopoly profit-maximizing condition and $Q^* = Q_M$. But, because of agency costs, $C_2 > 0$, and it follows from equation 2' that

$$P + (dP / dQ)Q < C_1, \tag{3}$$

or the cartel's marginal revenue is less than the standard marginal cost of production. If, as is almost always the case, the marginal revenue decreases in output, then equation 3 implies that $Q^* > Q_M$. The output that maximizes cartel profits is greater than the output that maximizes the profits of the standard monopoly.

On the other hand, if the cartel is worth forming, its profit-maximizing output will be less than the competitive output level. At Q_C if the cartel marginally reduces output it loses marginal revenue of $P + (dP/dQ)Q_C$, but it gains the marginal costs of $C_1 - C_2$. Since $P = C_1$ at Q_C it follows that if $(dP/dQ)Q_C < -C_2$ (or $-(dP/dQ)Q_C > C_2$), then cartel profits are increased by reducing output below Q_C. The possibility exists, of course, that $C_2\ (Q_C, 0) > -(dP/dQ)Q_C$.[13] If this is the case

$$P + (dP / dQ)Q_C > C_1 - C_2 \quad (4)$$

at the competitive output level and the loss in revenue from a marginal reduction below Q_C is greater than the reduction in costs. Therefore, there is no motivation to reduce output, and nothing to be gained from forming a cartel.[14]

[1] Implicit in the graphical depiction of the dead-weight loss is the assumption that the competitive supply curve is the same as the monopolist's marginal cost curve

[2] See Browning and Zupan (1996, chap. 12).

[3] Our analysis is grounded in Coase's classic work on the theory of the firm (1937) and the considerable literature on institutional/organization economics spawned by Coase's work. Tullock's work on bureaucracy (1965) is an early part of this literature, a literature that despite the date of Coase's original contribution really didn't begin flourishing until the late 1970s.

[4] For discussions of the impact of group size on incentives, see Tullock (1965), Olson (1967) and Radner (1987). For example, Tullock (1965, p. 132) states "Yet most of the members of the hierarchy may be doing things that are either opposed to [the principal's] desires or, at best, neutral. The difficulty here arises because in a large hierarchy—that is, the persons within it—will be doing far more things than can be ordered by any one man, regardless of his rank, diligence, and ability. Those orders that he directly issues will represent only a very small part of the total 'output' of the organization, which must, by necessity, operate on the basis of established decision rules."

[5] See Tullock (1965), Alchian and Demsetz (1972) and Fama (1980) for a discussion of the role of shirking and other forms of agency costs in organizational theory.

[6] Granted, in imperfectly competitive markets, agency costs might exist. Still, we would expect agency costs to rise with the monopolization of the market, given that the agency problems become more severe with more people in the one firm and with a shift in the roles that are played by firm members. Also, monopolies have less information on what minimum cost can be than do competitive firms that can compare, at least indirectly, cost with each other. This lack of information increases the scope for principle-agency problems within the monopoly firm.

[7] Johnson and Libecap (1989) evaluate the issue of salary growth in protected markets in the context of highly protected government monopolies. Ed Zajac, in a communication to us transmitted through Price Fishback, argued that, based on his experience at AT&T and Bell Labs, "Parkinsonian bloat was a bigger problem than shirking . . . ."

[8] Jensen (1986) recognizes the efficiency problems that are bound to arise as monopoly profits (which will be realized in the form of "free case flow") emerge with curbs in production.

[9] Pay rules that tie pay in law firms to years seniority, not to market or productivity (Gilson and Mookin, 1985) or that reduce the dispersion of pay of among academic workers have been explained as means of reducing internal organizational rent seeking; and Pfeffer and Langton, 1988).

[10] We would like to thank Price Fishback for calling our attention to this possibility.

[11] Gurbaxani and Whang (1991) discuss the various ways computers and communication systems have improved monitoring and reduced monitoring and agency costs.

[12] Since maximizing cartel profits requires equalizing the marginal production costs over all members, it is common to assume that cartel agreements satisfy this condition with output allocations. We also incorporate this assumption in our model, with the understanding that production costs now include the agency costs of enforcing whatever level of compliance is associated with the cartel's output.

[13] This possibility is remote when the competitive output occurs in the inelastic portion of the market demand curve. In such cases, since the marginal revenue curve is negative at Q_C, the marginal agency cost would have to be large enough to cause the cartel's marginal cost also to be negative (less than the negative marginal revenue) at Q_C. Marginal agency cost is unlikely to be this large for the first little bit of output reduction below Q_C.

[14] The condition in equation 4 appears to suggest that profits could be increased by expanding output above the competitive level. But this is not the case. The inequality in (4) only holds in one direction: for reductions in output. In the other direction (an increase in output) there is no marginal agency cost ($C_2 = 0$) and the inequality in equation 4 is reversed.

REFERENCES

Alchian, Armen A., and Harold Demsetz (1972). "Production, Information Costs, and Economic Organization." *American Economic Review* 62, pp. 777–95.

Browning, Edgar K., and Mark A. Zupan (1996). *Microeconomic Theory and Applications*. New York: Harper Collins.

Coase, Ronald H. (1937). "The Nature of the Firm." *Economica* 4, pp. 1–44.

Fama, Eugene F. (1980). "Agency Problems and the Theory of the Firm." *Journal of Political Economy* 88, pp. 288–307.

Gilson, Ronald, and Robert Mnookin (1985). "Sharing Among Human Capitalists: An Economic Inquiry into the Corporate Law Firms and How Partners Split Profits." *Stanford Law Review* 37, pp. 313–92.

Gurbaxani, Vijay, and Seungjin Whang (1991). "The Impact of Information Systems on Organizations and Markets." *Communication of the ACM* 34, pp. 59–73.

Jensen, Michael C. (1986) "Agency Costs of Free Cash Flow, Corporate Finance, and Takeovers." *American Economic Review: Papers and Proceedings* 76, pp. 323–29.

Jensen, Michael C., and William H. Meckling (1976). "Theory of the Firm: Managerial Behavior, Agency Costs and Ownership Structure." *Journal of Financial Economics* 3, pp. 305–60.

Johnson, Ronald N., and Gary D. Libecap (1989). "Agency Growth, Salaries and the Protected Bureaucrat." *Economic Inquiry* 27, pp. 431–51.

Olson, Mancur (1965). *The Logic of Collective Action: Public Goods and the Theory of Groups*. Cambridge. MA: Harvard University Press.

Pfeffer, Jeffrey, and Nancy Langton (1988). "Wage Inequality and the Organization of Work: The Case of Academic Departments." *Administrative Sciences Quarterly* 33, pp. 588–606.

Radner, Roy (1987). "Decentralization and Incentives," in Theodore Groves, Theodore, Roy Radner, and Stanley Reiter (eds.), *Information, Incentives, and Economic Mechanisms : Essays in Honor of Leonid Hurwicz*. Minneapolis: University of Minnesota Press.

Tullock, Gordon (1965). *The Politics of Bureaucracy*. Washington, D.C.: Public Affairs Press.

______ (1967). "The Welfare Costs of Tariffs, Monopolies, and Theft." *Western Economic Journal* 5, pp. 224–32.

FREE RIDERS AND COLLECTIVE ACTION REVISITED

Richard L. Stroup
Department of Economics
Montana State University
and
Political Economy Research Center
Bozeman, MT
U.S.A.

PUBLIC GOODS AND THE FREE RIDER PROBLEM IN THE PRIVATE SECTOR

The free rider problem associated with public goods was recognized by David Hume, even before the time of Adam Smith's writings. Each citizen who can enjoy the benefit of a public good has the incentive to try to lay the whole burden of provision on others, whenever the exclusion of non-payers is costly or impossible. Hume recommended in 1739 that government could provide the goods in question, such as bridges (Musgrave [1985] 729). Two and a half centuries later, economists typically recommend a similar solution (Arrow [1970], Atkinson and Stiglitz [1980], Auerbach and Feldstein [1985], Cornes and Sandler [1986], Nicholson [1989], and Samuelson [1954]).

The public provision prescription is seldom questioned, although today's economists and policy analysts, having been exposed to public-choice logic and empirical analysis, do recognize that government is an imperfect institution. Provision of public goods by the public sector, it is conceded, will not be free of problems. (Schleifer [1998]) For example, rational voter ignorance is widely recognized, and so too is the disproportionate influence of organized special interest groups. Lobbyists, and their campaign contributions, are the facets of the problem receiving most attention.

Even though the imperfection of government is commonly recognized, it is seldom noted explicitly that the root of those problems is precisely the same as the free rider problem associated with private-sector production of public goods. The formation and successful control of a public sector program in the public interest, for any reasonable definition of that nebulous term, is itself a public good. As in the private sector, provision of a public good in the public sector is subject to the free rider problem. Who will pay the price in time, effort and other lobbying costs to originate a program and to produce control that is in the interest of the general public? Does efficiency in serving the public have a constituency? Adam Smith pointed out long ago that no individual can be expected to seek the public interest; markets work to exhaust the gains from trade and cooperation because it is in the interest of each individual to find and capture any and all such gains. But of course when free riders can enjoy a public good without payment or trade, production and the potential gains from it may never occur. And so it is with efforts to originate government programs and to control them in the public interest. As Gordon Tullock (1971) put it:

> *The public decision-making process is a procedure for generating a public good; and the persons involved in it, whether they are the voters, judges, legislators, or civil servants, all can be expected to treat it as any other public good.*

Tullock recognized the point very clearly.[1] He recognizes the likelihood of shirking, in the form of spending too little time and effort in researching the issue of any public decision, and in the form of utilizing the decision maker's own preferences rather than the interest of the public in general. For these reasons, public decisions will not necessarily promote the well-being of the general public. Indeed, a program justified in the name of producing a public good may in fact be utilized by special interests to help themselves and to harm the public in the process. Analyses of programs gone awry are common, but the free rider problem that surely causes many of these problems is seldom mentioned. Tullock's observations, though published in a prominent economics journal, seem not to have made a large impression on policy-relevant discussions by economists since that time. The problem of free riding seems to this day to be discussed almost entirely in the context of market failure.

One constructive use of Tullock's basic insight can be in systematic side-by-side comparisons of the incentive problems built into private provision of public goods on the one hand, and those built into every case of public provision of any good (and of public regulation), on the other hand. This is the sort of comparison called for by Buchanan, by Schepsle and Weingast, and by Komesar in his recent book.[2] A careful and realistic evaluation of the incentives facing participants in the public policy process—that is, the free rider problem inherent in all politically directed public activity—would in fact be useful in comparing alternative institutions whether the *output* of the public policy is in fact actually a public good or not, and whether a change in policy might provide a superior result. In using Tullock's insight, we can in fact build upon it and say more. Expanding the usefulness (and the use) of the basic insight is the purpose of this chapter.

PUBLIC PROVISION OF PUBLIC GOODS: SOLVING THE FREE RIDER PROBLEM OR EXPANDING IT?

Economists who discuss public goods and the free rider problem use many examples. Among the most common are national defense, public health measures such as mosquito abatement, and roads and bridges (Varian [1984] 253, Atkinson and Stiglitz [1980] 486–87, and Nicholson [1989] 727). Each is subject to the most common problem cited: the lack of any producer's ability to exclude beneficiaries in a low-cost fashion, a condition that generates the free rider problem, resulting in an expectation that the good will be under-provided. Public provision of the good, through purchase or production, or public subsidy to private provision are the standard solutions offered for this problem. Each of these, however, introduces a large set of free rider problems of its own.

The production of goods and services, whether in the private sector or public, is a complex undertaking. A starting point, in meeting the demand for a good, is to define specifically the quantity and the qualities of the good to be provided.

Decisions on What to Produce and How to Produce it

Consider the case of national defense. What is the proper type and level of national defense? What sort of fleet should the navy have and support, and how large should it be? Where should the ships and their support be based, in order to provide the best defense for a given expenditure? Similar questions must be answered about the air force and its airplanes, and about the army and its forces. Each of these decisions has intensely important ramifications for suppliers to the military, and for units within the military bureaucracy. The interests of each of these groups is likely to be well represented in the decision process, both directly and in lobbying. Members of Congress and relevant members of the current administration will be strongly lobbied on behalf of each supplier group, and probably by each bureaucratic unit.[3] Who, on the other hand, will persistently lobby for the diffuse interest of the general public, by for example identifying and then lobbying for the most cost-effective package of resources, or deployment of those resources, to deter potential foreign aggressors? Citizens who are employed by defense contractors, or who live in an area where a defense contract is locally important, may become active when their specific issue is being debated. The search for cost effectiveness, rather than economic benefits for them and their localities, will surely be secondary for them. But certainly the firms, the chambers of commerce and other organized interests will lobby intensively, often with large budgets to do so, as the narrow issues of specific interest to them are being considered.

Most citizens, and most groups, however, are not apt to be involved when a specific defense procurement or deployment issue is settled. Each may well recognize that the plethora of decisions on defense procurement and deployment are important; but for each person, the cost of learning the issue and becoming involved is borne privately by the citizen, while the payoff to better decisions on behalf of cost-effectiveness is spread among the general public. The classic free rider problem is present very strongly, even in the case of decisions about the *goals* of public provision of national defense.

The same problem appears in complex decisions on public provision of mosquito abatement. Which wetlands should be treated? Should aerial spraying of mosquitos be utilized? Which chemical pesticides are acceptable to reduce mosquito populations? Which is best in each situation? Again, those with income directly at stake, or with strong views on one side or another of these questions will probably be heard. But by whom will the general public's diffuse interests be strongly and persistently represented? Each ordinary citizen is likely to act as a free rider when the level and description of provision by the public of a public good is being decided. And such decisions are only the beginning of the public provision process.

Control of the Production Process

A large literature in economics shows that in the private sector, where minimizing the cost of producing anything (of a chosen quantity and description) is necessary to maximize the profits of a firm, organizing for cost-minimizing production nonetheless remains a complicated process. Thrainn Eggertson, in his review and extension of this topic, lists the following activities that typically must be undertaken in the production of a good in a modern economy (Eggertson [1990] 15); each is applicable to production or regulation by the public sector:

4. The search for information about the distribution of price and quality of commodities and labor inputs, and the search for potential buyers and sellers and for relevant information about their behavior and circumstances (Who might be the low-cost provider of each good and service needed?)
5. The bargaining that is needed to find the true position of buyers and sellers when prices are endogenous (What prices can actually be negotiated on behalf of the public?)
6. The making of contracts (What specifications and stipulations should be included to reduce future performance problems while controlling costs?)
7. The monitoring of contractual partners to see whether they abide by the terms of the contract (Is the contract being faithfully followed?)
8. The enforcement of a contract and the collection of damages when suppliers fail to observe their contractual obligations (When should contract problems be renegotiated? When should they be taken to court instead? How should these matters be handled, once decisions are made?)
9. The protection of property rights to goods and resources against third-party encroachment (When should the rights of suppliers and those regulated be respected? How should they be protected, and at whose cost?)

To carry out each of these activities successfully requires thoughtful and diligent action, good judgment, and intelligent responses to the recognition of mistakes and changed situations. How will each unit of a bureau be organized to allow each decision maker the latitude to operate intelligently in changing circumstances, while reducing the ability to shirk or to act opportunistically under pressure on behalf of external interests or of the bureaucratic unit's own narrow concerns or even venal interests?[4]

Entrepreneurship is a key to efficiency in a world where technology and relative prices change rapidly. Private-sector firms are constantly adjusting their own organizations to meet changing problems and opportunities. The carrot or incentive for them is profit, and the stick or penalty for failure is failure to survive under competition. Feedback to them from the product market tends to be constant. And for leaders in publicly traded corporations, there is constant feedback from the stock market as well, concerning both current practices and decisions about the future of the corporation. Each buyer has a personal stake in monitoring the product in order to seek better products and to avoid payment for inferior goods. The capital market imposes similar information feedback and the incentive to heed that information. Each investor providing capital to a firm, or holding its stock, has an incentive to monitor that firm's policies (or to pay a specialized investment advisor to do so) in order to buy a larger stake if good things are about to happen in the firm, or to bail out by selling ownership rights (e.g. stock) if a bad trend is sensed. There is no such personal incentive for efficiency, and no such monitoring and feedback, typically, in the public sector. Each voter has a voice, but exit from tax payment is usually difficult or costly, even if the taxpayer studies and disapproves of the government agency's policies or its products.

Who will oversee the efficiency of the day-to-day and year-to-year operation of each unit of government in the public interest? Ultimately, voters are in charge. But the individual as voter, unlike the same individual as buyer of a product or of corporate stock, can seldom benefit *personally* from obtaining better knowledge, and applying it more diligently. The individual buyer in a market can easily exercise an option such as selling stock, or buying a different product, with information gathered on the details of how a product will work or how a private-sector corporation is being run.

The same individual as voter has a more serious problem. Rational voter ignorance is a well-known and well-documented phenomenon. Voters tend to be free riders on the vigilance of others, on any issue that is not of unusually concentrated personal interest to them. And there is no capital market that constantly assesses the performance, or the plans for the future, of a government program. Instead there is constant pressure from special interests, tending to mold each program and its operation to serve their narrow interests.

Some of these problems can be made smaller by partially "privatizing" provision–using tax finance and low-bid private sources of supply–or with more "local" provision of goods, so that citizens can more easily choose to "vote with their feet" (Tiebout [1956]) in search of better government outcomes. Neither of these eliminates the free rider problem in the public sector, but each can reduce it by introducing competition enforced by the possibility that buyers, periodically at least, can exit.

REGULATION: CONTROL OF REGULATORS AS A PUBLIC GOOD

We have seen how, when a bureau or a government program is established and given access to the public purse through the budget process, control of the program in the public interest is a public good and subject to the free rider problem. When the bureau is also given broad regulatory powers, control can be even more difficult. In addition to setting the specific program goals and the general methods of achieving those goals within a budget, regulators are often able to utilize methods that increase costs to others but do not force the spending of the bureau's own funds.

We can expect narrow bureaucratic interests, backed by specific constituencies, and possessing "tunnel vision"[5] to attempt to expand their activities well beyond those desired by the broader public. They see and value the benefits to their program, but do not see, or they have no reason to value, the alternative goals given up to gain increments to their own program. Regulators who can order costly measures to be undertaken, without the check of a budget, will also utilize costly methods, failing to economize except to enhance their own program. No check on cost, other than political pressure, is present. In contrast, seeing and valuing only costs and gains to their own program has direct costs to the owners of a competitive firm. And competition in government can produce much the same result, when tax base (and thus budget) follows citizens as they vote with their feet. But competition of the sort that eliminates waste is seldom present in government. Further, the presence of bureaucratic rule, or "red tape," which is needed because the zeal of an owner or a residual claimant is not present to force cost control, further reduces the ability of bureau leaders to streamline procedures and reduce costs. And as we noted earlier, because the control and monitoring of government action in the public interest is a public good, the potential controllers and monitors—voters and their elected representatives—tend to free ride rather than to zealously protect the public interest.

As a result, government programs can often impose very high costs on society, even when the programs imposing the costs produce little in the way of demonstrable, intended benefits.[6] In fact a bureau can go so far as to cause negative results for the overall goal of its own program. One example is the program to enforce the Endangered Species Act.

The Endangered Species Act

Animal species listed as endangered or threatened are generally protected by the U.S. Fish and Wildlife Service (FWS) under the Endangered Species Act (ESA). The ESA as now written and interpreted gives the FWS the responsibility and authority to preserve the listed species, and its habitat, without regard to cost. Any habitat, public or private, declared to be important to threatened or endangered species, is in effect placed under constraints dictated by FWS project biologists, without regard to cost to the land's private or public owner, and without compensation to the owner. FWS habitat decisions may be extremely expensive to private resource owners or to other agency missions, but the cost is exempt from the deliberations of the congressional budget process. No compensation is paid. Congress, which took the credit for helping to save species in passing the ESA many years ago, declines to monitor the program's true costs and benefits. Some members say that they had no idea, when they voted for passage, that the costs on landowners would be so great. But few have even attempted to revise the ESA. Most are, understandably, riding free while taking credit where they can.

At least three consequences flow from this arrangement. The first was, according to the courts, intended by the Congress: there is no limit to the land that may be devoted to the biologist's mission to preserve land from any use other than habitat for a listed species. The second is presumably unintended: land, logically treated by the project biologist as having zero price, will be substituted for other, on-budget factors of production, such as professional services, that could be utilized to find less costly conservation plans. The cost of other factors of production is borne by the FWS, while land costs are borne instead by the landowner. In effect, factor prices for the production of habitat protection are severely distorted. Tunnel vision precludes each program leader from seeing and fully valuing the total social cost of the program's elements. They too ride free. Control of the program in the interest of the general public is, as always, a public good.

The third result, exacerbated by the cost imposed on landowners by the first two, is that prior to being contacted by the FWS, private landowners have an incentive to manage their land in such a way that listed species will not find the land attractive. When no members of the species are present on or near his land, the ESA is unlikely to become costly to the landowner. Landowners also can gain by cooperating with their neighbors to learn and teach such techniques for preemptive habitat destruction, and even by applying social pressure for those nearby to apply the habitat-modifying techniques. That is true even when, as is frequently the case, the species themselves do no harm and would have been welcomed on the land absent the uncompensated financial harm imposed by the ESA.

There is increasing evidence (Stroup [1997] and Lueck and Michael [1999]) that preemptive habitat destruction is important. Lueck and Michael, for example, find statistically that when a colony of the listed red-cockaded woodpecker (RCW) is near a forest, costly measures are taken by the landowner to make that forest less attractive to other colonies of RCWs. The birds like old-growth forests for their nests, so the forest owner is more likely to harvest the forest prior to the normal harvest age.

The unintended negative effect of preemptive habitat destruction by landowners has been noted by close observers of habitat preservation for some time. The effect could be mitigated by putting land use acquisition on budget for the FWS. That would cause the program biologists and their supervisors to face market prices for land, restoring both the total cost and the true land cost as a factor of production, to program decision makers. Less costly and more effective strategies for habitat preservation could logically result.

A second unintended negative effect of the ESA program is serious harm to voluntary programs that have previously been successful over the past several decades. Long before the ESA, wood ducks on the eastern flyway were saved from threatened extinction partly by the voluntary placement of nest boxes by landowners. Eastern bluebirds were saved in a similar way. More recently, the preservation of wetlands habitat in the form of prairie potholes has been done very economically by soliciting landowner cooperation at very low cost, again expanding available habitat for important wildlife. These and many other successes would be exceedingly expensive, if not impossible now in the case of listed species, due to landowners' fear of the uncompensated takings that might easily result under the ESA.

Changing the ESA to avoid uncompensated takings would eliminate both of these unintended negative effects. However such a change is opposed by environmental groups, perhaps because the current arrangement is a powerful tool for another use: to stop the use of certain tracts of land for timber harvest, development, or even for intensive agricultural use. The free rider problem severely reduces the incentive of most voters and elected politicians to effectively monitor the actual results of this and other programs, and to demand changes that would make them more effective in reaching their stated goals, or to minimize their cost.

When the Benefits are Less Public and More Concentrated: State Forest Management

When the benefits of the good produced in the public sector are concentrated on a few beneficiaries, and thus have less of the public-good characteristic, the beneficiaries have a strong incentive to monitor the program. This happens, for example, in state land programs that are intended to make money for the public school system of a state. The public school establishment then has an incentive to monitor the state lands programs. Their task is made easier by the fact that the program goal is simple: make money for the schools.

Under those conditions, state lands programs that sell timber have been shown to be run much more economically than the national Forest Service program, which is supposed to produce benefits of many kinds for the general public in the national forests. Leal has shown that the several state programs he examined make money whereas the Forest Service timber sale program, on similar sites nearby, operates at a substantial loss (Leal [1996]). Leal also showed that in Montana, which conducts environmental audits on both state and federal timber lands, the state forests were more environmentally sound as well.

State programs that are ordered simply to make money for the schools are easier to monitor than their federal counterparts; they did or did not make money. And watching them are specific interest groups who capture the benefits when the state programs operate more efficiently. The gains they make are concentrated on an organized beneficiary: the public school system. The good the state programs produce, in other words, has less of the public-good aspect than the federal program, where proceeds go to the federal treasury. It may seem ironic that public provision of goods that are less public and closer to private goods should logically be better monitored and thus more efficient. Leal's evidence is consistent with that logic.

PUBLIC GOODS AND PUBLIC BADS: THE POTENTIAL FOR HARMS BEYOND RESOURCE WASTE

The fact that control of a government program in the public interest is a public good implies that groups with far narrower interests may gain control. Their agendas may not only cause resource waste (from the general public's viewpoint) in the presence of voter shirking by free riding in the political and bureaucratic processes; in addition, control by those with narrow agendas may cause positive harm. That can easily be true for regulatory agencies, as we saw in the case of the ESA. But it can also be true for public goods provision.

The classic public good is the military, in the form of a large standing army. It is intended to protect citizens against threats from hostile foreign nations. But it may be used in ways that increase, rather than reduce, the likelihood of citizens dying at the hands of hostile foreign nationals. One of the controversial questions surrounding the Vietnam War is whether tens of thousands of Americans would have died at the hand of foreigners if the large standing military force had not been available for quick deployment to serve the aims of the administration sending them. More recently, is the likelihood of terrorist attacks within the U.S. increased by use of our military abroad? With smaller provision, that particular risk is reduced. Most citizen-voters, including this writer, cannot know whether a larger standing army is more protective or more risky, without far more study than we will ever put into it. Will a large standing military increase or decrease the public good of reduced risk from foreign aggressors? Given Tullock's basic insight, who will answer this question on behalf of the general public (if indeed that can be done) and then lobby strongly, against the interests of military suppliers for example, for adoption of the answer that best serves the general public, in defense policy?

Production of public goods to reduce natural risks can also result in greater risk, when free riding on control of the program leaves decisions in the hands of narrowly interested parties. Another public good, mosquito abatement, is a case in point. Is a reduction in mosquitos worth the risk of extensive aerial spraying of the sort that is so controversial in California? Is it worth disturbing wetlands ecology? Few citizens have sufficient knowledge to vote intelligently on the issue, even if given a chance in a referendum. Public provision of mosquito abatement, however, unlike private abatement, generally means that the official decision maker is not personally liable if that official's program damages affected citizens. The standard of care is likely to differ as a result of public provision[7]. Once again, it is easily possible that fighting one danger by establishing pubic provision makes others worse. The free rider problem among voters, and the poor oversight that results, makes public provision of "protection" from a specific risk potentially dangerous.

IMPLICATIONS OF THE FREE RIDER PROBLEM FOR PUBLIC POLICY AND VOLUNTARY ACTION

The free rider problem, and its resulting reductions in the efficiency and effectiveness of the public sector, has important implications. Better understanding of it could lead to improvement in institutional choice by society generally as well as by individuals as they choose which institutions to support voluntarily.

Some goods with public-good aspects are provided by a variety of institutions —private individuals, private clubs, and government agencies. For example, wilderness or habitat for endangered species can be provided by individuals, clubs like the National Audubon Society or the Sierra Club, and government agencies.

Whether private or public, each kind of provision requires individuals who are sufficiently well paid or passionate to work hard or make other sacrifices to cause production of the public good. In other words, public provision requires voluntary private sacrifices. For example, establishing public-sector habitat protection in the first place requires strong lobbying from clubs such as the Audubon Society or the Sierra

Club. To maintain such programs, lobbying must continue to keep them from being defeated by those seeking other goals from the federal budget and federal lands.

The clubs mentioned in fact spend most of their time and money in lobbying for public sector provision. But would their efforts be more productively spent organizing and campaigning for individual private landowners to help? Or instead, on a campaign seeking help from individuals for the private club's efforts to obtain and administer such lands as owners?

The theory of clubs suggests, and observation confirms, that club decisions tend to be made by like-minded individuals who have come together drawn by shared preferences.[8] For that reason, decisions about how the good will be defined and managed will be made by those like-minded individuals, rather than by a median voter in the public sector, by politically sensitive (and compromising) politicians, or by bureaucratic decision makers under political control. In contrast, public-sector provision must, at least formally in a democracy, be "controlled" by voters—few of whom are likely to be as passionate and motivated, and thus knowledgeable about the good to be provided, as are the self-selected, dues paying members of a club.

Expanding the responsibility for provision to the level of the general public gains tax support from all taxpayers only by trading off the ability to retain the focus and intensity of like-minded club members. Whether the tradeoff is worthwhile can be debated. However, there is at least some empirical evidence, discussed briefly below, suggesting that voluntary provision is qualitatively different and can be qualitatively superior.

Each institutional approach mentioned above requires at least partial defeat of the free rider problem to obtain cooperation among enthusiasts. Each requires work and sacrifice. Public sector efforts may be the most effective means for some individuals and some groups, who are especially good at lobbying and other forms of political action relative to their ability to act privately. For them, formation of a club that amounts to a special interest lobbying group may yield the highest return to their resources.

Yet even when they win public sector action, so that provision of the good is assigned to a bureaucratic unit, continuing provision is not guaranteed. Defense of that unit's budget, and control of its actions in service to specific desired goals, is a never-ending problem. Public sector victories are never bought—only rented. Whether majoritarian interests (and the median voter, who typically is uninformed about provision of the good) prevail or minoritarian special interests (such as those of contracting providers) prevail instead, the battle is never fully won in the public sector, for the courts have consistently held that one legislature cannot bind the next. In the words of one environmental leader, whose specialty is preserving land for wild habitat, "You know what I like? A deed in the courthouse."[9]

The analysis above suggests that for an enthusiast wanting to expand the provision of a public good, the same amount of organizational and fund-raising effort might be more successful when directly applied to seeking private provision of that good. It is also true that the analysis does *not* indicate that such will *necessarily* be the case. Depending on the circumstances, the shortfall in payments from some who benefit, and thus the shortfall in provision, caused by the free rider problem in private provision may or may not be a smaller problem than the reductions in the value (reduced quantity and quality delivered by public provision) due to the multiple free rider problems in the public sector. Even with the tax-revenue advantage, public provision may still provide a lesser amount of the good, as the following example illustrates.

Case Study: When Public Provision of Religion Became Private

Consider an actual case study, comparing the provision of religious services, investigated by Kelly Olds (1994). Two centuries ago, when Connecticut and Massachusetts were considering disestablishment (ending the subsidy to each state's respective established church), the case was made that without taxpayer support, religion would wither. From Adam Smith forward, the case has been argued that the church provides positive benefits to the community, beyond those provided to church goers. On this view, those who participate in religion become better neighbors, more upstanding citizens, and more honest market trading partners as well (Olds [1994] 280). These public good aspects, it was claimed, justified taxpayer subsidies. To this day, many industrial nations have an established (*i.e,* state-supported) church.

Olds's study, however, found that when disestablishment occurred in Massachusetts and Connecticut, and all subsidies were stopped, indicators of religious activity rose rather than fell. The statistical evidence indicates that church membership and the demand for preachers both rose rapidly (Olds [1994] p. 277). Many churches prospered, and the methods of finance varied. The services provided undoubtedly had changed. Church leaders, after all, needed now to appeal more to individual congregations and less to legislators and state voters as a group. Whatever the reason, the results showed impressive increases in the provision (and the diversity) of church services. Church membership rose in the United States as a whole for nearly all of the nineteenth and twentieth centuries (Iannaccone [1998] 357) Further, the United States, having no established church, experiences greater church attendance and a greater percentage of citizens proclaiming themselves to be religious, than any of the industrialized nations which provide public funding for their religion (Iannaccone, Finke, and Stark, [1997]).

It appears that in some cases at least, private provision allows and encourages appeals to more niches than a public provider, bound as it is by the need for support from median voter (or from the most powerful interest groups), is able to do. And it may be that public provision undercuts private support for an activity by replacing it, as it seems to do dollar for dollar, in the case of private support for higher education in public universities (Becker and Lindsay [1994]). In either case, increased public provision of the good in question is not an unalloyed benefit to the mission supported, and may on balance harm that mission.

CONCLUSION

Gordon Tullock first pointed out that the existence of the free rider problem *in the public sector* is important. Recognizing it should reduce our expectation that when the private sector imperfectly provides a good, citizens will have the option to utilize the public sector in a way that approaches an ideal delivery of the good. The public sector approach is one candidate among several as an institutional way to deal with the provision of a particular public good, but the free rider problem in that sector has several implications:

1. Establishing a public sector program to provide a public good requires voluntary private effort. Keeping the program funded requires continued voluntary private effort.
2. Control of the public sector program in the general public's interest requires voluntary private effort in competition with the many narrow interests that will seek to control that program.
3. When taxpayers fund a program, the product will be different from a private effort when the preferences of voters as a committee of the whole differ from those of those with the greatest zeal and the strongest interest in the activity; the latter will control a private effort but must compromise with those having less interest, when public provision is utilized.
4. Private clubs and other private providers have more freedom to choose their methods and full financial responsibility for the cost, so we can expect them to be more efficient in what they provide
5. In light of points 1 to 4, there is reason to think that private provision may produce more and/or better-quality public goods; and some data exist to support that notion in specific cases such as provision of religious services.

No human institution works perfectly. When a decision about public provision of a specific good in a specific case is to be made, each available institutional alternative should be realistically compared.[10] To look only at one sector and point out its weaknesses, and hence to opine that when that sector is weaker, another sector will be superior, is not justified. The same factors that make one sector weak may weaken an alternative sector. When an externality involves many people and the costs or benefits are not concentrated on a few, the market may be weak, but so may the public sector. The insight that "public decisions are public goods," first brought to light by Gordon Tullock, and the related expansions noted here should be borne in mind as institutional arrangements are compared.

The research assistance of Charles Steele and Matthew Brown is gratefully acknowledged, along with research support from PERC (the Political Economy Research Center) in Bozeman, MT.

[1] That article in fact spurred the thinking that has gone into this chapter, which seeks to push the analysis further and to make it somewhat more concrete.

[2] See Buchanan (1987), Schepsle and Weingast (1984) p. 417, and Komesar (1994).

[3] The rent-seeking literature points out the costs to society of competition among special interests to control various aspects of public policy (Rowley et al. [1988]).

[4] Niskanen has shown (Niskanen [1971]) that under certain circumstances, the bureaucratic unit may, due to a monopoly on cost information, be able to put the legislature, at budget time, on an all-or-none demand curve so as to maximize the unit's budget. Today that is generally thought to be an extreme case, even by Niskanen (see Andre Blais, Stephane Dion, eds. [1991]); but the tendency, and some ability to indulge it, may be present nonetheless.

[5] "Tunnel vision" is the term utilized by U.S. Supreme Court Justice Stephen Breyer to explain why each regulatory agency tends to go well beyond any social optimum in its activities. It does not experience the opportunity costs of its actions, and avoids many ordinary constraints in the exercise of regulatory powers granted by the legislative branch (Breyer [1995]).

[6] A concise overview of the high-cost–low-benefit nature of much federal environmental regulation is in Crandall (1992).

[7] It was precisely this problem that helped generate the Love Canal hazardous waste problem in Niagara Falls, New York, and that led to the creation of the Superfund program. Recognition of potential liability had caused the chemical company to carefully isolate the buried wastes. When a public-sector unit (the local school board) purchased the property, it was explicitly warned of dangers from the waste, but proceeded to utilize "tunnel vision" in managing the land, ignoring the chemicals and by digging through the containment walls, allowing them to seep out (Stroup [1996] 5–6, and Zeusse [1981]).

[8] The theory of clubs addresses these issues; it originated with Buchanan (1965) and is discussed in Mueller (1989).

[9] Brent Haglund, executive director of the Sand County Foundation, quoted by Anderson and Leal (1997), p. 52.

[10] The case for comparative institutional analyses is made in an important book by Neil Komesar (Komesar [1994]). He stresses that analysis should center on comparison, under alternative regimes, of 1) how concentrated the payoffs are in each case, and 2) how many parties are importantly involved.

REFERENCES

Anderson, Terry L., and Donald R. Leal (1997). *Enviro-Capitalists*. Lanham: Rowman and Littlefield.

Arrow, Kenneth J. (1970). "The Organization of Economic Activity: Issues Pertinent to the Choice of Market Versus Nonmarket Allocation." in Robert H. Haveman and Julius Margolis, *Public Expenditures and Policy Analysis*. Chicago: Markham Publishing Co.

Atkinson, Anthony B., and Joseph Stiglitz (1980). *Lectures in Public Economics* (Chapter 16: "Public Goods and Publicly Provided Private Goods"). New York: McGraw-Hill.

Auerbach, Alan J., and Martin Feldstein, eds. (1985). *Handbook of Public Economics*, vols. 1 and 2. New York: North-Holland.

Bagnoli, Mark, and Barton L. Lipman (1992). "Private Provision of Public Goods Can Be Efficient." *Public Choice* 74, 59–78.

Becker, Elizabeth, and Cotton M. Lindsay (1994). "Does the Government Free Ride?" *Journal of Law and Economics* 37 (April) 277–96.

Blais, Andre , and Stephane Dion, eds. (1991). *The Budget-Maximizing Bureaucrat : Appraisals and Evidence*, Pittsburgh: University of Pittsburgh Press.

Breyer, Stephen (1995). *Breaking the Vicious Circle*. Cambridge, MA: Harvard University Press.

Buchanan, James (1965). "An Economic Theory of Clubs." *Economica* 32, 1–14.

______ (1987). "Constitutional Economics." in *The New Palgrave: A Dictionary of Economics*, Vol. 2, p. 585

Cornes, Richard, and Todd Sandler (1986). *The Theory of Externalities, Public Goods, and Club Goods*. New York: Cambridge University Press.

Crandall Robert (1992). "Why is the Cost of Environmental Regulation So High?" St. Louis: CSAB, Policy Study 110 (24 pp.).

Davis, Otto A., and Morton I. Kamien (1970). "Externalities, Information, and Alternative Collective Action." in Robert H. Haveman and Julius Margolis, *Public Expenditures and Policy Analysis*, Chicago: Markham Publishing Co.

Eggertson, Thrainn, (1990); *Economic Behavior and Institutions*, Cambridge: Cambridge U. Press.

Haveman, Robert H., and Julius Margolis (1970); *Public Expenditures and Policy Analysis*; Chicago: Markham Publishing Co.

Iannaccone, Laurence R., (1998). "Introduction to the Economics of Religion." *JEL*, Vol. XXXVI (Sept.) 1465–1496.

Iannaccone, Laurence R., Roger Finke, and Rodney Stark (1997). "Deregulating Religion: The Economics of Church and State." *Economic Inquiry*. XXXV (April) 350–64.

Komesar, Neil (1994). *Imperfect Alternatives: Choosing Institutions in Law, Economics and Public Policy*. Chicago: University of Chicago Press.

Layard, P. R. G., and A. A. Walters (1978). *Microeconomic Theory*. New York: McGraw-Hill.

Leal, Donald R. (1996). "Turning a Profit on Public Forests." PERC Policy Series PS-4. Bozeman, MT:

PERC. (Available online at www.perc.org)

Lueck, Dean, and Jeffrey Michael (1999). "Preemptive Habitat Destruction Under the Endangered Species Act." (unpublished paper presented at seminars at Brigham Young University, Montana State University, North Carolina University and Stanford University.)

McMillan, John (1979). "The Free-Rider Problem: A Survey." *The Economic Record* 55, 95–107.

Mueller, Dennis (1989). *Public Choice II*, Cambridge: Cambridge University Press, pp. 150–54.

Musgrave, R. A. (1985). "A Brief History of Fiscal Doctrine." in Auerbach and Feldstein, *Handbook of Public Economics*, vol. 1, pp. 1–59. New York: North-Holland.

Nicholson, Walter (1989). *Microeconomic Theory: Basic Principles and Extensions*, 4th ed. Chicago: Dryden Press.

Niskanen, William A. (1971). *Bureaucracy and Representative Government.* Chicago: Aldine Press.

Oakland, William H. (1985). "Theory of Public Goods." in Auerbach and Feldstein, *Handbook of Public Economics*, vol. 2, pp. 485–535. New York: North-Holland.

Olds, Kelly (1994). "Privatizing the Church." *JPE* 102 (no. 2) 277–97.

Pommerehne, Werner W., Lars P. Feld, and Albert Hart (1994). "Voluntary Provision of a Public Good: Results from a Real World Experiment." *Kyklos* 47, 505–18.

Rowley, Charles K., Robert D. Tollison, and Gordon Tullock (1988). *The Political Economy of Rent-Seeking*, Boston: Kluwer.

Samuelson, Paul A. (1955). "Diagrammatic Exposition of a Theory of Public Expenditure." *Review of Economics and Statistics* 37 (Nov.) 350–56

_____ (1954). "The Pure Theory of Public Expenditure." *Review of Economic and Statistics* 36, (Nov.) 387–89.

Schepsle, Kenneth, and Barry Weingast (1984). "Political Solutions to Market Problems." *American Political Science Review* 78, 417

Shleifer, Andrei (1998). "State versus Private Ownership." *JEP* 12 (no. 4, Fall) 133–50.

Steiner, Peter O. (1970). "The Public Sector and the Public Interest." in Robert H. Haveman and Julius Margolis, *Public Expenditures and Policy Analysis.* Chicago: Markham Publishing Co.

Stroup, Richard L. (1995). *The Endangered Species Act: Making Innocent Species the Enemy.* PERC Policy Series PS-3, Bozeman, MT: PERC. (Available online at www.perc.org)

_____ (1996). *Superfund: The Shortcut that Failed.* Policy Series PS-5, Bozeman, MT: PERC, (May). (Available online at www.perc.org)

_____ (1997) "The Economics of Compensating Property Owners." *Contemporary Economic Policy*, Vol. 15 (Oct.) 55–65.

Tiebout, Charles M. (1956). "A Pure Theory of Local Expenditures." *JPE* 64, 416.

Tullock, Gordon (1971). "Public Decisions as Public Goods." *JPE* 79 (no. 4) 913–18.

Varian, Hal R. (1984). *Microeconomic Analysis*, 2nd ed. New York: W. W. Norton & Co.

Zeckhauser, Richard (1970). "Uncertainty and the Need for Collective Action." in Robert H. Haveman and Julius Margolis, *Public Expenditures and Policy Analysis.* Chicago: Markham Publishing Co.

Zeusse, Eric (1981). "The Truth Seeps Out." *Reason* 12, (no. 10).

GORDON TULLOCK: HIS DEVELOPMENT AS AN UNCONVENTIONAL ECONOMIST, 1947–1962

Gordon L. Brady
Center for Study of Public Choice
James M. Buchanan Center for Political Economy
George Mason University
Fairfax, VA 22030
U.S.A.

It is quite ironic that Tullock, the lawyer, sought to apply economic analysis while Buchanan, the economist, initially preferred the perspective of the moral philosopher.

INTRODUCTION

This essay examines Gordon Tullock's early career and his intellectual interaction with a number of well-known scholars.[1] It describes the period from his graduation at the University of Chicago Law School (1947), through his time with the U.S. Department of State (1947–1956) and his early years in academia (1958–1962), to the publication of *The Calculus of Consent* (1962). It includes examination of his relations with Colin Campbell, Warren Nutter, Richard "Dixie" Walker, Karl Popper, Anthony Downs, Duncan Black, and James Buchanan during these years.

LAW SCHOOL AND AN ABORTED LEGAL CAREER

Gordon Tullock began his undergraduate education at the University of Chicago in 1940, and after three years of "undistinguished" military service (Tullock's word), received his D.J. degree from the University of Chicago Law School in 1947. During the 1930s, law schools in the Midwest consisted of three years of undergraduate education including "pre-law" courses and three years of formal legal training. The University of Chicago had a different approach, which allowed two years of undergraduate courses to be combined with four years of formal law. Tullock in fact completed this program in five years because, upon completion of specific courses, he was allowed to enter the law school after one year. The baccalaureate degree which required payment of a five-dollar fee would have been awarded after two years at the law school, but Tullock's decision not to pay this small sum created the basis for endless speculation regarding his credentials as well as fueling the myth of the self-taught economist.

Tullock's short legal career was initiated and completed with a small but expensive downtown Chicago law firm. Tullock handled what he described as two rather simple cases. One case he won, when he should not have won. The other he lost, when he should have won. In both cases the expected probability of success was so low that he was dispatched with little instruction by the senior members of the firm. To make matters a bit worse, in the case he won, the client had been told by a senior attorney not to pursue the case and the senior attorney thought that Tullock had done something improper. In the case he lost, Tullock not only lost, but was reproached by the court. The combination of the two cases following closely on each other determined in Tullock's mind that he would be better off in another profession.

TULLOCK'S YEARS WITH THE U. S. STATE DEPARTMENT, 1947–1956

So, after five months as a law clerk, Tullock decided to build upon his interests in law and foreign affairs by pursuing a career in the diplomatic service. He enjoyed travel and adventure and thought the U.S. Department of State would provide the perfect venue for a serious Midwesterner who had seen Europe through the U.S. Army. He therefore joined the State Department in the fall of 1947. After a two-month initiation course at the Foreign Service Institute in Washington, D.C., he received an assignment as vice consul at Tientsin, China, where, in his own words, he was in charge of "odds and ends." Nevertheless, it was an important assignment, which allowed him to gain experience in economic matters by writing cables and reports. It also allowed him to explore the China that he had read about as a youth.

His two-year duty station was punctuated by the Communist seizure of the city in January, 1949, whereupon he returned to the United States and was sent to Yale (1949–1951) and Cornell (1951–1952) for advanced study in Chinese. In late 1952 he joined the mainland China section of the U.S. Consulate General in Hong Kong. It was there that Tullock observed, in respect of Chinese monetary history, the world as being at variance with economic theory (although he says he did not know much theory). He often pondered economic theory while taking long walks on the Hong Kong water supply network, which he described as level and making for pleasant walks. Nine months later, he was transferred to the political section of the U.S.

Embassy in South Korea. Finally, from January 1955 until his resignation in the fall of 1956, Tullock was assigned to the Office of Intelligence and Research at the State Department in Washington, D.C., where he worked on Korean affairs. During this period, he had few academic contacts, but became acquainted with other foreign service officers in his area of expertise. His social life centered around drinking and he now says that he did more of it than he would like to have thought he had done.

TULLOCK LEAVES THE U.S. STATE DEPARTMENT, 1956

According to Tullock, he resigned from the State Department because he concluded that he was accomplishing very little and would be better off undertaking other employment. However, Tullock also had other good reasons to be cynical about a career in diplomacy. According to Richard "Dixie" Walker, upon the fall of China Tullock had been instructed to destroy cash held by the Department of State. Tullock performed exactly as instructed, but an unfortunate chain of events left him in a difficult position. To his astonishment, he later received a bill for $55,000 because the financial reports he had filed months earlier were lost by the Department of State, and as the accounting officer, he was held responsible. Did "justice triumph" because the truth finally came out? Hardly, all of this was resolved by political means. Tullock's step-father happened to be a good friend of a high ranking member of the United States Senate. In addition to what he learned from this episode about bureaucracy, the resolution through political means provided a grim insight in how the government actually operates and the role of politicians as brokers. However, in building upon this critical insight in his theory of candidates and political parties, Tullock was criticized as cynical.

That said, in 1956 he had no desire to become an academic. Nor did he even consider it an option. His choice of pursuits was influenced by his interest in the Far East, which had been cultivated by his parents' and grandparents' gifts of books on history, travel, and culture. Many of these books emphasized successful campaigns of warfare as well as the nobility of combat and the savagery of victors. And one might suppose that he desired the trappings that good fortune and hard work had brought his family throughout his youth. At the time of his leaving the State Department he considered work either in international trade or with an international agency in Thailand. However, he pursued no serious negotiations for such positions and decided to write a book on bureaucracy, about which he had acquired many insights through his work at the State Department and through his observations of historical and contemporary Chinese bureaucrats. While his romanticism for the Far East had been tempered by the reality of having spent time in China, his position at the State Department insulated him from the more mundane aspects of the old Chinese bureaucracy. He found Chinese bureaucrats overly educated for the work they did and very competent, although their high educational attainments were not necessary for the work that they had to do. Once he had completed the book which became *The Politics of Bureaucracy* (1965), he intended to go off to work in the Far East. Interestingly, during this period, he started his insect book, which focused on the economics of coordination in the absence of command,[2] as well as completing a lengthy monograph on the history of fisheries management in which he argued for privatization of what was a common property resource.[3] In an interview with Tullock, he indicated this came about as a result of his interest in the subject of fisheries and common property resources and had not been an offshoot from his earlier work.

To return to his immediate plans, his choice of Thailand was based on several factors. First, the language was similar to Chinese, which he could handle reasonably well despite his tone deafness that made it difficult for him to speak the language like a native. Second, while Tullock had not visited Thailand, he had read a great deal about the country. Tullock's personal library contained many books about the Far East and its explorers and adventurers, and he was very knowledgeable—as the following anecdote illustrates. I once showed him a Chinese scroll which depicted a "crowd scene" with Chinese ciphers whereupon he quickly explained that it depicted the traditional celebration for those who passed the very difficult civil service examination. Tullock also considered Burma and Vietnam, but rejected them because both countries were involved in civil wars. The Philippines were also considered, but he did not consider that country an attractive place to live, viewing it as an "incomplete outpost" of Europe.

BETWEEN THE U.S. STATE DEPARTMENT AND ACADEMIA, 1956–1958

Tullock's transition from the State Department to an academic career was influenced by the associations that he had forged while at the University of Chicago. Upon leaving the State Department, he chose to renew and build upon his Chicago connections. As I show below, these contacts and connections subsequently became important to his intellectual development. It is well known that Tullock was profoundly influenced by Henry Simons,[4] from whom he took his one and only class in economics while at the law school prior to induction into the military. Much later in the 1960s, Tullock published the syllabus of that course.[5]

It was Colin Campbell who was one of the first people to recognize Tullock's scholarly potential. Tullock first met Campbell one Christmas when Campbell, then a doctoral student in economics at the University of Chicago, was visiting his fiancée, whose brother was a friend of Tullock. Colin Campbell influenced Tullock's views on monetary theory and encouraged his interest in economics. In a casual conversation, Tullock came to discuss Chinese monetary history with Campbell and was surprised with Campbell's interest as he did not think that what he had observed was unusual. Fortunately, Campbell immediately recognized that what Tullock had seen did not fit the orthodox theory. Tullock's collaboration with Campbell produced three papers, two on Chinese monetary history (Tullock and Campbell [1954], Tullock [1956]) and the other on the Korean monetary system (Tullock and Campbell [1957]), and was Tullock's initiation into scholarly publishing. It is important to note that Tullock's work with Campbell came into being because of Tullock's observations of events around him, and at this time Tullock was not theorizing in a formal way or developing his new approaches to economics. By helping Tullock to understand what he had observed in China and to fit it into a scholarly framework, Campbell gave Tullock the confidence that he too could be a successful economist.

For the two years from 1956 to 1958, Tullock was engaged in various writing and consulting assignments, including that of research director of the Princeton Panel, a subsidiary of the Gallup organization. In a letter to Walker dated September 26, 1957, Tullock provides insights into his time at the Princeton Panel and the reason for his departure:

> Dear Dick:
>
> As I think I told you last time I saw you, I took a part time research job last February. This summer the people for whom I was working asked me to come east, and after I got to Princeton they talked me into working 3/4ths time instead of 1/3rd. Since I was trying to finish up my book [on the politics of bureaucracy], this put considerable pressure on me, and a series of family crises running through the summer made things even worse. About a month ago all three of these pre-occupations suddenly disappeared. The one indispensable and irreplaceable employee at the place where I was working had a heart attack, and the organization folded like an Arab tent, my mother recovered from her second heart attack, and I finally finished the second draft of my book. As a consequence I decided to use my new freedom by moving to New Haven. I intend to put the final polish on my book, renew my Chinese, and write another book for Fred Praeger on the modern history of Korea. The last item is not as important as it might seem since I do not consider myself much of an expert on the area and am writing only because there is simply nothing literate now in print on the subject.

His association with the Princeton Panel was an important episode for Tullock and came about more or less by accident. He had met Claude Robinson, a partner to Gallup, while Robinson was setting up the panel. The Princeton Panel gave Tullock an exposure to broader public policy issues and allowed him to apply his unique insights to the economic relationships which he observed. During his time at the Princeton Panel, Tullock worked on a number of projects including a statistical study of labor unions, which exposed him to the realities of interest group politics.[6] Later, with Robinson's death the panel came to an end. Tullock then left for Yale with the intention of writing a modern history of Korea, which was still fresh on his mind.

KARL POPPER

Sometime immediately prior to working for the Princeton Panel, Tullock met Karl Popper and assisted him in writing the postscript to *The Logic of Scientific Discovery*. In the late 1930s, Popper had left Vienna for the University of New Zealand at Christ Church and had come to the London School of Economics in 1946 as the result of Hayek's influence. Both Popper and Hayek were born in Austria and both were students of Ludwig von Mises, although Popper, of course, was not an economist but a philosopher of science. Tullock's first encounter with the work of Karl Popper was during a visit to Hong Kong when someone mentioned *The Open Society and Its Enemies* and Tullock bought a copy. He remembers that he was much impressed with the book and, quite atypically, read it several times. Later a foundation sponsored a meeting on sociology, and Tullock, although not a sociologist, was invited to attend. Popper was one of the speakers and Tullock took the opportunity to talk with him. Popper informed Tullock that he would be spending time at the Institute for Advanced Studies in the Social Sciences at Stanford University. So, after leaving the Department of State in 1956, Tullock drove cross-country in his MG with the idea of writing a book on bureaucracy. There at Stanford, Tullock helped Popper on what was projected to be a postscript to the English translation of *The Logic of Scientific Discovery.*[7] Tullock's role was limited to insuring that Popper's English was properly idiomatic. In the process, Tullock learned a great deal about Popper's philosophy of science and came to like him very much. The feeling was apparently mutual as Popper later referred to Tullock as one of his disciples. And, as one might expect, this greatly pleased Tullock.

Popper's influence was considerable on Tullock's views of how to conduct research. Consequently, Tullock became an advocate of statistical testing, although he never did the testing himself. Indeed, Tullock's two works, *The Organization of Inquiry* (1966) and *The Logic of the Law* (1971), advanced hypotheses which Tullock hoped would be tested by others. Many of his other works have provided insights that others might test. Popper also contributed to Tullock's knowledge of Greek philosophy and physics although neither subject had much to do with what Tullock ever did. Tullock remembers Popper as a stimulating person, although he found him very impatient. One of the last letters Popper wrote prior to his death in 1994 was to Tullock. He reviewed some of Tullock's writing and appeared to show a genuine interest in his work.

HOW TULLOCK MET BUCHANAN

In 1958 Tullock was awarded a research fellowship by the Thomas Jefferson Center for Studies in Political Economy and Social Philosophy at the University of Virginia. It was here that he renewed his acquaintance with G. Warren Nutter and James M. Buchanan, and developed a new set of colleagues and friends. Tullock had first met Nutter when both were members of the student debate team at the University of Chicago.[8] Nutter introduced Tullock to Buchanan at the annual meetings of the American Economic Association in Philadelphia in December 1957, and Tullock gave Nutter and Buchanan copies of his manuscript on bureaucracy which both then read before they decided to offer Tullock the post-doctoral fellowship.[9]

Nutter did pioneering work on Soviet economic growth, and found that the USSR was not growing as rapidly as was generally thought. This did not make him popular in the academic community that supported the ill-conceived notion of the superiority of central planning. Nutter's work and his involvement with Republican politics in the 1960s also encouraged negative scrutiny of the Virginia School of Political Economy.

Nutter was much different from Tullock in both his demeanor and his research orientation. Tullock reports that there was some degree of personal friction between Nutter and himself, which subsequently Tullock deeply regretted. Nevertheless, Nutter passed Tullock's manuscript on bureaucracy to Leland B. Yeager, who in turn sent copies to other people. One might wonder whether these were efforts simply to pass along promising work or to get rid of it because did not know exactly what to do with it. While at the University of Virginia, Tullock shared many research interests with William Breit, James Buchanan, and R. H. Coase, as well as with Nutter and Yeager. Tullock also mentioned John Moes as having a considerable influence on him.

THE THOMAS JEFFERSON CENTER

The Thomas Jefferson Center for Studies in Political Economy and Social Philosophy was established in 1957. Although the door sign was never changed, the name of the Center was eventually shortened to The Thomas Jefferson Center for Studies in Political Economy. According to Tullock, the abbreviated name reflected the movement away from philosophy towards an emphasis on economics. At one point William L. Duren, dean of the College of Arts and Science, mistakenly referred to the Center in several official letters as the "Circle of Political Economy and Social Philosophy." The Center was established as an independent entity within the College of Arts and Sciences as a community of scholars dedicated to the preservation of a social order based on individual liberty. The objective of the Center was to encourage students to understand the philosophical as well as the technical issues raised by problems of social organization.

The organizational material filed by Buchanan with the University of Virginia was clear about the four goals of the Center. First, it was to create an intellectual environment that would generate discussion of the basic ideals of Western civilization and of the solutions to social problems most in accord with those ideals. Second, it was to encourage scholarship in broad problems of political economy and social philosophy, as opposed to narrow disciplinary specialization. Third, the Center was to stimulate the permanent faculty and the graduate and undergraduate students to an awareness of the basic social issues of the times. And, fourth, it was to encourage research on particular problems of political economy and social philosophy. The staff was composed of faculty and scholars in economics, history, philosophy, and political science who wanted to extend their competence and interests beyond the narrowly technical subject matter of their particular discipline.

The Center sought to bring in scholars from outside the University of Virginia. A number of outstanding scholars were mentioned as being of the caliber which they anticipated would hold this appointment: F. A. Hayek, John Jewkes, Lionel Robbins, George J. Stigler, Milton Friedman, David McCord Wright, P. T. Bauer, Michael Polanyi, Karl Popper, O. H. Taylor, Wilhelm Ropke, Gottfried Haberler, George Hildebrand, W. H. Hutt, F. A. Lutz, Leo Wolman, and A. A. Alchian. Their first Distinguished Visiting Scholar was Frank H. Knight (1957–1959). The Center's lecture series in 1957–1958 included P. T. Bauer (Cambridge University); R. H. Coase (University of Buffalo);[10] and Charles E. Lindblom (Yale University).[11]

An important objective of the Center was to nurture promising young scholars by providing residence at the Center for one year. A post-doctoral fellowship was awarded each year to an "outstanding young scholar of proven competence who has demonstrated an interest in advanced study of some general problem of social policy." The award carried a stipend of $5,500 to enable the recipient to pursue independent research along the lines of his indicated interest, and to participate informally in the intellectual activities of the Center. Three pre-doctoral fellowships of $2,500 were awarded to advanced graduate students from economics, history, philosophy, political science, and other related fields, who were completing their formal course of study. Five graduate fellowships of $1,500 plus tuition were to be awarded to first-year or second-year students. The Center also established a program of research associates to encourage work in social policy by established scholars in other departments and institutions. The first Research Associate of the Center was D. Rutledge Vining, Professor of Economics and Statistics, at the University of Virginia.

James Buchanan envisaged that the organizational structure of the Center would be simple. The executive director was to act with the advice and counsel of the dean of the College of Arts and Sciences and the dean of the Graduate School of Arts and Sciences. The chair of the Department of Economics or a representative designated by him was to serve as the executive director. Buchanan was the first executive director and Nutter was associate director. Yeager, then an assistant professor, was executive secretary. The advisory committee consisted of Colgate W. Darden, Jr., president of the University of Virginia, William L. Duren, Jr., dean of the College of Arts and Sciences, and Lewis M. Hammond, dean of the Graduate School of Arts and Sciences, all of whom served as *ex officio* members. Charles C. Abbott, dean of the Graduate School of Business Administration, Rowland Egger, chair of the Department of Foreign Affairs and Political Science, and Hardy Dillard, professor of law at the University of Virginia, served as the working members of the committee. From its beginnings the Center was interdisciplinary and had a clear idea of its intellectual enterprise. At that time it was contemplated that the bulk of the support for the Center would be from foundation grants-in-aid from the Thomas Jefferson Memorial Foundation and the William Volker Fund. The Relm Foundation provided the funds for office space and equipment for the Center together with five graduate fellowships. The plan was for the university to pay a small allowance for operating expenses and the initial provision of salary for one clerical assistant.[12]

TULLOCK'S YEAR AT THE THOMAS JEFFERSON CENTER, 1958–1959

Tullock's year at The Thomas Jefferson Center played a crucial role in his intellectual development and it was significant for the Center that Tullock was the Center's first post-doctoral fellow. Tullock has reminded me on several occasions that his stipend of $5,500 was a lot of money in 1958. To provide proper perspective one need only note that it was 220 percent of the $2,500 received by pre-doctoral fellows, 367 percent of the $1,500 received by graduate fellows, but only 37 percent of the $15,000 received by the Distinguished Visiting Scholar.

In the fall of 1958 Tullock arrived at the University of Virginia to assume his post-doctoral fellowship. During his year there, Tullock learned a great deal from Buchanan, and it was then that they began a most fruitful collaboration for which we are grateful. Each morning at the Thomas Jefferson Center began with tea at the Colonnade Club. Also, at that time, Tullock was in the habit of working with his office door open, which served as an invitation to conversation, particularly since the coffee-maker was outside his door. And, most importantly, his congeniality fostered productive scholarly conversations with his colleagues. However, it was only after Tullock had assumed his teaching position at the University of South Carolina in the fall of 1959 that he and Buchanan decided to collaborate on what was to become *The Calculus of Consent*. Buchanan wrote Tullock that he thought they could produce a joint book, Tullock agreed wholeheartedly, and the rest is history.

Tullock's post-doctoral fellowship at the University of Virginia gave him first-hand experience with economics and consequently he underwent a major change in his views. When he came to the University of Virginia, he describes himself as antagonistic (at best) towards welfare economics. Tullock credits Buchanan with greatly improving his knowledge of economics and providing him with an appreciation of the Paretian framework. However, it is quite ironic that Tullock, the lawyer, sought to apply economic analysis while Buchanan, the economist, initially preferred the perspective of the moral philosopher.

As a student of Frank H. Knight, Buchanan had a natural interest in philosophy, and one might argue that Buchanan played a role in Tullock's intellectual development similar to that which Knight had played in Buchanan's. Buchanan described Knight as a teacher who "gave us who bothered to listen the abiding notion that all is up for intellectual grabs, that much of what paraded as truth was highly questionable, and that the hallmark of a scholar was his or her courage in cutting through the intellectual haze. The willingness to deny all gods, the courage to hold nothing as sacrosanct—these were the qualities of mind and character that best describe Frank Knight."[13] Most would agree that this account applies equally well to both Buchanan and to Tullock. Buchanan further described "Knight as the inveterate puzzler; but his thought process probed depths that the scholars about him could not realize even existed. To Knight, things were never so simple as they seemed, and he remained, at base, tolerant in the extreme because he sensed the elements of truth in all principles . . . . Knight left us with the awful realization that if we did not have the simple courage to work out our own answers, we were vulnerable to victimization by false gods."[14] Again, this description is equally applicable to both Buchanan and Tullock. How these two kindred scholars interacted is important to understanding their collaborative work.

Tullock did a good job at providing puzzles and nontraditional perspectives on the real world economics that he observed. Tullock's contact with Buchanan and the Virginia school, then in its early development, was fortuitous for him and for the group of scholars that it brought together. Once at the Center, it was Buchanan who recognized Tullock's potential for a scholarly career. Perhaps Buchanan recognized Tullock's insights on majority voting as unusual and framed them in the language of economics. Buchanan's reading of Wicksell led him to focus on the question of super-majorities. The interests and personalities of Buchanan and Tullock fitted together well and Tullock credits himself with focusing their work on the task of applying economic reasoning to a political problem. Tullock brought to Buchanan the somewhat naive optimism of the natural economist that economics could be applied fruitfully to understanding political problems. Buchanan was a neoclassical economist (e.g., his work on public debt). After getting to know each other's views, they collaborated successfully to write *The Calculus of Consent*.

As we have seen, Tullock was antagonistic to Paretian welfare economics, and this was due to a mistaken view, which he harbored, about what it involved. Like many non-economists Tullock took its name at face value and confused it with such government programs as the social security system and various other welfare programs. Indeed, Tullock admits that with the exception of voting, he became a strict Paretian. In the case of voting, Tullock thought that in practice voting could not be made unanimous. When Tullock arrived at the University of Virginia he had in his early drafts of the bureaucracy book the argument that logrolling deserved the condemnation that it normally gets. Buchanan, on the other hand, argued that that was not true because of involuntary trade. This prompted Tullock to think about the matter and he then realized that, while it was a voluntary trade, the bargain implicit in logrolling did not include all the people who were involved in the decision and thus the minority were not included. This in turn may have affected Tullock's work on the problems with majority voting. It was this recognition that led him to compare the cost of getting the wrong conclusion with the cost of getting a decision made, a concept highlighted in *The Calculus of Consent*. Tullock credits Buchanan with clearing up his confusion.

ANTHONY DOWNS AND DUNCAN BLACK

Tullock met Anthony Downs while Downs was in the naval air force stationed near Orlando, close to where Tullock's mother then lived in Winter Park. Tullock had already read *An Economic Theory of Democracy* (1957), although he did not read Downs's 1956 article in the *Journal of Political Economy* until sometime later. Tullock does not think Downs's work heavily influenced *The Calculus of Consent* except in so far as they were writing in the same field: Tullock was interested in the application of economics rather than the specific arguments in Downs's analysis. Later, Tullock sent a draft of his own book to Downs, who offered extensive editorial advice. Indeed, Downs's comments were almost as long as the book itself. Although Downs was, and remains, strongly opposed to Public Choice, Tullock was very grateful for his suggestions.

Tullock became aware of Duncan Black through Downs's review of Black's *The Theory of Committees and Elections* (1958) which appeared in the *American Economic Review*. Tullock ordered five copies of Black's book for distribution at the Thomas Jefferson Center. Tullock then acquired a copy of Black and Newing's *Committee Decisions With Complementary Valuation* (1951). As was the case with Downs's work, Tullock's interest was not so much in Black's approach, but rather his choice of subject matter.

Tullock elaborates on the intellectual roots of *The Calculus of Consent* in Appendix 2, "Theoretical Forerunners," of that book. He notes that economics and probability theory are the major sources of their analysis. However, he also attempts to explain their debt to what he refers to as a series of investigations in a poorly defined field called the "strict theory of politics." He first discusses the efforts of mathematicians to solve strategic games in which the outcome is indeterminate because the rules of the game make it possible for players to conceal their strategies. He further notes a set of cases, involving large numbers of players, in which the individual player's attempts to adjust to strategies chosen by other players lead to a determinate result, called a "saddle point," or equilibrium. He indicates that their theoretical apparatus is grounded in modern economics and game theory begun by Von Neumann and Morgenstern. He explained that there are three major guidelines in their investigation. First, modern utility theory, developed largely by economists but having benefited greatly from the work of game theorists, led Buchanan and Tullock to concentrate on the calculus of the individual decision-maker. Second, game theory and their economics background led them to search for "solutions" to well-defined "political games." Third, political economy and the search for criteria in modern statistics led them to search for an "optimal" set of "political rules of the game," as conceived by the utility-maximizing individual.[15]

The discussion of the role of game theory in their analysis lays the groundwork for discussing "the strict theory of politics" and the contributions of Duncan Black. Tullock divides this little-known field into three areas: the theory of committees and elections by Duncan Black; the theory of parties and candidates; and the theory of constitutions. Tullock chooses to emphasize the contributions of Duncan Black, whom he credits with reviving the subject. Tullock notes the early contributions of Borda, Condorcet, and Nanson as well as the lesser known theorists, George H. Hallet and Francis Galton. C. L. Dodgson (Lewis Carroll) is credited with original work on the topic and Black with discovering Dodgson's contribution. Tullock's work on majority voting reflects Buchanan and Tullock's efforts to deal with the puzzle of finding a system of voting that would lead to a majority decision which could reasonably be regarded as the genuine will of a majority of the group. Black demonstrated that many issues are decided in a manner which can legitimately be called majority rule, but that there still remained those issues which were not "single-peaked" and which led to the problem of cyclical majorities. Arrow's work argued that the difficulties, which Black and his predecessors sought to avoid, simply could not be avoided. Buchanan and Tullock were addressing a different set of issues and chose to focus on the problem as laid out by Black.

Tullock indicates his debt to Downs and Black in developing his theory of candidates and parties which treats politicians as entrepreneurs and parties as corporations or partnerships. Parties are voluntary coalitions of politicians organized for the purpose of winning elections and serve as the vehicle by which politicians get elected or re-elected. Tullock indicates that his theory was built upon the contributions of a number of modern economists. Hotelling and Schumpeter made contributions, but the basic theory was developed by Anthony Downs and Tullock. He cites Downs's book and his own manuscript "A General Theory of Politics" as the two principal works in the area. He credits the formal theory in this field largely to Duncan Black's concept of a single-peaked preference curve. He notes that both he and Black discuss other possible structures but focused on the left-right continuum of the conventional political scientist. Tullock tried to simplify the analysis by confining his attention to a few examples based on the incentive for politicians to take similar positions.

TULLOCK'S YEARS AT THE UNIVERSITY OF SOUTH CAROLINA, 1959–1962

Richard "Dixie" Walker, who had been victimized by the backlash in academia against Senator McCarthy and his perceived supporters in the early 1950s, saw the great potential in Tullock and arranged for him to become an assistant professor at the University of South Carolina.[16] Walker had left Yale and had settled at the University of South Carolina. (Later he became ambassador to South Korea during the Reagan administration.) Tullock got along well with the Walker family and greatly admired Walker's ability to speak Chinese like a native. Tullock made friends easily and soon had assembled a "coffee klatch," which served as his mid-morning sounding board. Tullock's circle of colleagues included Milledge Broadus Seigler, professor of English Literature.[17] In 1958 when Walker invited Tullock to join the faculty at the Department of International Studies at the University of South Carolina, Tullock agreed without hesitation, and it was there that Tullock served as assistant, and later associate, professor. However, when Warren Nutter offered him a one-year post-doctoral fellowship at the Thomas Jefferson Center for Studies in Political Economy at the University of Virginia, Walker, much to Tullock's amazement, graciously let him postpone taking up his professorship at the University of South Carolina. This was indeed fortunate for Tullock and the Public Choice movement because, had he not seized the opportunity, it is unlikely that he would have had meaningful exposure to the personalities and physical setting of the Virginia School of Political Economy, then in its infancy and awaiting the fresh ideas and energy that someone like Tullock with his very different background could bring.

While at the Department of International Studies at the University of South Carolina, Tullock focused on bringing his long-time interest in science and interdisciplinary research to bear on the topics of science and foreign policy, games of strategy and international politics, and problems in Asia.[18] As part of his duties, he lectured on all of these topics. While at the University of South Carolina, he achieved a reputation as a political theorist and one of the country's leading authorities on the application of mathematical techniques to problems in the social sciences. He was also a regular contributor to a series of articles on foreign affairs sponsored by his department that appeared in South Carolina newspapers.[19]

While at the University of South Carolina, Tullock also published a new edition of what has become known as *Walsingham's Manual,* which he had first come across in the university library.[20] In the preface, he examined the motives of the author, readers, and publishers, and the publishing history of the book. Tullock observed that, since it was written as a manual for the courtier hoping to rise to a position of power and influence at a royal court, the author would not want his identity to become known. "The book is too faithful a portrait of the ambitious and unscrupulous courtier to bear inspection by his prince. If the name of the author had not been concealed, his career could have been ruined by any one of his rivals who took the trouble to read a few selected passages to his ruler." (Tullock [1961], vii)

"TULLOCK THE NEEDLE"

We have all heard about "Mack the Knife," but what of "Tullock the Needle"? Bill Breit once referred to Tullock's ability to administer the carefully crafted but "studied insult."[21] Tullock's keen mind remained ever ablaze with mischief as evidenced by his 1962 correspondence with R. Sargent Shriver, then director of the Peace Corps. Tullock's letter of June 1, 1962 to Shriver is provided in its entirety below to insure that justice is fully served.

Dear Mr. Shriver:

In accordance with your advice I wrote to Mr. Grubb [a youthful Peace Corpsman whose photograph adorned a recruiting poster]. A copy of the rather distressing reply is enclosed. Apparently someone in your office, probably Mr. Nelson, sent him a complete file of our interchange. The result was that he not only replied to the question I had asked him, but he also commented extensively on the matters which were covered in our correspondence. From his remarks it is clear that almost everything you told me in your letter of March 2nd is incorrect. He is not making a rail fence, but rabbit "huts." (How he succeeded in making hutches out of logs of the size shown in the picture I have difficulty imagining. What part the chisel played in the process is even more mysterious.) Far from having a degree in economics, he is only semi-literate. I trust that those members of the Peace Corps who engage in teaching English have been more carefully screened for spelling and grammar.

Although I must admit that my original letter to you was more in the nature of a "needle" than a request for information, I have become interested in the specific projects of the Peace Corps. Could you recommend to me a member of your Corps who is not only well-motivated, but also reasonably well-educated and economically sophisticated and who would be willing to answer questions about some specific projects with which he is connected?

Sincerely,
Gordon Tullock
Associate Professor

Tullock's letter must have been lost at the Peace Corps. Receiving no response, Tullock sought to close the matter with the following letter also provided in its entirety.

Dear Mr. Shriver:

According to today's *New York Times* you have a sign on your office door saying: "There is no place in this club for good losers." Presumably this does not mean that you want bad losers, but winners. Sticking to the game analogy, it might be contended that you have lost in our correspondence so far, but simply refusing to answer my letters is no way to win. Surely there is at least one of your corpsmen who has enough discretion so that you can trust him to correspond with me.

Sincerely,
Gordon Tullock
Associate Professor

PS: Also according to the *New York Times*, Davis (sic) Grubb "took a bus into Bogota, called on the Minister of Public Works and came back with a bulldozer, which his village used to build an eight-mile road to market." Zipacon is more or less a suburb of Bogota, and has regular rail service. Improved transportation to markets must be much more necessary elsewhere in Columbia.

HOW *THE CALCULUS OF CONSENT* CAME TO BE WRITTEN

The year at the University of Virginia was filled with fruitful discussions and debates which led to *The Calculus of Consent.* The bits and pieces which emerged during that year represent the origin of many of the specific parts of the work. Tullock does not remember reading any of Buchanan's work prior to arriving at the University of Virginia. Upon reflection, he thinks that he may have read some of Buchanan's journal articles, but was not explicitly aware of his work.

In an interview in April 1999 with the author of this essay, Tullock stated that *The Calculus of Consent* was entirely the work of Buchanan, with the exception of Chapter 16 on the bicameral legislature which originated from a forty-page monograph written by Tullock. He describes Buchanan as writing the initial drafts and passing them along to him for comments. However, Tullock's contribution is described rather differently in the preface to *The Calculus of Consent.* One might argue that the preface reflects Buchanan's recollection of what had just occurred and therefore may be more accurate than Tullock's reflection on the matter nearly forty years later. Tullock's mimeographed research paper entitled "A Preliminary Investigation of the Theory of Constitutions" contained the first elements of the central analysis of the entire book. An additional preliminary manuscript was completed in the summer of 1959. Buchanan's "Economic Policy, Free Institutions, and Democratic Process" was delivered at the annual meeting of the Mont Pelerin Society in September 1959 at Oxford. This paper contained many of the ideas that had been jointly discussed by the two authors during Tullock's post-doctoral fellowship.

As we have seen, Tullock moved to the University of South Carolina as assistant professor in September 1959, and the bulk of the book was written during the academic year 1959–1960. Tullock initially developed the arguments of Chapter 10 ("Simple Majority Voting"). When Tullock showed him the problems with majority voting, Buchanan became quite excited by this insight as well as being intrigued by the prospect of crossing traditional disciplinary boundaries. It was during the fellowship that Tullock wrote his seminal article "Problems in Majority Voting"[22] which began the field we now call Public Choice. To this day, Tullock expresses surprise that this article was accepted for publication without much difficulty. This preliminary analysis of logrolling in democratic government, submitted to the *Journal of Political Economy* in June 1959 and published that December, became Chapter 10 of *The Calculus of Consent.* Tullock went on to produce further work on majority voting which resulted in an eighty-page monograph. This insight became a critical part of *The Calculus of Consent.* One of Buchanan's principal contributions was to provide an exposition of the public finance framework. This constituted the first four chapters of *The Calculus of Consent* and explains the need for government provision of certain public goods.

According to the preface of the book, Buchanan should be given credit for the emphasis upon the unique position occupied by the unanimity rule in democratic theory, which was developed in Chapter 7 ("The Rule of Unanimity"). Tullock is responsible for stressing the necessity of placing some quantitative dimension on the costs of decision-making which was discussed in Chapter 8 ("The Costs of Decision-Making"). Buchanan developed the initial version of the analytical framework discussed in Chapter 9 ("The Organization of Human Activity"). He was also responsible for the applications of game theory and theoretical welfare economics that are contained in Chapter 11 ("Simple Majority Voting and the Theory of Games"), Chapter 12 ("Majority Rule, Game Theory, and Pareto Optimality"), and Chapter 13 ("Pareto Optimality, External Costs, and Income Redistribution"). Ideas for the remaining substantive chapters of Parts II ("The Realm of Social Choice") and III ("Analyses of Decision-Making Rules"), with the exception of Chapter 16, were jointly derived. Their approach was first to discuss, then draft, critique, and revise.

As I have mentioned earlier, Tullock felt that his influence on Buchanan was to convince him that economics offered a legitimate approach to politics, whereas Buchanan leaned more toward philosophy. Buchanan has at various times described himself as a "born again" economist who had once been a libertarian socialist with a strong individualist thrust, but a socialist nevertheless because he did not know how the economy worked. He learned from Knight how the economy worked and came to realize that in order to change the outcomes in politics, one must change the rules, including a shift away from simple majoritarian towards more inclusive voting rules.

CONCLUDING COMMENTS

Buchanan, having worked with Tullock on *The Calculus of Consent*, brought him back in 1962 as an associate professor where he remained until 1967. As is well known, the university administration three times refused to promote Tullock to the rank of full professor because of his lack of a degree in economics and what were perceived to be his conservative political views. The rejection of Tullock's superior scholarship provides an example of the shortsightedness of a major institution, but that is another story of which this is but a small part.

APPENDIX: TULLOCK'S VITA, 1947–1962

1947–1956: Foreign Service, U.S. Department of State.

1954
Tullock, G., "Hyper-Inflation in China, 1937–40" (with Colin Campbell), *Journal of Political Economy* 62 (June 1954), pp. 237–45.

1955
Tullock, G., "The Fishery: Methods of Sole Ownership" [1955] [published as a pamphlet].

1956–1958: Research and Writing Consultancy at the Princeton Council, a subsidiary of the Gallup organization

1956
Tullock, G., "Paper Money: A Cycle in Cathay," *Economic History Review* 9 (June 1956), pp. 393–407.

1957

Campbell, C., and Tullock, G., "Some Little Understood Aspects of Korea's Monetary and Fiscal System," *American Economic Review* 47 (June 1957), pp. 336–40.

Translated into Korean and published in Seoul National University's *Economic Journal.*

"Reply," *American Economic Review* 48 (September 1958), pp. 661–62.

Tullock, G., "Japanese Modernization and the West," *Prod* 1 (November 1957), pp. 28–29.

Tullock, G., Comment, "Increased Rents From Increased Costs: A Paradox of Value Theory."

1958–1959: Post Doctoral Fellow, Thomas Jefferson Center, The University of Virginia

1959

Tullock, G., "Publication Decisions and Tests of Significance: Comment," *Journal of the American Statistical Association* 54 (September 1959), p. 593.

Tullock, G., "Sources of Union Gains", University of Virginia, Research Monograph 2 [1959]. 65 Pages.

Tullock, G., "Korea," *Collier's Encyclopedia Yearbook for the Year 1959 (1960)*, pp. 371–73.

Tullock, G., "Problems of Majority Voting," *Journal of Political Economy* 67 (December 1959), pp. 571-79.

Reprinted in Kenneth Arrow and Tibor Scitovsky (eds.), *Readings in Welfare Economics* (Homewood, IL: Richard D. Irwin, Inc., 1969), pp. 169–78.

Translated "Problemi del voto a maggioranza," in Francesco Forte and Gianfranco Mossetto (eds.), *Economia del Benessere e Democrazia* (Milano: Franco Angeli Editore, 1973), pp. 459–71.

Reprinted in Thomas Schwartz (ed.), *Freedom and Authority: An Introduction to Political Philosophy* (Encino, CA: Dickenson Publishing Co.).

Tullock, G., "An Introduction to Logical Models," *Prod* 3 (November 1959), pp. 9–11.

Tullock, G., "The Sources of Union Gains," Research monograph (Thomas Jefferson Center for Political Economy, University of Virginia, 1959).

1959–1962: Assistant and Associate Professor, University of South Carolina

1960

Tullock, G., "Aphorisms for the Ambitious," *American Behavioral Scientist* 4 (December 1960), pp. 36–38.

Tullock, G., *"Welfare Economics and Ethics: a Comment."*

Tullock, G., "The Proletarian's Burden."

1961

Tullock, G., "The Historic Figure: Why Study Ignorance," *American Behavioral Scientist*, 5 (November 1961), pp. 25–26.

Tullock, G., "Korea," *Collier's Encyclopedia Yearbook for the Year 1960 (1961)*, pp. 351–54.

Tullock, G., "Reply to a Traditionalist," *Journal of Political Economy* 69 (April 1961), pp. 200–03.

Tullock, G., "An Economic Analysis of Political Choice," *Il Politico* 16 (1961), pp. 234–40.

Tullock, G., "Utility, Strategy, and Social Decision Rules: Comment," *Quarterly Journal of Economics* 75 (August 1961), pp. 493–97.

Tullock, G., "Our 'Other-Directed' Foreign Policy," *Foreign Policy Bulletin* 1 (November 1961), pp. 1–2.

Tullock, G., *A Practical Guide for the Ambitious Politician*, (Columbia, SC: University of South Carolina Press, 1961).

1962
Tullock, G., "Political Realism in Economics," 1962 *The Exchange*.

Buchanan, J. M., and Tullock, G., "A Note of the Theory of Charitable Gifts," [1962].

Buchanan, J. M., and Tullock, G., *The Calculus of Consent: Logical Foundations of a Constitutional Democracy* (Ann Arbor: University of Michigan Press, 1962).
Paperback, 1965.
Spanish Translation, 1980.
Japanese Translation, 1980.

Tullock, G., *Entrepreneurial Politics.* Research monograph #5 (Thomas Jefferson Center for Political Economy, University of Virginia, February, 1962).

Book Reviews

Soviet Economic Warfare, by Robert L. Allen. In *Journal of Politics* 23, No. 4 (November 1961), pp. 760–61.

Conflict and Defense, by Kenneth E. Boulding. In *Southern Economic Journal* (October 1962). box 151

Silent Spring, by Rachel Carson. In *National Review* (November 1962).

Awakened China, by Felix Greene. In *Virginia Quarterly* 38 (Winter 1962), pp. 170–73.

This paper was presented at a conference in honor of Gordon Tullock, 22 May 1999, University of Arizona, Tucson, Arizona. At the time this paper was written, the author was Director, Law and Economics Center, George Mason University School of Law. He is a student of Gordon Tullock, has published a book of Tullock's previously unpublished papers, and has worked closely with Tullock over the years since graduate training at Virginia Polytechnic Institute and State University.

[1] For a discussion of Tullock's life and work, see Gordon Brady and Robert Tollison, *On the Trail of Homo Economicus: Essays by Gordon Tullock*, Fairfax: George Mason University Press (1994) and "Gordon Tullock: Creative Maverick of Public Choice," *Public Choice*, (1991).

[2] *The Economics of Non-Human Societies*, Tucson, Arizona: Pallas Press, 1994.

[3] *The Fisheries: Some Radical Proposals*, Bureau of Business and Economic Research, Columbia: University of South Carolina Press, Feb. 1962

[4] Henry C. Simons, *Economic Policy for a Free Society*, Chicago: University of Chicago Press, 1948.

[5] Simons's Syllabus.

[6] *The Sources of Union Gains*, Thomas Jefferson Center for Political Economy, Charlottesville: University of Virginia, 1959, Research monograph.

[7] The Postscript was written mainly during the years 1951–1956, at the time when *Logik Der Forschung* was being translated into English as *The Logic of Scientific Discovery*. The different volumes were originally intended as a series of appendices to *The Logic of Scientific Discovery*, where Popper would expand, correct and develop its ideas. But one group of appendices grew into a work far exceeding *The Logic of Scientific Discovery*, so it was decided to publish these as a separate work called *Postscript: After 20 years*. But no sooner had the text been set in typed galley proofs in 1956–1957, when the project came to a halt because Popper had to have operations on both of his eyes. When he had recovered, Popper did do a great deal of work on the book, but other projects took over (completely after 1962) and the *Postscript* lay unpublished for decades. The three volumes can be read separately, but form a connected series of arguments with each volume attacking one or another of the subjectivist or idealist approaches to knowledge.

[8] As an aside, John Anderson, the 1980 Independent presidential candidate, was a member of the debate team with Tullock at Rockford High School, but not someone with whom Tullock chose to keep in touch.

[9] Tullock, G., "A General Theory of Politics" (privately circulated, 1958). This was eventually published in a somewhat modified form as *The Politics of Bureaucracy* (Washington: Public Affairs Press, 1965).

[10] Now called the State University of New York at Buffalo.

[11] At a later period, Ford Foundation executive Kermit Gordon suggested that Lindblom might be an appropriate addition to the faculty to provide broader perspective for the Economics Department.

[12] Letter and Enclosure 1 from James M. Buchanan to William L. Duren, Jr., 25 March 1957.

[13] Buchanan, James M., *Better than Plowing and Other Personal Essays*, (Chicago and London: University of Chicago Press, 1992), 75–76.

[14] Ibid., 76.

[15] *The Calculus of Consent*, 326.

[16] Tullock actually called Walker by the nickname "Dick."

[17] Seigler received his MA (Duke University,1936) and Ph.D. (Duke University, 1942). His master's thesis was "Gothicism in Poe's Short Stories" and his Ph.D. dissertation was "Milton's Prosody." Research indicates that he published one jointly authored paper entitled "Peter Freneau, Carolina Republican"*The Journal of Southern History*, 13, no. 3 (August 1947). His co-author was Richard Beale Davis.

[18] Tullock wrote several papers on this subject during this period, e.g., "Science and Foreign Policy" (no date).

[19] Examples include: "Exports Without Imports" (no date), "Mussolini and Mao," (no date), "Sino-Soviet Split?" (no date), "Thoughts Before the Election" (October 9, 1962), and "Schism in the Party" (no date).

[20] Tullock's edition was published as *A Practical Guide for Ambitious Politician; or, Walsingham's Manual* (Columbia: University of South Carolina Press, 1961).

[21] *Breit, William, "Creating the 'Virginia School": Charlottesville as an Academic Environment in the 1960s," Lectures on Virginia Political Economy, Center for Study in Public Choice, George Mason University 1986.*

[22] *Journal of Political Economy*, Vol. XVII, No. 6, December 1959, 571–79.

INDEX

Index

MIX
Papier aus verantwortungsvollen Quellen
Paper from responsible sources
FSC® C105338

If you have any concerns about our products,
you can contact us on
ProductSafety@springernature.com

In case Publisher is established outside the EU,
the EU authorized representative is:
Springer Nature Customer Service Center GmbH
Europaplatz 3, 69115 Heidelberg, Germany

Printed by Libri Plureos GmbH
in Hamburg, Germany